The Bob Verga Shift

How One Man's Illness Changed History and Saved Duke Basketball

THE BOB VERGA SHIFT

How One Man's Illness Changed History
and Saved Duke Basketball

Michael B. Layden

Torchflame Books
Vista, CA

Copyright © 2024 by Michael B. Layden

All Rights Reserved. No part of this publication may be reproduced, stored in or introduced into a retrieval system, or transmitted in any form or by any means (electronic, mechanical, photocopied, recorded of otherwise), except as permitted under Section 107 or 108 of the 1976 International Copyright Act, without the prior written permission of both the copyright owner and the publisher of this book, except by a reviewer who wishes to quote brief passages in connection with a review written for insertion in a magazine, newspaper, broadcast, website, blog or other outlet. For information, address Top Reads Publishing Subsidiary Rights Department, 1035 E. Vista Way, Suite 205, Vista, CA 92084, USA.

ISBN: 978-1-611532-41-8 (paperback)
ISBN: 978-1-970107-47-0 (ebook)

Library of Congress Control Number: 2024901515

The Bob Verga Shift is published by: Torchflame Books, an imprint of Top Reads Publishing, LLC, USA

For information about special discounts for bulk purchases, please direct emails to: publisher@torchflamebooks.com

Cover design: Jori Hanna
Book interior layout: Teri Rider

Printed in the United States of America

Permissions Granted: Photographs of Texas Western basketball team from the University of Texas at El Paso used with permission, Mark Brunner, UTEP Athletics. Photographs from *Durham Herold Sun, Raleigh News & Observer*, used with permission, Scott Sharpe. Photos of the University of Kentucky basketball team used with permission, Jason E. Flahardy, UK Libraries Special Collections Research Center. Official individual or team photographs from Duke University used with permission, Jon Jackson, Duke Athletics.

Author's note:
Every effort has been made to give credit for photos and art shown in this book. We apologize for any errors or omissions and will gladly make corrections on subsequent editions.

Dedication

This book is dedicated to my daughter, who in her younger days enjoyed reading books, especially by Dr. Seuss.

CONTENTS

Chapter 1 | Durham and Duke in 1966 | 1

Chapter 2 | Kentucky and the SEC in 1966 | 25

Chapter 3 | The Texas Western Team | 48

Chapter 4 | Race Relations in America in 1966 | 60

Chapter 5 | Bob Verga's Illness: The Verga-Conley Matrix | 82

Chapter 6 | The 1966 Final Four | 94

Chapter 7 | What If for Duke and Durham | 133

Chapter 8 | What If for Duke Basketball | 152

Chapter 9 | What if For Kentucky | 176

Chapter 10 | What If for Black Athletes and Black America | 191

Chapter 11 | The Rematch: Duke-Kentucky 1992 | 210

Chapter 12 | Changing the Verdict of History | 236

Acknowledgements | 253

Notes | 255

Bibliography | 275

About the Author | 279

CHAPTER 1

DURHAM AND DUKE IN 1966

Let's start from home, which is where one usually starts when they begin a journey. In 1966, Durham, NC—as it was for about eighty thousand other people—was my home. It was a considerably smaller city back then, with a considerably smaller Duke University too. It didn't have a freeway through the middle of town; to get there, you had to drive in up 15-501 business into the center of town. There was a Sears downtown with TVs and lawn mowers for sale and a big motel, the Jack Tar (later renamed the Durham Hotel), which was demolished in 1975 in a giant implosion which covered all of downtown in a cloud of dust. The old, decaying public library had a children's room downstairs where we used to check out books. You could buy a new car for two thousand dollars at Alexander Ford or Carpenter's Chevrolet back then. The owner of the latter, Skip Carpenter, doubled as the local weatherman back then. (If Skip said it was going to be sunny, it was a good idea to pack an umbrella.) In summer, the Single-A Bulls played in Durham Athletic Park, in front of maybe five hundred or a thousand fans sitting on rickety, wooden benches (later immortalized in the movie *Bull Durham*, which turned the Bulls from a single A to a triple A team in the late 1980s; attending a Bulls game was just like in the movie, where a player could hit a baseball through a tire in the outfield and win a new set of radials). In 1966, my father backed his new Chevrolet—just purchased from

Carpenter's—into a tree, taking the family to a Bulls game. In winter, we had a Christmas parade with a Santa that reminded me of the one from *A Christmas Story*. It was a different place than it is today.

When visitors arrive in Durham today via Raleigh-Durham International Airport, they must drive through the Research Triangle to get to the city. They drive by numerous laboratories filled with high paying, quality jobs. Then they drive through downtown Durham, which, surprisingly, doesn't look all that much different than it did in 1966. There are a few skyscrapers and other buildings, some dating from before 1966, the aforementioned nice baseball park, and some old tobacco factories which have been renovated and turned into various small businesses. They may see a few nice restaurants and bars where local college students hang out. And then, they might visit the Duke Medical Center, which is now a world class institution, or stop by Cameron Indoor Stadium to see the place shown on so many Duke basketball telecasts. It is indeed a progressive and pleasant area to live, often regarded as one of the best places to live in the country.

But Durham, back in 1966, was a very different city. In 1966, Durham was a tobacco town. In North Carolina, growing and harvesting tobacco was a way of life that had existed for nearly three hundred years. When visiting downtown Durham back then, the now abandoned or renovated tobacco factories were humming, working year-round to ensure that the rest of the country was amply supplied with the product that satisfied their nicotine addiction. Downtown, when the wind was blowing the right way, the smell of tobacco filled the air. It permeated everything.

Driving from Durham into eastern North Carolina, you could see where the tobacco in the Durham factories came from. Places like Smithfield and Goldsboro were an ocean of tobacco. Miles of it, in every direction. Hundreds of thousands of acres of land dedicated to growing an addictive, poisonous, life ruining crop. This was the economic foundation of central and eastern North Carolina in 1966.

It was an alien and strange world to me back then, as I peered out into it from my groovy little enclave in West Durham, where jacked up cars bobbed up and down like little boats on an ocean of tobacco, and where rednecks with slicked back hair who listened to Conway Twitty and Loretta Lynn went to tent revivals and (sometimes) Klu Klux Klan rallies. In 1966, the Klan was very strong in North Carolina. As Julius Erving—"Dr. J," the Hall of Fame ballplayer—recalled, Black visitors driving in from the North would get a friendly greeting at the state line as to where they had entered. "There would be a big sign when you got past Virginia and into North Carolina that said, 'Welcome to Klan Country.'"[1] And in case they forgot, there were other Klan signs around to remind them. The one outside of Smithfield along US route 70, which I used to see on the way to the beach, was particularly famous. It exhorted drivers to "Help fight communism and integration," showing a white hooded rider on a horse. It was finally removed in 1977.

Since the Klan Country farm folks grew tobacco, they would tune in to WRAL in Raleigh at noon to see the farm report (the price of tobacco was quoted daily). And, in the later part of the program, they could hear a political commentator as well. It was none other than the executive vice president of WRAL television, Mr. Jesse Helms. For several minutes at lunch each day, you could hear Mr. Helms pour on racist hatred and bigotry. He had a special way of sneering and being sarcastic that seemed to endear him to his tobacco growing viewers. He was not known for being a fan of Dr. Martin Luther King Jr. My mother and I used to throw things at the screen when he came on. But the people who owned tobacco farms seemed to like him a lot; they elected him a US Senator a few years later. After I left North Carolina, I often felt compelled to apologize to people out of state about him when sharing that I grew up there.

If you looked out into the tobacco fields more closely as you drove by, you could see the people out growing and harvesting it (which was just where the tobacco farmers and Mr. Jesse Helms wanted them to be). Most of them, as they had been for the last three hundred years, were Black. People whose ancestors were brought to America chained to the decks of slave ships, forced into servitude before the Civil War, and who for nearly a hundred years since, had been forced to live in segregated communities. A great many of them had left the South years before. But in 1966, there were still a huge number of Black laborers working out in the sun, fertilizing, priming, and cutting tobacco (since, historically, White people had had little inclination to do it). It's indeed a product and a way of life which are not looked on today with any particular nostalgia. But that was the way of life in much of eastern North Carolina in 1966.

Tobacco labor was low paid and degrading. According to Jennifer Wells, prior to the 1960s, the majority of leaf house workers were Black, with 75 percent comprising Black women under White male supervisors. Working conditions were abysmal: twelve-hour shifts of backbreaking labor with low pay. The atmosphere was "dangerous, dirty, and deeply marked by racism and sexism."[2] The working conditions were so bad in the 1940s that the tobacco industry could not get White workers to work there even during strikes. During a strike in 1943, it was rumored three thousand White workers were assigned to jobs normally undertaken by Black workers, but they could not handle the intense physical labor the jobs required.

And that was the world inhabited by many of my future classmates in Durham, where conditions in the factories and fields were the same as they had been in the 1940s. However, in 1966, when much of this book is set, things were starting to change in North Carolina. The world of tobacco and racism—in which central and eastern North Carolina had lived for nearly three hundred years—was, for the first time since the Civil War, being seriously challenged on both fronts. In 1964, the surgeon general had published a famous report which had statistically linked smoking to lung cancer and emphysema. Now, for the first time, the nation had clear cut proof of what people had long suspected; tobacco smoking was indeed harmful to your health.

In 1964, people smoked like chimneys. Smoking was just at its peak then; more than half of men and nearly a third of women smoked in 1964 (the total has declined now to about one-fifth of the total population). People smoked in cars, in restaurants, at home, everywhere. Everyone had ash trays in their homes. A pack of cigarettes in Durham cost twenty-five cents, and, of course, in North Carolina, there were no taxes on the local product. This was one reason Northerners would fill up their trunks with cigarettes when they visited the Carolinas back then (and still do). There were cigarette commercials on television constantly, and who wouldn't want to light one up after seeing the handsome cowboy calmly smoking a Marlboro: "Come to where the flavor is. Come to Marlboro country!" with the theme music from *The Magnificent Seven* playing in the background? Never mind that one actor who portrayed the Marlboro cowboy later died of emphysema. When you went to a basketball game in Cameron Indoor Stadium, the cigarette smoke was often so thick it was hard to see the people on the other side of the stadium through the blue haze.

When the surgeon general's report came out in January 1964, this was indeed a major blow to the North Carolina economy. People had long believed that smoking was bad for your health, but it had not been quantified with any level of accuracy before. The report's conclusions were simply staggering, even viewed today, and were even more devastating when they first came out. When they showed the actual death rates from smoking, the numbers seemed incredible. The report stated: "For men who smoke fewer than 10 cigarettes a day, the death rate from all causes is about 40 percent higher than for non-smokers. For those who smoke from 10 to 19 cigarettes a day, it is about 70 percent higher than for non-smokers; for those who smoke 20 to 39 cigarettes, it is 90 percent higher, and for those who smoke 40 or more, it is 120 percent higher."[3] It also specifically examined the incredibly higher death rates from each of an array of smoking induced illnesses, including emphysema, heart disease, bronchitis, lung cancer, and a number of other illnesses.

The report had a huge impact. It proved without a doubt what people had long known; smoking was indeed deadly. This report was the beginning of the long, slow decline of the tobacco industry. As more and more people realized the damage that cigarettes could do to their health, people began the difficult process of breaking their nicotine addiction and quitting smoking. In addition, now armed with evidence to prove what they had long suspected, the long legal battle to hold the tobacco industry responsible for marketing an addictive, dangerous product to minors had begun, one which the tobacco industry was ultimately destined to lose. The decline of the tobacco industry was starting to become visible.

The second blow to the tobacco industry in 1964 was the passage of the Civil Rights Act. For the first time, Black workers found themselves free to travel and work wherever they were able to. With the end of segregation, new economic opportunities were opening up for Black workers who, heretofore, had found themselves relegated to a life of low paid field labor. The labor force on which the tobacco industry depended could now find other, better opportunities. The entire central and eastern North Carolina way of life was being seriously threatened.

One upshot of these two challenges was that eastern North Carolina's way of life was going to have to change, and so was Durham's. The twin foundations of the local economy were under siege, and the area was going to have to make the transformation to another way of life. In Durham and the surrounding area, this change was just beginning. Governor Luther Hodges, in 1958, had established the research triangle, surrounded by the three major local research universities in the area: Duke, UNC, and NC State. In 1959, the Research Triangle Institute became its first occupant. As a result of the considerable efforts of Wachovia Bank president and State Senator Archie Davis, a few more laboratories had moved in by the mid-1960s; the year before the game, both IBM and the US Department of Health Education and Welfare National Environmental Health Science Center announced moves into the park, with more tenants expected. This was the beginning of the eventual transformation of the triangle area into the huge pharmaceutical and research center it is today, with around forty thousand jobs in dozens of laboratories and facilities (along with accompanying annoying traffic jams on I-40, which wasn't built until 1974), forming the economic foundation of the area.

The 1964 Civil Rights Act had ushered in tremendous changes in race relations: segregation was now banned in public facilities such as churches and restaurants. However, the school desegregation battles were still to come. There was some change in that people were now given some choice as to where they attended school, but they were largely still segregated. Children of different races spent little time together in the segregated North Carolina of the mid-1960s. I attended an (almost) all-White school on the west side of Durham, while future Attorney General Loretta Lynch attended an all-Black school on the other side of town. (We were later to meet in the middle as classmates in sixth grade.)

Even though outright segregation was banned a few years before, Durham in 1966 was still very racially divided. Black and White people lived in different neighborhoods in different parts of town, went to different churches, attended different schools, and did not socialize particularly extensively. It almost seemed as if we lived on different planets. This difference also extended to the two universities in town as well; North Carolina Central University (then known as North Carolina College), a public university on the southeast side of town, was almost all Black, while Duke University, the other larger and better-known private school on the west side of Durham, was almost all White.

Despite segregation, the Black side of Durham had established a fairly substantial middle class. Durham had a tradition of Black entrepreneurship and business development which were atypical of the South overall. Surrounding NCCU, the Black side of Durham had produced a thriving and successful middle class, who prospered in spite of the obstacles of racism and segregation. This had produced successful businesses such as Mechanics and Farmers Bank and the NC Mutual Life Insurance Company (which became the first Black billion-dollar business in 1971). Overall, the Black part of Durham was viewed as fairly successful and considered one of the best places for Black people to live in the South.

On the White side of town, Duke University was an island near the western edge of the sea of tobacco. It was an enclave of educated, well-paid scientists, researchers, teachers, and doctors, which stood in considerable isolation from the rest of North Carolina and the rest of the South. Even back in those days it was considered a fairly liberal, enlightened place to live. Folks there prided themselves on being progressive on racial and social matters, while conveniently ignoring the rather obvious fact that the entire university in which they worked had been built on an economic foundation of tobacco and Black labor in central and eastern North Carolina.

Every cent of Duke founder James B. Duke's fortune had come from tobacco; his American tobacco company was the industry leader in the late nineteenth and early twentieth centuries. Tobacco magnate Julian Carr, who promoted Bull Durham Smoking Tobacco, donated the land in Durham which became Duke's original home on East Campus. Carr's racial legacy endures at Duke even today. Carr, who grew up in the Antebellum South and fought with the Confederacy (he was with Robert E. Lee at Appomattox) was a known supporter of the Klan and White supremacy. He supported lynchings and the murder of sixty Blacks at the famous Wilmington massacre of 1898. He was the single largest donor to a famous Confederate monument at UNC known as "Silent Sam." According to Carr, "The whole world admits that it was a mistake to have given universal suffrage to the negroes."[4] Carr, who remembered the pre-Civil War South, even regularly argued that African Americans were better-off enslaved. His racist legacy was so strong, even by the standards of his day, that Duke recently had to remove his name from buildings on the Duke campus at the request of much of the student body.[5]

Despite its racist origins, Duke was already in the process of becoming a top national university. Being well known for its educational excellence, it became known as a top regional university, not yet on a par with the Ivy League but improving steadily in that direction. Its faculty of arts and sciences was well regarded nationally, and many of its departments were highly ranked. Duke was, and still is, a beautiful campus. Its gothic architecture, chapel, and gardens (of 1920s vintage) are famous for their well laid out attractiveness, hiding the racist exploitation which had produced the wealth to pay for them.

The medical center, while not yet quite world class, was moving up in stature as well. Back in those days, the irony of the medical center was that the illnesses of many their patients were directly attributable to the product manufactured on the other side of town, namely cigarettes. I used to joke that Durham was a one-stop cancer center; you could buy cigarettes from one side of town to give you cancer and then drive to the medical center on the other side of town to treat it. I also used to joke that the best way for the Duke Medical Center to treat cancer would be to hire the Air Force to drop a couple of five-thousand-pound bombs on the tobacco factories across town. *That* would do something to prevent cancer, but then, of course, the medical center would have fewer patients to keep them busy. It wouldn't have been good for business on either side of town! But despite the Duke medical center's somewhat schizoid relationship with the tobacco industry—or maybe because of it—they became quite good at treating all the cancer patients the tobacco industry created. Perhaps James B. Duke felt guilty about how many people his products had killed and left some money for the Duke hospital to treat the cancer he helped create.

Prior to 1963, like most institutions of its time, Duke had been segregated. When you walked around the beautiful campus of Duke University back in the 1960s, what you saw was mostly White people. When you went to homecoming in the fall of 1966 and saw all the floats at the fraternities, you saw almost all White people there, looking back at you as you toured the floats. There weren't many Black folks at Duke back then, except maybe working at the hospital. Until only a few years before the 1966 Final Four, Black students could not attend the very university which their families' low paid labor had helped finance and create. Duke, like other prestigious, private Southern schools in that era, had *not* been a leader in desegregation;

racist labor practices in the tobacco industry had been too much a part of the reason for its very existence.

There was an obvious reason for that however segregation had also been a huge part of the community that Duke inhabited. Back in the 1940s, segregation was strictly enforced in Durham, to the point where it was considered dangerous for White residents to venture into Black parts of Durham. In Durham, before the Civil Rights Act, according to Segal, "Legally mandated segregation permeated all areas of life where white and black people might come into contact."[6] Everything from marriage to morgues, libraries to churches, hospitals to jails, and emergency services were all strictly segregated.

In 1944, word had gotten around at North Carolina College that the Duke medical school had an excellent basketball team filled with former college players getting ready to go overseas to fight WWII. Duke student Jack Burgess, who had played guard at the University of Montana, decided he wanted to play the NC College players despite local segregation. Burgess abhorred Jim Crow. He was once chased off a Durham city bus at knife point for telling the driver off about the seating arrangements.[7] The medical school team was supposedly better than the Duke varsity squad, which was the current Southern Conference champion. John McLendon, the North Carolina College coach, wanted his team to play them. His team ran an up-tempo, high-speed game and had only lost once all year. According to McLendon, "We could have beaten anyone."[8]

But for a White squad to play a Black team was a dangerous proposition in segregated Durham in 1944, which also had an active KKK. Both sides agreed to play anyway, which they did in a game later known in legend as "The Secret Game." The game was held at 11:00 a.m. on a Sunday morning, a time when most of Durham would be attending church. Everything was done under a cloak of secrecy. There were no spectators, and the Duke players took a serpentine route through town and covered their car windows with blankets so as not to be seen or followed driving to the Black side of town. They entered the gym through the women's dressing room, hiding their heads under their jackets. Once the players and the referee were all inside, the gym was locked.[9] Playing a style that wouldn't be widely seen for another two decades, the North Carolina College team won 88-44. According to Burgess, it was an all-around enjoyable game, "and when the evening was over, most of them had changed their views quite a lot."[10]

But this was typical of things in the 1940s, when the first attempts at integrating Duke began; changing people's views wasn't easy. The first attempt to desegregate Duke began in 1948 with a petition to the divinity school to admit Black day students. The petition, appropriately enough, stated, "We, the undersigned, students of The Divinity School of Duke University, would welcome the fellowship, stimulation, and fuller Christian cooperation that we feel would exist here if Negro students were to join us in our common Christian study as ministers of the Gospel."[11] The petition, as expected, was denied.

In 1949, Duke inaugurated a new president, Hollis Edens. Edens was deliberately bland and noncommittal about integration during the beginning of his tenure. His response to the question of Black admissions in 1950 was to lament what a complicated problem it was, with no clear or easy solution. "It is easier to crystallize one's personal attitude in this matter than to obtain a workable solution in society."[12]

The problem with which he was confronted was actually quite simple; the local population and the university board of trustees, most of whom had lived their whole lives with segregation, were against integrating the university. Similarly, other Southern private university presidents in that era, such as Emory, Rice, and Vanderbilt, also faced considerable resistance to integration from both their boards of trustees *and* the surrounding local White populations. In early 1954, Edens said, "I cannot foresee the necessity at any time in the foreseeable future of admitting Negroes at the undergraduate level."[13] Edens' position on the issue was typical of the time.

However, the Brown vs. Board of Education decision in May 1954 completely changed the situation. The pressure was now on all public universities to desegregate. UNC, the state school ten miles away, was now under legal pressure to accept Black students. The first three—from my own high school, Durham Hillside—were enrolled in 1955. (The experience at another university was described by one Black racial pioneer as being "drowned in a sea of whiteness.") Other public universities in the region were also required to admit Black applicants. Students and faculty at Duke—especially the divinity school—began pressuring Duke for change, even though, as a private university, the ruling did not specifically apply to Duke; only the board of trustees could make the final decision to admit Black students.

Hollis Edens, who actually was as ambivalent about the issue as his publicly stated positions, took note of the situation and began to change his position. Edens recognized that Duke's position as a regional leader—a topic of considerable debate among the faculty at the time, as some wanted it to be a regional school while others wanted it to become a nationally prominent research university—was now endangered by its segregated status, as well as its ability to attract quality faculty, who were turning down job offers from Duke due to disapproval over segregation, as more state schools started to integrate. In the mid-1950s, Edens began to pressure the Duke board of trustees to admit Black students. The board of trustees was, of course, comprised exclusively of older White men. Most of them grew up in the South in the later nineteenth and earlier twentieth centuries surrounded by people like Julian Carr; some of whom were even Civil War veterans. They were not likely to change their minds on race relations at that point in their lives, and also resented outside incursions into their Southern way of life.

By the late 1950s, the changes around them were becoming noticeable. In 1959, much of the younger Duke faculty and students were from the North and accustomed to living in non-segregated areas, and they started coming out in favor of admitting Black students. A petition was submitted that year with nearly three-quarters of the graduate students signing and more than half of the faculty. This put the board of trustees at odds with the younger, largely non-Southern student body and a majority of the faculty as well. But the Duke board refused to even consider it, stating that having already previously discussed the matter thoroughly, "the best interests of the University are not served by having the matter brought up again at this time."[14]

But by this time, Duke was clearly starting to get behind the more progressive parts of North Carolina. Racial barriers were starting to fall across the whole region. By the early 1960s, the Duke student body and much of the faculty, both of whom had spent years fighting the trustees to finally integrate Duke, had become allies of the local Black community in trying to combat racial injustice. They came from parts of the country that had been desegregated before the 1960s. When Northern Duke students came to Durham and saw segregated facilities in the era before the Civil Rights Act and saw that Duke itself had no Black students, many of them found this to be an injustice that was clearly unacceptable.

During the protests, sit-ins, and lunch counter boycotts of that era, Duke students and faculty had worked hand in hand with the local Black population to eliminate the injustice of segregation. Duke students had taken an active role in the struggle to integrate public facilities in the early 1960s, such as the Carolina Theater and the local Woolworth's restaurant. At the Woolworth's sit-in, which actually originated in Greensboro in 1960 but quickly spread throughout the area, Dr. King himself had shown up at the White Rock Baptist Church in Durham to speak to a crowd of a thousand people. Both White and Black people heard King's call: "Let us not fear going to jail if the officials threaten to arrest us for standing up for our rights."[15] He publicly acknowledged the importance of college students (many of them from Duke): "What is new in your fight is the fact that it was initiated, fed, and sustained by students."[16]

But the university itself persisted in segregation into the early 1960s, even as Duke students and faculty participated in civil rights protests outside the university. Duke was segregated in a manner typical of most Southern universities. Its hospital had segregated wards and separate lobbies (activist Howard Fuller remembers having to sit in the segregated lobby in 1965). The chapel had segregated wings; Blacks were only permitted to sit in the South transept, and Blacks were not permitted to preach or lead religious services in the chapel. The football stadium had a separate section at the corner of the end zone. The Duke golf course did not allow Black golfers, and they were not permitted to see basketball games at Cameron Indoor Stadium (a local Black coach asked to see a game and was told he could attend if he dressed as a waiter). At Page Auditorium, Blacks sat in a restricted mezzanine area.

Duke's treatment of Black employees was even worse. In 1964, of 1,666 officials and managers, only seven were Black, while of 1,230 laborers and service workers, 1,059 (86 percent) were Black. Prior to Duke's actual integration, according to Oliver Harvey, Black workers were treated as less than humans. "I never worked at a place as bad or as racist. You talk about slavery, it was absolutely so at Duke, because people almost had to beg to keep their jobs when they were the least little bit aggressive."[17] In 1965, Duke's typical wages for service employees were eighty-five cents per hour, well below the federal minimum of $1.25. They had no holidays or sick leave and could be asked to work more than forty hours a week at no additional pay at their manager's discretion. They had no job security even if they had worked there for ten or twenty years.

So, even as Duke faculty and students participated in civil rights activities off campus, the University itself lagged behind in integration. In 1960 and 1961, as lunch counter sit-ins and protests were occurring throughout the area, the new Duke president Daryl Hart—realizing that change was now inevitable and that Duke was clearly in danger of losing its leadership position—tried again to integrate the school. And this time, he had an even stronger argument; Duke, like other segregated schools of the time, was now in danger of losing its federal funding, due to requirements in new civil rights legislation, which was a large part of its revenue. The president presented the trustees with a report which recommended desegregation primarily for this reason, and *deliberately* omitted any mention of the obvious injustice of the racial situation, assuming that the trustees would never admit it. Finally, in 1961, facing loss of much of the university's federal funding, the trustees relented, and admitted Black graduate students to Duke in 1962. Undergraduates were admitted a year later in 1963, a few months after an all-White Duke basketball team had lost to a largely Black Loyola of Chicago team in the NCAA Final Four. After a nearly *fifteen-year* struggle, the Duke trustees had finally capitulated.

The first Black students to attend Duke in 1963 were Gene Kendall, Mary Mitchell Harris, Wilhelmina Reuben-Cooke, Nathaniel White Jr., and Cassandra Rush Smith. Harris and White, like the three first students at UNC, were also Hillside graduates; Harris had been valedictorian. All of them went on to have exemplary careers; Kendall went on to be a rear admiral in the Navy, while White went on to be president of Hayti Development Corporation. They knew they were pioneers: Reuben-Cooke stated years later, "Our perception was that people would make decisions about a whole race of people based on how we performed and what we did."[18]

Unfortunately, these pioneers received the same treatment at Duke University as did its Black employees. It admitted only five Black students in 1963, eleven in 1964, and fourteen in 1965 out of a student body of five thousand. According to Black student Bertie Howard, her freshman English teacher "would be surprised when I wrote a good paper, but would never find a reason to give me an A."[19] The first Black basketball player at Duke, C. B. Claiborne, and three of his fellow Black students took an engineering class and asked for clarification, because they wanted to get an A on an assignment. The White professor stated, "Don't worry, you won't get an A".[20] William Turner actually turned in a paper from a White student that had previously gotten an A, and received a C. Between 1966 and 1968, nearly half of the Black students at Duke left after just one or two semesters. When the Duke band played Dixie, Nathaniel White noted that it was "practically the national anthem because everyone would stand up and sing along. People went wild over that song."[21] The confederate flag was also displayed at Duke events; some Black students returned to their dorm rooms to find confederate flags on the doors with "n---- go home" written on the door. In the time preceding the 1966 Final Four game, Duke University had done *very little* to endear itself to the Black community of Durham, despite the civil rights activities of some of the faculty and students.

After Duke finally decided to desegregate, Duke students and faculty participated in massive demonstrations at Howard Johnson's in 1963 where four thousand people came out to demonstrate against segregation in Durham public facilities. My mother, a Duke faculty wife, wrote in 1964 about the demonstrations at Howard Johnson's.

> *In the summer of 1964, I and my family, including my mother-in-law, were eating lunch at Howard Johnson's on Chapel Hill Boulevard. We had all three children with us. As we were eating, a large group of black college students from the N.C. College, the black school in Durham, had gathered on the sloping front lawn and began to sing freedom songs. When a few tried to enter the restaurant to be served they were refused admittance. . . . I was also upset but because I knew that the students were right to demand access to public facilities and if I had been black, I would not have been sitting there enjoying a Sunday dinner.*[22]

Unlike many other parts of the South, the civil rights protests in Durham had been largely peaceful. Racial violence in that era primarily occurred in areas with large disparities in wealth. That was not the case in Durham. Durham had a large, educated, and prosperous elite on *both* sides of town. Durham, in the era after World War II, had been known as the capital of the Black middle class. The people at Duke and in the Black community near North Carolina College were not predisposed to violence. Consequently, most racial change in Durham had been accomplished relatively peacefully. When Dr. King spoke at Duke in Page Auditorium after the Civil Rights Act had passed in 1964, he said, "You can't legislate integration, but you can legislate desegregation; you can't change the heart, but you can restrain the heartless."[23]

The civil rights struggle had consumed the better part of ten years, from the late 1950s until the time of the 1966 game. Much of the Duke student body in that era had *not* especially endeared itself to the surrounding local White population in North Carolina, whose attitudes on race tended to be much more in line with the rest of the South. So Duke and Durham had a complex relationship with regard to racial issues; even as Duke students helped further civil rights activities *outside* the school, *inside* the school itself, the administration had treated Black students and employees very poorly, resulting in Duke University overall being not particularly well liked by the Black community of Durham.

But the changes that had come to Duke University had not yet come to the Duke varsity men's basketball team. In the few years prior to 1966, Duke had started being known for excellence in college basketball, but with teams that were all-White. In the years between 1985 to 2022, Duke Basketball, under head coach Mike Krzyzewski, became known as a top-quality program, producing top ranked and championship level teams on an annual basis. The words "Duke Basketball" today denote All-Americans, winning teams, national championships, the Cameron crazies, shoe company logos, and endless (and often annoying to the non-Duke supporters) appearances on television. It can be argued that, along with the University of North Carolina (that *other* program in Chapel Hill), the Duke program is probably the most successful college basketball program of the last three decades.

However, in 1966, that tradition of excellence had begun only a few years before. Duke had good teams in the 1950s, under coach Hal Bradley, but had never been considered a top basketball power. At that time, the Duke basketball teams were still pretty isolated from what was going on in the South. Duke basketball player Pete Moeller describes the situation in the '50s for players as being fairly disciplined and disconnected from external events off campus, something which was also true at the 1966 Final Four when the Duke players had little understanding of what was happening in North Carolina. He remembers life back then being simple: he went to class, went to practice, and studied a lot. He remembers Duke and North Carolina College having a close athletic relationship, especially in track and field. He was not all that aware of what was going on in the South around him.[24]

Under coach Vic Bubas, who became Duke basketball coach in 1959, the Duke Blue Devils were becoming a national basketball program. He built a program which was, from his first year in Durham, at or near the top of the Atlantic Coast Conference (ACC) for most of his time at Duke. He brought in dancing cheerleaders and started the Duke pep band (now famous for its TV appearances). He had his assistants tirelessly selling the program not only to recruits but also to the surrounding population, who were naturally more likely to cheer for the nearby state schools. He was a tireless promoter and innovator who worked hard to fill Duke's large and previously half-empty building, Duke Indoor Stadium—now the famous Cameron Indoor Stadium seen on hundreds of college basketball telecasts. When Adolph Rupp and Kentucky (who Duke was to play in the NCAA Final Four semifinal game in 1966) played at Duke right before Bubas's arrival, according to Moeller, Rupp famously told Duke that he would not be coming back because Duke had disrespected him by not selling out the stadium,[25] which, with its original capacity of 8,564, was the largest stadium south of Philadelphia when it opened in 1940, and still one of the larger ones at that time.

Bubas scoured the country for quality players, recruiting them from as far away as Montana, where he met 1966 Duke center Mike Lewis, after a very queasy plane ride across the mountains to a small airport. Lewis had previously turned down Adolph Rupp, stating that he didn't want to waste Rupp's time and money going that far from home, but Bubas sold him on going to Duke anyway. He recruited great players such as All-Americans Jeff Mullins (taking him from under Rupp's nose in Lexington) and Art Heyman (stealing him from North Carolina *and* Rupp). Duke was well represented on the all-ACC teams of that era as well, and Heyman had been Duke's first National Player of the Year in 1963. When Rupp recruited him, he told Heyman's mother that Art should come to play for the best basketball coach in the country. To which Heyman's Mom replied, "And who's that, dear?"[26] Duke, for the first time ever, made the Final Four, in 1963 and again in 1964, and played for the national championship in 1964, in the game that also kicked off UCLA's twelve year run of ten national championships. Duke finished in the top ten for six straight years. From 1961 to 1967, Bubas's teams had the best record in the nation: 159-37. Duke was good enough to be televised often on the local C.D. Chesley ACC game of the week in the 1960s, where the commercials for Pilot Life Insurance Company invited you to "Sail with the Pilot, at the wheel, on a ship serving from its mast to its keel."

Back in those days, there were no pro sports teams within about three hundred miles of the Triangle area. In addition, ACC football was—and still is—relatively weak. College basketball had the state pretty much to itself back then. The intensity locals felt about their college basketball teams in North Carolina in those days was truly remarkable. Back then, all four North Carolina ACC teams were pretty good, including NC State and Wake Forest—and some of the out-of-state ACC teams, such as South Carolina, were sometimes pretty good too. And of course, there was the perennial arch-rival North Carolina, only ten miles away, which produced unbelievably intense and competitive games then, much as they still are today.

All three major college basketball programs in the Triangle Area—Duke, North Carolina, and NC State—had great coaches that put all three on the national map before or at the time of the 1966 Final Four. NC State had great teams with Everett Case in the 1950s in its large, elongated stadium with extra seats on the end. The University of North Carolina had Frank McGuire in the 1950s and early 1960s, who had won the state's only national college basketball championship in 1957 with an undefeated team in triple overtime against Wilt Chamberlain, in what was (and remains today) the

The Bob Verga Shift

greatest sports story in the history of the state of North Carolina. Right before the 1966 game, they had just moved into their friendly new stadium, Carmichael Auditorium, which would be the scene of many happy Duke memories in the following nineteen years (Duke never beat Carolina in Carmichael at that time). And Duke had, as has been just mentioned, a great program with Vic Bubas starting in 1959. At that point, college basketball in Durham, and the rest of the triangle area, was basically the only game in town; the local college basketball teams were virtually unchallenged by anything else nearby for fan interest.

There was another factor that contributed to the popularity of college basketball in North Carolina (and also, not coincidentally, in Kentucky a few hundred miles away, which also had no professional sports teams then either). The weather in North Carolina during the winter is such that there is almost *nothing* to do outside between December and March. Usually, the temperatures in the region are in the thirties to forties range. It also rains *a lot*. So, it's usually cold enough to keep people from doing anything outside, but it's not cold enough to snow. There are almost no winter sports to divert interest away from basketball: no ice skating, no cross-country skiing, no hockey, almost nothing to do outside, away from the mountains. To a lesser extent, that is also true in Kentucky, where it is slightly colder but snows about the same amount. Therefore, not only were there no local pro sports in 1966, but almost nothing to do outside either. That being the case in both North Carolina and Kentucky, college basketball was almost the only thing happening, which was a main reason why it took such a hold of the populations there; it had their undivided attention during the winter.

When I was a kid in Durham back then, I lived and died with every Duke basketball game. When Duke lost (which wasn't often), it was sometimes an occasion for tears. But Duke usually won, giving me many childhood memories of great Duke victories. One particularly legendary victory occurred in 1968, when Duke beat Carolina in triple overtime. Duke player Fred Lind, having done almost nothing his entire career, came off the bench after center Mike Lewis had fouled out and won the game with sixteen points in triple overtime. He was then carried across West Campus on the shoulders of the students.

I hung out at Duke a lot back then. We had swimming lessons at the old pool on West Campus, which usually had too much chlorine in it, from a swimming coach named Jack Persons, who was the scariest guy to ever terrify a six- or seven-year-old kid in the water. When swimming was done, we kids hung out in Card Gym next door, where they had a jukebox. When you walk into a supermarket or hardware store today, a lot of the music you hear is from that era. But back then, it was all new. You could push B13 on the jukebox and hear "Walk Away Renee." Push C12 and hear "Happy Together." Or maybe a new Beatles song would be on it, so you would push D21 and hear "Yellow Submarine." And since Card was right next door to Cameron Indoor Stadium, occasionally one of our heroes on our beloved Duke basketball team would stroll through, eliciting awe from all the kids gathered around the jukebox.

We used to shoot baskets at Card Gym back then too. In those days, of course, we all dreamed of growing up to play for Duke, as a player from my high school, John Harrell, actually did, starting for the 1978 Duke Final Four team. But for me, that was never an ambition that I could ever seriously even think about. When I was seven years old, barely able to grip a leather ball, the last kid off the bench on my church league team, watching as the other kids ran past me on my skinny junk legs and bony knees, that was simply laughable. A movie about my basketball career would *not* have been "Glory Road". The extent of my basketball career was, "Okay kid, now there's a minute to go, we're ahead by twenty points. *Now* you can play. If by accident you get the ball, quick pass it before they foul you, because not only can you not dribble, you can't hit free throws either!" A few years later, I was also the last kid picked at Pete Maravich's basketball camp (where Harrell was the first). Pistol Pete could do things that I'd never seen anyone do: Throw the ball into the rafters and catch it behind his back. Hit you with no-look passes at full speed. Swish 'em from almost anywhere inside thirty feet. It was incredible. So instead I lived my childhood vicariously, worshipping the players on my beloved Blue Devil basketball team, knowing he could never remotely approach what the Duke players and Maravich did.

We kids were not usually disappointed by Duke basketball; in 1966, the team was loaded. The 1966 team would mark Bubas's fourth ACC championship and third (and last) Final Four appearance. Bubas thought it was better than the 1963 and 1964 Final Four teams: "That was our strongest team. I thought overall that was the toughest team to beat that we had."[27] It had three eventual All-Americans on it (two during the 1966 season), two future NBA players (one of them Jack Marin, a six-foot-seven forward and an excellent shooter who went on to a long career with the then NBA Baltimore Bullets (now Washington Wizards)), and three future ABA players, two of whom, burly 235 pound six-foot-eight center Mike Lewis and six-foot-one guard Bob Verga, were future ABA all-stars. Verga was an amazing shooter, who was both an NBA and ABA player (he was actually traded by the Kentucky Colonels of the ABA for none other than Pat Riley of Kentucky, who is a central figure in this book, after Verga was drafted in 1967) and who could score from almost anywhere. He was a clearly better shooter than 2010 NBA player and former Duke great J. J. Redick, with a career college field goal percentage of 49 percent versus Redick's 43 percent. Six-foot-six forward Bob Riedy, an excellent glue player on a team with four other main scorers, was the perfect complementary player to the other four, averaging almost ten points a game. The team was anchored by six-foot-one guard senior captain Steve Vacendak, also a future ABA player, famous for taking charges and diving for loose balls—when Bubas first met him, he saw him dive for loose balls on an *asphalt* court; Bubas asked him about it, and Vacendak said "That's the only way I know how to play."[28] In a tribute to his all-around toughness and hustle, he was named ACC Player of the Year in 1966 even though he had *not* been voted onto the All-ACC first team at his position. He was a personal favorite; I used to pretend to be Vacendak in the back yard when I shot baskets.

But like most of Duke, the Duke basketball team in 1966 was also all-White, as was almost all of the rest of the ACC. That was how it had been since Duke University began. The Duke staff of Vic Bubas, Bucky Waters, and Chuck Daly (future NBA championship coach with the Detroit Pistons) were just beginning the process of bringing in quality Black players to play for Duke. Its first Black player, C. B. Claiborne, had just joined the freshman team as a walk on. Claiborne himself was an outstanding student and had actually earned a national scholarship for academics; he went on to earn an engineering degree from Duke.

But recruiting Black players was not easy for Duke, for two reasons. First, back in those days, college basketball players were actual college students. They were expected to attend class, stay four years, and graduate. In addition, they were not eligible to play as freshmen; they had to play on special freshmen teams their first year on campus, the exact opposite of the current situation of one-and-done freshmen players. They were not the AAU rent-a-players seen today at Duke and Kentucky who spend little of their time in class but a very large amount of their time playing basketball and traveling. They had to meet the same academic standards as the rest of their classmates. Consequently, finding quality players of either race who could complete their classes and compete in the ACC was always a difficult task for Duke. The Duke recruiting pool back then was relatively small. That's why Vic Bubas had to cast such a wide national recruiting net to be successful; it was hard to find enough local players to go to Duke who were not going to go to other nearby schools with lower academic standards.

The second reason, of course, was that the tradition of Duke being a historically segregated campus in a historically segregated part of the country alienated potential quality Black players. Back then, when Duke played other Southern schools, there were racist fans that often abused Black players. Consequently, while the Duke staff was doing their best to integrate the program, they were having a hard time attracting Black players to come play for Duke.

As a result, in 1966, the Duke men's varsity basketball team was still all-White. So, when Duke was to compete in the NCAAs, the Duke program did not yet represent racial progress, as many other programs of the time did, which would ultimately have historical significance in the 1966 Final Four.

And so, this was Durham and Duke in 1966. A still largely segregated community, split into Black and White communities, with kids who attended separate, largely unequal schools. A world where Black and White children sometimes (but not often) played together. A world where tobacco still reigned supreme as the king of the local economy, and where college basketball was the only game in town. And a world that was just beginning the long process of becoming the national center of research excellence that it is today. That was the world we lived in back then, for better or worse. And that was the world in which the all-White Duke University men's basketball team played in 1966, as they played their way toward the fateful 1966 Final Four.

CHAPTER 2

KENTUCKY AND THE SEC IN 1966

Duke is just the first team of the three teams that would make history in the 1966 NCAA Final Four. The other two teams were the University of Kentucky and Texas Western (now University of Texas, El Paso). As we examine each of the three main protagonists in this drama, any one of whom could actually have been champion in 1966, we see that each of these programs had different social and political situations in which they operated, which greatly contributed to the significance of the Final Four games and the greatly differing social outcomes of the games, depending on who played. For Duke, the issue was that their program was located in a tobacco producing area experiencing significant racial change and unrest. For Kentucky basketball, the issue was that Kentucky still did not have any Black players, and that the team itself was also the leader of the still-segregated Southeastern Conference (SEC), which was what ultimately made the actual 1966 finals so significant.

Now, the overall social and economic context of Kentucky in 1966 was significantly different from the one in North Carolina. Kentucky had a diversified economy, featuring coal, manufacturing, horse raising, and also (some) tobacco. Kentucky overall was still economically behind much of the rest of the country after WWII, but in the decade before the game, it had started to catch up some. This gave Kentucky basketball a somewhat chippy attitude; the people in Kentucky back then had something of an inferiority complex compared to more advanced urban areas in the Northeast and Midwest. According to Michael Lindenberger, Kentucky college basketball was king—especially during the Great Depression, in an era of bad roads. poverty, and in many areas, deep isolation, where news of wins and losses were experienced like wartime reports from loved ones at the front. "The winning tradition in Lexington was the single most unifying force in the state."[1]

Kentucky in 1966 had a much smaller Black population than North Carolina, less than 10 percent of the state population, and most of it was concentrated in the cities. It did not form as much of an essential element of rural labor as it did in North Carolina and the rest of the Deep South. This introduced a significant difference in race relations between the two states. Kentucky did not possess as much of the combustible mix of economic dependency on low-paid Black labor and racist resentment that existed in North Carolina. The main difference between Kentucky and North Carolina was that in Kentucky, racism was a *cultural* issue, but in North Carolina it was an *economic* issue. This was why race relations in North Carolina had traditionally been much more openly contentious; the local economy had, for a very long time, depended on low-paid Black field and factory labor. Consequently, North Carolina was much more likely to experience significant racial disturbances as a result of a championship game between an all-White and all-Black team than was Kentucky.

Kentucky, like most of the Border South, had actually had a tradition of racism that actually extended back before the Civil War, during which Kentucky was neutral. Kentucky had Jim Crow laws requiring segregation of public facilities since the late nineteenth century until the 1950s, along with the states further south. Segregation in public accommodations was finally banned in Kentucky in 1961 a few years before the federal Civil Rights Act. The Kentucky Civil Rights Act, which passed in

1966, was the first passed by a state south of the Mason-Dixon line. It became a model for many other Southern states and was duly lauded by Dr. King at the time of its passage as being the strongest civil rights act passed by any Southern or border state. Civil rights activities in Kentucky were led by such pioneers as Georgia Davis Powers, who played a key role in enacting the Kentucky Civil Rights Act, and John Jay Johnson. Racism in Kentucky, though not completely woven into the entire economy the way it was in North Carolina, was still culturally prevalent in 1966 and very much a part of the way people at the University of Kentucky saw things.

University of Kentucky (UK) was, as it is now, the northernmost member of the SEC, the Southeast Conference, which was formed in 1932, during Adolph Rupp's third year as Kentucky's coach. The university is actually geographically closer to many of the Big Ten schools further north, such as Indiana University or University of Illinois, than it is to many of the Southern schools, such as University of Alabama or University of Mississippi. Big Ten schools had started integrating nearly fifty years before, around the beginning of the twentieth century, as much of the North had. If Kentucky had joined the Northern Conference instead of the SEC, it might have integrated much sooner. UK actually desegregated in 1954 (nine years before Duke and twelve years before the 1966 Final Four). In Kentucky, being a border state, the change had come fairly peacefully, unlike at universities further south where the change had been often accompanied by violence. The first Black graduate student, Lyman T. Johnson, had enrolled there in 1949, after winning a lawsuit. In 1954, after the Brown vs. Board of Education case, the main campus was integrated, helped by future Senator Mitch McConnell's mentor, future Senator John Sherman Cooper. Like most Southern and border schools of that time, that had only been done with difficulty and through considerable legal challenges, but it had finally been accomplished. But UK was still an almost all-White school in 1966, with only a handful of Black students at the time of the 1966 Final Four.

In 1966, twelve years after Black students first appeared at University of Kentucky, there were still none on the UK basketball team. And this was clearly noticeable as well; Kentucky at that time played many Northern teams in Lexington with good Black players who clearly had superior athletic skills. So their exclusion from the UK team was becoming more and more obvious; it was clear that including them would significantly improve the team, as it did for the teams that they played against. At the time, Black players were still being excluded from the SEC, which was typical of Southern and border schools back then. This was to change in 1967, largely as a result of the 1966 Final Four. But UK was not willing to be the first team in the SEC to include Black students when the Deep South teams in the conference were still actively resisting it.

One Deep South SEC team, Mississippi State, had even gone so far as to refuse three NCAA bids in 1959, 1961, and 1962 because the state didn't want their team even *playing* Black players. In fact, the team that had taken their place to represent the SEC had been Kentucky, the SEC runner-up each of those three years. Mississippi State first team All-America forward Bailey Howell, who went on to become an NBA Hall of Famer, earning six NBA All Star appearances and two NBA championships against such Black players as Oscar Robertson, Bill Russell (he was a Russell teammate for his titles), and Wilt Chamberlain was bitterly disappointed that his own racist state government took away his only chance as a White player to compete against outside competition in the year 1959. Howell graciously hid his disappointment, saying years later, "Back then, you did what you were told. . . . But what's disappointing is we didn't get to see how good we really were."[2] Mississippi State did not go to the tournament even though the students had voted by nearly a 6-1 margin for the team to attend. But this shows how Deep South schools in the SEC saw integration of basketball teams in that era; the racism of that era had a huge negative impact on the White players too.

One player on the 1962 Mississippi State team, Dan Gold, went to Iowa City to see Kentucky play in the NCAAs in their place. According to Gold, "That's the first time I really understood. We could have been there. We deserved to be there."[3] Doug Hutton, another Mississippi State player that year, thinking of how he could have played against Big Ten champion Ohio State with great players such as John Havlicek, Jerry Lucas, and Bobby Knight, said "When we saw who Kentucky was playing, I'm sure we all thought, *Boy, what a treat that would be, to see how good we were compared to them.*"[4]

Mississippi State finally played in the NCAA tournament in 1963, after the first Black students had enrolled at Old Miss. The governor, Ross Barnett, a known racist, had stated that he was against the team going; however, the university board of regents voted to let them go anyway. A Mississippi state senator obtained an injunction forbidding them from leaving the state to play the game, but the Mississippi dean of students and the Mississippi state coach got wind of it and snuck across the state line the night before the summons was to be served. Not knowing if the summons mentioned the team, Coach James McCarthy, sent out a team of scrubs and managers to the airport in case they were met with the summons there, with the main team scheduled to drive across the state to Columbus if the team was mentioned. As it turned out, the summons mentioned only the coach and the dean, who were already gone, so the players got on the plane and finally got to play in the NCAAs the last year they were SEC champions. They lost to Chicago Loyola (with four Black starters, who also played an all-White Duke team in the NCAAs that year) in the regional semifinals in the famous so-called "Game of Change."

By 1966, twelve years after the University of Kentucky was integrated, the SEC and Kentucky still did not have integrated teams. The Kentucky coach in 1966, the defacto leader of SEC basketball, was Adolph Rupp, "The Baron of the Bluegrass." Rupp was one of the greatest college basketball coaches of all time. He started coaching in 1930 and coached for forty-two years. When he retired in 1972, he had the record for the most wins of all time by a coach, 876, with a lifetime winning percentage of better than 80 percent. He won four NCAA championships, all in the 1940s and '50s, two more than anyone else at the time of the 1966 Final Four, (the UCLA dynasty, which was soon to surpass him, had just started in the two years prior to 1966) and a couple of Helms national championships too. His teams were very successful, year after year, winning nearly two-thirds of all SEC championships during his tenure, a total of twenty-seven in all, making them the standard bearer for the conference, and consistently finishing in the top eight nationally even when they were not national champions. Rupp was famous for being able to win with virtually any group or size or players. After thirty-five years of winning, Adolph Rupp was viewed as a virtual deity in Kentucky; the stadium at University of Kentucky, Rupp Arena, is named after him.

Rupp himself played a huge role in making college basketball into a national sport. When he first started in the game in the 1920s (his coach at Kansas, Phog Allen, was taught the game by James Naismith himself), basketball was considered a minor sport, not anywhere on a par with baseball or even football, which was then becoming popular. But Rupp decided he was going to help change that. He had no doubts as to his abilities even then. When Rupp, then a twenty-nine-year-old high school coach, interviewed for the University of Kentucky job, he was asked why he should be hired. "Because I'm the best damned basketball coach in the nation," Rupp replied.[5]

In the subsequent forty years, he would prove what he said was true. Rupp started at Kentucky as a young coach at the beginning of the Great Depression in 1930. He worked tirelessly to promote the game in his first ten years and succeeded effectively. In 1930, college games were written up in the papers as mere afterthoughts, but by 1941, Rupp had turned his Kentucky program and college basketball games into significant media events. Rupp worked on making the game appealing to fans by playing entertaining, up-tempo basketball. Many teams back then played a slower, rougher, less exciting style; they still had jump balls after every made basket until 1936. His fast-paced teams scored far above the average and won consistently. He was famous for his hard practices; his players hated and feared him when they played for him and loved him later on.

The era after World War II was the golden age of Rupp and Kentucky basketball, when he won three of his four championships in 1948, 1949, and 1951. (This was also an era where Kentucky was involved in some significant gambling scandals involving point shaving as well.) Rupp, along with Hank Iba (who coached Texas Western coach Don Haskins, described in the next chapter), played a huge role in the transformation of basketball into a major sport, as post-WWII America was booming. Rupp's success had forced Kentucky into building an eighty-five-hundred-seat facility in 1950, Memorial Coliseum, at a time when most of the other SEC schools played in small, bandbox size twenty-five-hundred-seat gyms. He was essentially both the founder and the leader of Big Blue Nation—the term for the Kentucky basketball community. Over thirty-five years of tireless work at Kentucky, Rupp had changed a minor college sport into a nationally played game, with a large media following. In a very real sense, college basketball, the way we see it now, *is* Adolph Rupp's invention.

By 1966, two generations of Kentucky fans had grown up with him. At the time of the 1966 game, he had built the most successful program of all time. His stature in the coaching community then was similar to what Duke coach Mike Krzyzewski's is today, if not greater. And as he built his program into a legend, he made sure that *he* was the program, not the players; more than any other coach in the country, Adolph Rupp was Kentucky basketball. He knew virtually every state leader and all the local media, and they understood the importance of being his friend. The media and the people in Kentucky accepted Rupp's word about virtually anything, which was to prove of considerable significance after the 1966 title game. As a later Kentucky coach Tubby Smith said in 1997, twenty years after Rupp's death, "I think people look at the Kentucky coach and they think that he's some idol figure."[6]

It was even more true when Rupp was alive and still coaching; Kentucky viewed Rupp as almost a deity back then, and Rupp was clearly happy to be treated that way. Home games were programmed to feed Rupp's ego. At the beginning of games, the Wildcat pep band would play the fight song. Then Rupp would walk out onto the floor alone to a deafening roar. It was expected that everyone would be on their feet as Rupp walked out in his trademark brown suit and waved to the crowd, and then the coliseum would go black as the spotlight trained on the American flag. Rupp was the undisputed king of Kentucky.

Back then, in places like Kentucky and West Virginia, the basketball coach essentially represented the entire state. When 1966 Duke coach Vic Bubas's assistant Bucky Waters became the coach at West Virginia University in 1965, he was told that he represented the aspirations of the entire state. At that time, the Mountaineers had produced players such as Jerry West and Rod Hundley and were nearly on a par with Kentucky. Waters was told that when miners were hurt in disasters that he was expected to go visit them, on behalf of the whole state of West Virginia.

That was what things were like in Kentucky, where Rupp's stature was far greater than that of Waters. Rupp had been in Lexington for thirty-six years at the time of the 1966 game, and he fit in well with what Lexington had been like for a long time. Prior to the mid-1950s, Lexington was a relatively sleepy backwater college town. It was primarily an agricultural and horse raising area with fairly rigid class and race distinctions. Although

Lexington's agricultural economy was not primarily supported by Black labor, most Blacks worked in lower-class service industries. It moved at a slow pace. It had very conservative fundamentalist religious values. So, during most of Adolph Rupp's reign in Lexington, he and Lexington were in agreement on many issues. Most of Rupp's championships, in the late '40s and early '50s, had occurred before Lexington had started becoming more modern.

But by 1956, Lexington had begun to change. New industry was moving into the community. IBM, Trane, Square D, and other companies moved in. A new medical center was built, along with housing developments, shopping centers, and apartments. New people and new jobs were coming in. A bypass was built around the town. What was once a sleepy backwater town was being transformed into a much more modern, fast-paced community, one which was changing significantly from the world Adolph Rupp had ruled for nearly three decades.

Unfortunately, Adolph Rupp was not changing with the times. As one of his players said, "He wanted to do the same thing every game".[7] It is important to recognize that the mid-1960s were precisely an era where change was occurring rapidly in many areas. As 1966 Kentucky player Larry Conley said, "It was such a chaotic time. Things were just changing all over the place."[8] There were changing attitudes on sex, music, drugs, government, the military (1966 was the beginning of the Vietnam protests), religion, and other values. Lexington was a relatively neutral campus compared to others, like Berkeley and University of Michigan. Lexington didn't have any anti-Vietnam protests until the Kent State shootings in 1970. At the time of the 1966 game, the first large-scale, national Vietnam protests were only a couple of weeks away.

In college basketball, Black players were making inroads at programs throughout the country and were starting to dominate in many areas. According to sports historian Lane Demas, the change in basketball from a more structured, coach-controlled, play-diagrammed type of game—which Rupp favored—to a more individualistic free flowing game in which the players made more decisions, was part of a general rebellion against authority in that era.[9] The Black style of play gave the players much more individual freedom and control on the court than in Rupp's old-fashioned, coach-controlled diagrammed approach.

The game was changing, but Rupp was not. In 1966, it had been eight years since Rupp's last NCAA championship. He was still considered a top coach, actually being voted National Coach of the Year, which he clearly earned by taking a team with no one taller than six-foot-five on the starting team to the Final Four. His teams still performed at a high level, but his program had faded some from its 1940s and 1950s peak. The 1966 team would be the last one Rupp ever took to the Final Four. Dave Kindred of the *Lexington Herald* noted how much Rupp wanted to win the 1966 national championship. "He was 64 years old. He might never get that close again. He loved that team, 'Rupp's Runts.'"[10]

The '66 game would, in fact, be Kentucky's last Final Four appearance until 1975, after Rupp had retired. In 1966, when Kentucky played non-SEC (and non-ACC) teams, there were often Black players on them. Kentucky usually played well against them, but they didn't always win. It was becoming clear that in order to compete in college basketball at the highest level, it was necessary to have quality Black players participate. Kentucky, like Duke, was about to be completely overshadowed during the peak of the Wooden-UCLA era, which prominently featured Black players (apparently adequately compensated by Mr. Sam Gilbert after 1967). Rupp himself famously pointed it out when he saw Duke and Kentucky near the top of the AP basketball polls in 1966. He told his players to take a long, hard look at the rankings. "One. Two. Three. Kentucky, Duke, Vanderbilt. All from the South. And all white. Read it and remember. You'll never see it happen again."[11] He was right. It would never happen again.

By 1966, Rupp had been coaching Kentucky for more than thirty-five years. Rupp had always mostly focused on basketball; he didn't pay all that much attention to the things going on around him. He was at an age where most people are set in their ways and not particularly open to changing their minds. His views had originated forty or fifty years before in a different time, and were typical of people from an earlier era, as had been the trustees of Duke University. Rupp had been immersed in the culture of Southern racism for a long time and had, not surprisingly, come to think like many of his colleagues further south.

Rupp, like many people his age, did not accept many of the changes going on around him, as they threatened his world and his world view. Rupp was known for being a solitary and stubborn person. According to Cawood Ledford, the longtime Kentucky broadcaster, "I don't think he had a close friend."[12] He kept his own opinion of things, regardless of what other people thought; he didn't change his mind because everyone else did. He was used to being hated because his teams won so much, so it didn't bother him like it would have someone else. He knew he had plenty of enemies, once saying, "I'd rather be the most hated winning coach in the country than the most popular losing one."[13] At that point he may have been the most respected man in Kentucky and had a very large ego. His attitude and social stature in Kentucky made him more immune to the change going on around him than he would have been otherwise.

But by 1966, college basketball was changing. While having once been an innovator and leader, Rupp didn't embrace the change in racial participation in basketball and the corresponding differences in playing style. Rupp actively resisted the changes that actually might have made his program better, which to other observers were clearly necessary in order to compete with integrated programs. His attitude toward recruiting was that *he* was making the choice, not the recruit—assuming that recruits wanted to go to Kentucky. He visited prospective Black players grudgingly, made little attempt to pitch his team to them, and mostly avoided dealing with them at all. He made little attempt to recruit players at the local Black high school, Louisville Dunbar, even though it was a known regional powerhouse with quality players. Jimmy Breslin, the New York columnist, stated that in the early 1960s, Rupp had asked him to kindly indicate Black high school players with an asterisk in his articles, so Rupp would know where *not* to send his recruiters.[14]

In 1966, Rupp was also getting old: he was sixty-four, with numerous medical ailments, so recruiting itself had become a chore. He had back problems, high blood pressure, diabetes, vision problems, and problems with his feet. His frequent bouts of anger caused him to be hospitalized several times. Rupp avoided traveling any distances when he could; he found climbing in and out of private planes and staying overnight in places where he couldn't sleep well wore him out. For Rupp, travel itself was hard enough. Having to travel with Black players on his team and deal with the racist abuse of the Southern fans would have been a huge headache, which he didn't want to deal with at his age.

Rupp was also known for watching recruiting budgets. On one trip, he decided to show Joe B. Hall how to reduce meal expenses, so he took a recruit out to dinner with him. Rupp ordered spaghetti and meatballs; the recruit, well over six feet tall, at the waiter's instigation, ordered a large steak *and* a rainbow trout, the two most expensive items on the menu, leaving Hall splitting his sides with laughter as they drove away.

Hall denies that Rupp was actually a racist. According to Hall, who knew Rupp more than thirty years, "I never once heard him be intolerant of anyone based only on that person's color, ethnicity, or religion."[15] In Rupp's defense, he consistently pointed out that there were legitimate safety issues with taking his players on the road in the SEC during the 1950s and early 1960s, before the Civil Rights Act had been passed. Having Black players on his teams would have made travel in the SEC considerably more difficult, and sometimes even dangerous, as many of the teams were in the Deep South where travel was segregated until the mid-1960s, requiring separate accommodations for Black players. Rupp also prided himself on how much his teams were hated as a measure of how successful they were, but he knew that it also created an additional safety issue for potential Black players on his team. Dick Gabriel, the sports manager for WKYT-TV in Lexington said, "[Rupp] said, 'Imagine what it's going to be like when we go down there with a black player who can't stay at the hotel where we stay, can't eat at the restaurants we eat?'"[16] Rupp knew how hard it would be to be the first Black player in the SEC to deal with racial issues further south, and this contributed to how particular he was in recruiting anyone (preferably a superstar) to do it.

And Rupp was clearly right about the situation. When the Loyola of Chicago team, which was mostly Black, visited New Orleans in 1962, one team member remembers trying to get into a cab with two other Black players and their White coach, George Ireland, the driver refused to take Ireland in his cab designated with a sign for colored people when he got into it at the airport. Ireland offered to pay the fine that the driver was worried about, but the driver refused. "No sir, you will not, I'll go to jail. I cannot drive you."[17] This was the sort of thing Black teams dealt with routinely when they played teams further south in the early 1960s. One of the Loyola players, Ron Miller wrote about that era fifty years later, reflecting on how the Founding Fathers had supported slavery and how many people never got their chances to participate in so many things because they were Black. "How could it have been like that? It almost doesn't seem real. How could it have been that bad?"[18]

It is possible that if Kentucky were not a member of the SEC that it might have integrated earlier than 1966. Rupp had been taking teams to the Deep South since the 1930s when there were still lynchings and was well aware of the attitude of most White Southerners back then. Other non-Southern teams with Black players were often unwilling to schedule games against Southern opponents before the mid-1960s, as they had to deal with both Jim Crow segregation and hostile fans. Fans in the stands often yelled racial epithets and threw ice and trash at the Black players. The Black players in the South received hate mail and death threats. Since there were at that time no Black players in the rest of the SEC, the first Black player at Kentucky would have to carry the burden of being the first in the entire conference to play in places like Alabama and Mississippi. And *that* was a very legitimate issue.

That role would require someone with a remarkable amount of toughness and self-control. As Dodgers owner Branch Rickey famously said to Jackie Robinson in 1947, "What I don't know is whether you have the guts. I'm looking for a ballplayer with guts enough *not* to fight back."[19] To have asked a potential recruit, like six-foot-seven, 240-pound Wes Unseld, to endure racist heckling in the SEC without retaliating, when he could have easily taken a courtside taunter and stuffed him into the nearest trash can, would indeed have been a tall order. Most Black players Rupp was recruiting, including Unseld knew what it would be like to be the first Black player in the SEC, and they didn't want to deal with it either.

The first Black player in the SEC, Perry Wallace, in the season after the 1966 Final Four, did not find it easy going. And there was no doubt about safety issues when his team traveled further south. James Meredith, the first person to integrate at the University of Mississippi, had actually been shot a few months after the 1966 Final Four, while starting a solo 270-mile walk that launched the civil rights demonstration March Against Fear. Wallace found the going in the South to be quite scary. The crowds would scream racist slurs and make verbal threats, hoping to intimidate them into defeat. In his first visit to Mississippi as a freshman, the fall after the 1966 game, Wallace remembered racist fans not only screaming insults but threatening to kill them. "Here they were, all these Mississippi bigots, so loud and so close, and it was harsh."[20] Hall described "the fears he [Wallace] had of being shot on the court or on the street. He tells about the death threats that were sent to his family."[21]

Joe B. Hall, known for being a good recruiter of Black players, had little success when recruits realized what they would have to deal with when they traveled further south. Prospect Cozell Walker told him he was not interested in pioneering the integration of the South. "I don't mind playing for Kentucky because I am from Kentucky, but I do not want to play in segregated places."[22] Hall had no success in the Rupp era recruiting Black players for Kentucky, even though he had them on all of his previous teams and had former Black players he had coached calling recruits for him. And much of it was clearly due to the racism of the rest of the SEC, not just Rupp. Northern coaches would tell potential Black recruits that if they played for Kentucky, they'd be going on the floor in Alabama, Louisiana, Mississippi, and Georgia, but if they came with them, they'd be going on the floor in Minnesota, Michigan, and Iowa.

So Rupp had been correct about the situation in the pre-Civil Rights Act South, where most of the SEC teams Kentucky played were located—it really had been that bad. And as Wallace showed a year later, it was still bad in 1966. But by 1966, racial barriers were coming down, and Blacks were starting to travel more easily in the South. Many were also hopeful that if Kentucky integrated first, being the northernmost school and the school with the best program, the rest of the conference and the South would have to follow. Butch Beard, Mr. Kentucky Basketball for 1965, said "They wanted Kentucky to be the first to integrate the SEC. They said if Adolph did it, everybody would."[23]

By 1966, teams in nearby Northern states that Kentucky frequently played had Black players, so the people in Kentucky were aware that the change was coming. And it was also clear that many of these players, such as Cazzie Russell at Michigan or

Oscar Robertson at nearby University of Cincinnati, were clearly better than the White players on the Kentucky team. There were meetings with local community leaders about getting Black players at Kentucky. And there had been petitions about it too.

In March 1964, the Lexington Committee on Religious and Human Rights had a meeting with Coach Rupp, bringing with them 150 letters urging him to integrate the team. But by 1965, there had been no action on it. In December 1965, Governor Ned Breathitt gave an order that there should be an all-out effort to desegregate the teams. The football team started playing two Black players in 1966: Nat Northington and Greg Page. Tragically, Page was killed at a Kentucky football practice when all the other players piled on him. Northington's mother, knowing the dangers of playing further south, told the coach, "If I find that his life is in danger by playing football in the Southern states, I will be forced to take action to haul him somewhere else where he won't be abused."[24]

Rupp did not adequately address the Black basketball players' parents' concerns either. According to Hall, concerned parents wanted reassurance that coaches would look after and protect their sons, and Rupp did not present the image of a caring father or kind grandfather "I don't think they got that feeling from talking with Coach Rupp."[25] Perry Wallace decided not to go to Kentucky when Rupp did not take the trouble to meet him personally.

Rupp's position also put him squarely against John Oswald, the university president. From 1963 to 1966, Oswald and Rupp clashed on the subject repeatedly. Oswald had heard that Rupp had called him a n----- lover. Rupp, after his first meeting with Oswald, said, "That son of a bitch is ordering me to get some n------ in here. What am I going to do?"[26] The university president, who was determined to integrate the program, pushed Rupp tirelessly to do something about it, having had meetings and issued demands, memos, and indirect pressure. Oswald hired Joe

B. Hall specifically to recruit Black players. He sent assistants on recruiting trips. Oswald even had Governor Breathitt helping out with recruiting Black players.

Oswald told Rupp that his lack of recruiting Black players was jeopardizing Kentucky getting $11 million in federal money. According to Rupp, Oswald said, demanding that Rupp get some Black players, "If we don't get this through, it's because basketball is the last segregated department that we have here in the university."[27] This was the same reason that the Duke board of trustees eventually capitulated to integration a few years earlier; they didn't want to lose their federal funding.

So even when urged by the governor of Kentucky and Oswald to do so, Rupp wouldn't make an attempt to seriously recruit local Black players (like Beard and Wes Unseld, who wound up together at nearby Louisville). It was simply too much trouble for him. He made only a grudging visit to Unseld (who was also personally visited by Oswald; Unseld was Mr. Kentucky Basketball for 1964), who was being pursued by one hundred schools. Unseld was a six-foot-seven future NBA Hall of Famer, picked number two in the 1968 NBA draft, and built like a block of granite. I remember watching Unseld's crushing picks, brutal rebounding, and incredible outlet passes in the NBA.

Some players, especially big men, are average in college, but blossom later in the pros. Not Unseld. He was a great player in both. Had he gone to Kentucky, instead of in-state rival Louisville, he might decisively have turned the outcome of the 1966 title game in Kentucky's favor by guarding Texas Western's taller front line. (He also might have even broken the arms of some of the Texas Western players blocking their dunk attempts!) According to Greg Hoard, a long-time sportswriter Unseld was the most impressive collegiate player he ever saw. Unseld had learned the game on Louisville's west side community centers, with chain nets and black top courts. He was a master of the outlet pass, turning in mid-air to throw passes to his fast-breaking teammates, and was able to throw a two-hand chest pass the length of the court. He was powerful and merciless when rebounding, but his intensity was reserved for the game alone. "His play was ferocious, but there was no rage in what he did on the court, just perfection and dominance."[28] This indeed was the player that could have helped win the national championship for Kentucky in 1966.

In his sophomore year, Larry Conley tried to get Wes to come to Kentucky: "Wes would have been an ideal guy to break the color line. He was such a class guy. A tremendous player."[29] Unseld told Conley that he didn't want to be the first. According to Louisville coach John Dromo, who was hiding in the kitchen when Rupp visited Unseld, Rupp wanted Unseld to be his first Black player, and Unseld's response was, "I don't want to be your first black player. I just want to be a basketball player."[30] Unseld also felt that, with as much power as he had, if Rupp had wanted to, he could have made it happen long before he made his lame attempt to recruit him. According to Unseld, "They never seriously recruited me, and those who say they did are not dealing with the facts."[31]

Rupp's attitude was in sharp contrast to the prevailing one with Dromo at nearby Louisville—where Beard and Unseld both wound up—which integrated in 1962. According to Perry Wallace, the first Black SEC player, "Whatever Louisville had been about in the past, it enthusiastically recruited those guys."[32] Beard had also gone to Louisville after concluding Rupp's efforts were mostly in response to Oswald. Oswald had Pat Riley escort Butch Beard (Mr. Kentucky basketball for 1965) around campus. According to Beard, Kentucky alums came by to visit his home practically every day his senior year. According to Beard, "We decided that Rupp was under pressure to recruit a black player but he didn't really want one."[33]

And so, the efforts of Oswald and the rest of the University of Kentucky were all to no avail. Oswald has actually been accused of tokenism by some more recent sources; he was more interested in having at least one Black player on the team for show than seriously integrating the program. According to Rupp, Oswald told him to get someone and just park him on the bench. Rupp refused. "I'm not going to put some kid on the end of the bench and hurt his feelings and his parents' feeling just so we can have a token."[34] He insisted that he always recruited guys who could really play. He always had excuses for why Kentucky couldn't get this or that player; it had to be a superstar, or he was going to sit on the bench, or he wasn't academically qualified, or he couldn't take them to Deep South schools, or some other reason would come up. Rupp said "So far we haven't found a boy who meets our scholastic qualifications. It's got to be a Kentucky boy or from a neighbor state."[35]

Even after the football team was integrated in 1965, Rupp *still* wasn't actively recruiting Black players. Rupp continually claimed he was unbiased, but the evidence contradicted him. According to Robert L. Johnson, a former head of athletics at Kentucky, "I think the feeling among a lot of people at the university was that Adolph was a racist who was never going to bring blacks onto the team."[36] Coaches who went to Rupp's summer school saw it that way too. In unguarded moments years later after he had been drinking, Rupp was once heard to say, "The trouble with the ABA is that there are too many n----- boys in it."[37] We'll never know for sure whether the predominant reason for his intransigence was the incredible difficulty of integrating the SEC, or whether Rupp was simply a racist. In the end, it was probably a combination of both.

That is what ultimately gave the 1966 title game such racial significance; Rupp had been so brazen about denying Black players the chance to play and fought so many university officials about it for so many years, that by 1966 he had become famous for it. In the end, Rupp and the SEC's eventual humiliation in the 1966 game was the fault of both himself and the conference. Having resisted almost *every* possible plea to integrate the program, they had no one to blame but themselves. By not seriously recruiting Unseld, he eventually gave his 1966 team little chance to win against Texas Western's taller, more athletic frontline. There could have been no more perfect foil for Texas Western than Rupp.

It wasn't until 1970 that Kentucky played its first Black player—three years after Black students at Kentucky had demonstrated against Rupp to get Black players—a seven-footer named Tom Payne, who Rupp had recruited grudgingly; the signing ceremony was singularly uncomfortable. Tom Payne played one year for Kentucky before turning pro near the end of Rupp's career.[38] In a final irony, Rupp lost his last game in 1972 to a team that had recruited two Black players from Louisville. At that point, he was seventy years old, and with his teams fading, was forced to retire by the mandatory university requirement.

When examining the 1966 Kentucky basketball team, the all-White composition of the team was historically the most significant aspect of it. But there was another aspect of the 1966 Kentucky basketball team that was also significant: it was quite short. There were no players taller than six-foot-five on the starting team. That is indeed very short for a college basketball team. They went by the nickname Rupp's Runts. Considered to be too small and having had a mediocre 15–10 record the season before, unusual for a Rupp team (the worst in his thirty years at the school), and having lost two of their best players, they had come into the season unranked. Contrary to legend, Kentucky did have one sizable player on the team in six-foot-eight, 230-pound Cliff Berger, who had a pretty good mid-range jump shot. He played significant minutes against Duke's Mike Lewis, a similar sized player in the semifinals, and often played significant minutes against bigger teams (he played in the championship game against Texas Western as well). However, lacking Lewis's better athletic skills, he was simply too slow to play many minutes on the Kentucky team under most conditions; he didn't fit into their style. Rupp always forced his players to compete for their positions. So Thad Jaracz, at six-five, both very tough and an excellent fast break player, beat out Berger to become the starting Kentucky center.

Surprisingly enough, despite their lack of size, they were still a successful team that year, as Rupp's teams usually were. Rupp was known for having very hard practices. In addition, he was also famous for his insistence that players successfully execute fundamentals properly, something that is not always done today. He would force his players to practice them over and over again until they were done correctly. And his practices paid off. His team shot and moved the ball extremely well, ran a disciplined offense, and worked hard on defense. The team had bonded by playing extensively together over the summer in Lexington pickup games, and also did weight training and running together, under a new conditioning program developed by Rupp assistant Joe B. Hall, a former player on one of Rupp's national championship teams. According to Hall, the Runts biggest asset was their unselfishness and teamwork, how well they passed the ball. "They developed into one of the most unified forces that shared the ball unselfishly and devoted themselves to winning the game."[39] "[They were] unselfish, good ballhandlers, good shooters, good on the run," writes Dave Kindred in the book *The Final Four*, "the very model of great Kentucky teams."[40] Rupp himself said that they were his all-time favorite team.

They managed to compensate for their lack of size with hustle, determination, and hard work. Kentucky had played multiple opponents with quality Black players, and they had successfully defeated all but one, including teams with considerably taller centers. They ran the floor well, and played an up-tempo game in which they attempted to outrun their opponents and score before their larger opponents could get back on defense. In fact, their offense was so good that they set the Kentucky scoring average record of eighty-seven points a game (done in an era without a shot clock *or* the three-point shot!). Player Larry Conley attributed their success to their quickness and ball handling; if the other teams didn't have guys who could guard them, they just went by them; they never slowed down. "We were very, very quick and a good team that really understood the game and how to play the game, the finesse and the skills needed to play at the height and size that we were."[41] They were good enough to beat good, bigger teams, including third ranked Vanderbilt with six-foot-ten All-American and reigning SEC player of the year Clyde Lee, in which they also outrebounded Vanderbilt 50-40. Vanderbilt's guard Keith Thomas said, "They shoot on the run and fire out on the court and they still wear out the net."[42] However, Kentucky's lack of size would play a crucial role in the outcome of the national championship game later that year, and in how people perceived it both in Kentucky and elsewhere.

There were five leading scorers on the Kentucky team: an athletic, hard playing swing guard/forward, six-foot-four Pat Riley; a six-foot point guard, Louie Dampier; six-five Thad Jaracz, a small forward who actually played center; another six-three guard, Larry Conley, who was an excellent passer; and six-five Tommy Kron, who was also a double figure scorer. Pat Riley went on to greater fame as an NBA coach and executive, where he won five NBA championships as a coach, and built two championship teams as general manager. Riley was an All-American in both football and basketball and had been recruited by legendary Alabama coach Bear Bryant to be his quarterback. They were a balanced team that moved the ball well; all five starters averaged double figures. Both Riley and Dampier were All-Americans. Rupp said Dampier was the finest college shooter he had seen in his thirty-six years of coaching. "He has a native basketball sense that a lot of players don't have."[43] Louie Dampier went on to have a very successful professional basketball career in the ABA, becoming the all-time leading ABA scorer and assist leader and leading the Kentucky Colonels to an ABA championship, although being only six feet tall. Larry Conley was not quite as good a player; however, after his college career ended, he went on to a very successful career as a basketball broadcaster for multiple networks, announcing more than eighteen hundred games. His illness in the semifinals would also have a significant effect on the Final Four.

The Kentucky team was also known for having style. They had a number of good-looking players. Riley, their top scorer, was handsome and a good dancer. After they beat Vanderbilt, just ahead of the 1966 championship tournament, they were featured in Time Magazine in a photo spread on "The Baron's Runts." Said sportswriter Billy Reed, "They were the darlings of college basketball. Clean-cut guys. Good-looking guys. It was impossible not to like them."[44] And that fact was not to be lost on Texas Western when they eventually played them.

That was the team Duke and Texas Western would eventually play in the Final Four. A short team that was well coached, tough, disciplined, and team oriented. A team that moved the ball well, shot well, ran the floor well, and played hard on every possession. They didn't look hard to beat on first examination, but they were one of the best teams in the country who had beaten almost every team they played the entire year—including a number of teams with quality Black players. Overall, given their lack of size and loss of talent from the previous year, Kentucky's run to the title game that year was almost as remarkable as Texas Western's. The fact that they were the team to ultimately play it instead of Duke was indeed to have significant repercussions, both for Kentucky and all of America.

CHAPTER 3

THE TEXAS WESTERN TEAM

The third team in this Final Four drama was Texas Western, now known as the University of Texas El Paso. Unlike the Duke and Kentucky teams, this team was of mixed race: there were seven Black players, four Whites, and one Hispanic on the team. However, the top seven players typically were the Black ones. Texas Western did sometimes play the non-Black players, but in the famous national championship game, the Black players were the only ones on the court, giving the game its historical significance.

Texas Western is located at the far end of West Texas in El Paso, Texas, on the US-Mexican border. In 1966, it was largely dependent on the local economy of cattle-raising. Being a border town, it had a tradition of being multicultural. El Paso was a mixture of Whites, Hispanics, and Blacks, where Blacks were not a substantial minority. Texas Western and El Paso therefore had relatively few Black-White racial issues; it was actually more than half Hispanic at the time of the game. Consequently, the outcome of the 1966 Final Four was not likely to have any significant racial implications in El Paso. When Texas Western won the championship, Ray Sanchez, the assistant sports editor at the *El Paso Herald Post*, noting that El Paso had always been on the forefront of civil rights, said: "Now we were looked at not only as champions, but as champions of civil rights too."[1]

El Paso is located nearly a thousand miles from most of the Old South. Unlike in North Carolina and Kentucky, Texas Western did not have to deal as much with prevailing historical local racism in building their team; they could recruit whoever was capable of passing their classes and playing for the team. Their geographical separation allowed them to be a pioneer in recruiting Black players. In 1957, at the time an all-White UNC team won the National Championship, Texas Western had already integrated in 1956 with two Black players, Charles and Cecil Brown. They were the only school in any of the former Confederate states to have any Black basketball players. Texas Western was even able to capitalize on the racism of many of the other Southern programs to recruit Black players that they couldn't have gotten otherwise. David Lattin became a Miner only because, in 1962, the University of Houston, soon to be the college of the legendary Elvin Hayes, wasn't quite ready to integrate the program when Lattin was ready to play college basketball.

The Texas Western coach was Don Haskins, a thirty-five-year-old former pool hustler, legendary in his ability to nonchalantly con unsuspecting pool players. Haskins grew up in Enid, Oklahoma, during the Great Depression, to a family of modest means. He lived in a segregated community and concluded that it was discriminatory. In high school, he was a pretty good basketball player, and was written up by the media as an all-state player. However, the best player in town, Herman Carr, who was Black, received little acclaim and no college scholarship offers, which Haskins thought was unfair.

When Haskins became a coach, he remembered the racial injustice of his youth and recruited players from both races to play for his team. In the movie *Glory Road*, Haskins was a rookie coach. In reality, he had already been at Texas Western for five years before the 1965-66 season. The first player he met there was Nolan Richardson, the future great Arkansas coach. Richardson, who modeled his practices on the ones he learned from Don Haskins, went on to be the first Black SEC coach to win a national championship in 1994, beating Duke in the title game.

Haskins recruited nationally. The fact that Texas Western had established themselves ahead of the field as recruiting Black players gave Haskins something of a recruiting edge. In 1966, Haskins had players from New York, Indiana, Michigan, Texas, and Missouri on the team. The team that Haskins built was more than half Black; four were White and one Hispanic, but the top seven rotation players were all Black. That was considerably more than the national average at the time of only about three, and more than 40 percent of all college teams (and almost all of the previously segregated schools in the South) still had no Black players at all.

However, the Texas Western team had their own issues to deal with. Unlike Duke and Kentucky, Texas Western was a school with almost no NCAA tradition. Texas Western only joined the NCAA three years before the 1966 game, whereas Kentucky and Duke had been in the NCAA for decades. That made recruiting truly top players difficult for the coach; they typically wanted to attend schools with more of a basketball tradition. The players that came to play there were not always considered to be the best recruits; many were big-city players with questionable academic backgrounds. In fact, when we examine the 1966 Texas Western team, the main question that *they* were dealing with was, were they, in fact, a real college basketball team with actual college students on the team? Consequently, the challenge that Don Haskins had to face was to convince his team that they could play at the highest level and also to prove to everyone else that his team was actually legitimate.

Fortunately for Texas Western, Haskins was able to instill in his players the belief that they could be a great team, and really could play at the highest level against established powers such as Kentucky and Duke. Looking back on the historical record,

Haskins accomplishment in doing that in 1966 is very unusual; in the annals of the NCAA, there are only a few examples of teams with little or no basketball tradition competing for a title. (Brad Stevens at Butler in 2010, whose team played Duke for the national championship, almost winning it, and also playing for it in 2011, comes to mind.)

But the success of the 1966 team was not quite unprecedented, at least for Texas Western. They actually had a very good team in 1964, only two years earlier. They started at 24-2 with a very good player, Jim "Bad News" Barnes, an NBA number-one pick in 1964, and were playing at a high level in the NCAAs. That team wound up losing to Kansas State in the regional finals, who lost a close game to UCLA in the Final Four semifinal. But Barnes had fouled out in that game, due to some highly suspect fouls, leading Haskins to believe that the game may have been fixed (or, since Barnes was Black, there may have been racial bias in the officiating); otherwise, Texas Western almost certainly would have won it. The game is also notable in that if Texas Western had won the game and made the Final Four, they had a very good chance of beating UCLA, which had a fairly small team (Barnes at six-eight could easily have dominated UCLA's six-five center), in the same way that they ultimately beat Kentucky in 1966. If that had been the case, the team they would have faced in 1964 for the national championship would have been Duke, which had 1966 players Jack Marin and Steve Vacendak on it. So 1966 would prove to be the *second* time in that events ultimately prevented Duke and Texas Western from meeting (although the 1964 Texas Western team did *not* start five Black players, preventing any such possible meeting from having the same racial implications as the 1966 game).

The following year, they had a slightly down year, finishing 16-9. So, at the beginning of the 1966 season, the Texas Western team was unranked. Nowadays, all the programs are subject to intense preseason scrutiny that was almost unheard of in 1966.

But back then, there weren't many games on television (Texas Western had not been televised during the regular season; there were no cable games back then, as cable was not yet available), so people didn't know as much about the other teams in the country. Rupp himself knew little about the team before the Final Four and did not consider them to be a threat to win the championship.

Texas Western's championship win in 1966 was not quite miraculous, as they had come close to winning a title two years earlier, but it was still remarkable. Regardless of the actual racial implications of the championship game, Haskins winning a championship with a virtually unknown team stands out in and of itself as a great accomplishment in coaching history—one that has almost never been duplicated since. For Haskins, it was the high point of his coaching career; although he coached until 1999, he was never able to replicate the success he had that one year.

The 1966 Texas Western squad that Haskins built was actually completely different from the stereotypes of Black basketball teams. Haskins had gone to Oklahoma State, where he played for Hall of Fame coach Henry Iba, Rupp's contemporary in the 1940s and '50s. Iba, who later coached the 1972 US Olympic team in the most controversial game ever played against Russia, was known for his insistence on tough defense and for having very hard practices. His insistence on defense and discipline had soaked into Haskins, who instilled it in his Texas Western team. Like Rupp, he was famous for having brutally difficult practices. His team played tough defense—often devoting three to four hours at a time practicing it—and rebounded well. They were especially well prepared to play the fast-breaking Kentucky team, as they worked very hard on transition defense with their fast backcourt players. Texas Western was actually the number one rated rebounding team in the country, and the third rated defensive team. And, of particular significance in the Kentucky game, they shot free throws well, a skill which today has sometimes been neglected, but which Haskins emphasized extensively back then, insisting that players hit ten in a row before leaving each practice. Haskins' mantra was that the free throw line was where games were won or lost. Against Kentucky in the 1966 finals, it was to be where the game was won.

Examining the accounts of that era, the Texas Western team is often described as being a rough team. Now, one of the problems with the media of that era is that a number of them wrote accounts of the game which fit into their preconceived notions of how Black basketball teams were "supposed" to be, so it's hard to say how true that was. One Baltimore paper famously wrote, "The Miners, who don't worry much about defense but try to pour the ball through the hoop as much as possible, will present quite a challenge to Kentucky. The running, gunning Texas quintet can do more things with a basketball than a monkey on a 50-foot jungle wire."[2] Now, in addition to being obviously racist, that description was also completely wrong. Their style was the exact opposite. They ran a rigid patterned offense and did not play stereotyped "black" basketball of running, shooting, passing poorly, and always driving to the rim, except of course when they ran in transition. In fact, the style of the all-White Kentucky team played closer to "black" basketball, with an up-tempo running and shooting game. It was Texas Western's slower pace, tough defense, and rebounding that made them so hard for Kentucky to play. Willie Worsley noting that his team's style of play was actually more White oriented, said, "We played the most intelligent, the most boring, the most disciplined game of them all."[3] But that was not what the media wanted to write. When reading media accounts of that era today, it's hard to determine how much of it was actually true and how much of it was written from preconceived racial bias.

But Haskins was not interested in having a team that conformed to racist stereotypes. He cared about winning basketball games, period. He was not actually particularly concerned with breaking

The Bob Verga Shift

any racial barriers; he simply put the Black players on the floor because they played better. In that regard, Haskins made an even more definitive racial statement, one that stands to this day; what actually matters most is winning. Remarkably enough, Haskins was the first coach to do that in the regular season too; before his team there had been no team that had *ever* started five Black players. He had first done it for a couple of games in the 1962-63 season where the fifth Black starter had been Nolan Richardson. The unwritten rule back then was that it was expected that there would be at least one or two White guys on the floor at all times. The 1963 national champions, Loyola of Chicago, had four Black starters, but had not played an all-Black team. By doing that, and breaking coaching convention, Haskins took a significant risk with his job at the time, with four kids to provide for. In 1966, Texas, a former slave state and member of the Confederacy, still had separate White and Black state high school basketball tournaments. If the team had been unsuccessful, he could have been fired.

Haskins, then, wasn't particularly aware that what he was doing in 1966 was historic; he just wanted to play the best players. His own university president suggested he start at least one White player in the custom of that time. He had put considerable pressure on Haskins a few years earlier to keep the number of Black starters down to three. But Haskins didn't think too much about the obvious racial implications of his team; he just wanted to have a team that won. And his 1966 team did win; they wound up going 23-1 in the regular season.

And his team agreed with him about who played. There was little racial tension on the team, even though there were five non-Black players, because everyone agreed that the best players should play according to the matchups and how well they were playing, White or Black. Ironically enough, Haskins didn't play White forward Jerry Armstrong in the finals, usually the second player off the bench, who had been effective against Utah's Jerry

Chambers in the semifinals, because he thought Kentucky's White players were too fast for him to guard. Armstrong easily bought into the concept of the best players playing. "I never gave it a thought you know, they were my teammates, they were great people."[4]

The Texas Western team was led by seven Black players: tough six-foot-seven center David Lattin; six-eight forward Nevil Shed; five-eleven guard Bobby Joe Hill, a good ball handler; six-one guard Orsten Artis, a good jump shooter; Harry Flournoy, a six-five forward who was an excellent rebounder; five-six incredibly quick guard Willie Worsley; and six-five forward Willie Cager. Each of these players had an interesting story to tell; they had all been recruited by Haskins from different locations and backgrounds.

Nevil Shed, the tallest player on the team, was from New York. Shed had grown up in the Bronx. He had originally attended the all-Black North Carolina A&T, about fifty miles away from Duke in still-segregated Durham, described in chapter one, and played as a freshman, but left after being suspended for missing curfew. According to Shed, who was there just before the Civil Rights Act was passed, "I wasn't accustomed to sitting on the back of the bus, having white and colored water fountains or going to the balcony at a movie and the back entrance of a restaurant."[5] So when Haskins offered Shed a scholarship at Texas Western—recruiting Shed by assuring his mom that Shed would finish and get his diploma—he took it. "I was a positive person in a negative environment," said Shed, "and I told myself, 'When you get a chance, don't you dare not take advantage of it.'"[6]

Willie Worsley and Willie Cager were from New York too. El Paso was a long way from the world they grew up in. They both had grown up in a tough neighborhood in the South Bronx and knew Shed when he was there. Worsley, at only five-six (he could dunk), was incredibly quick and had been a star at Dewitt Clinton High School, famously scoring thirty points in one half of a game before being sent home on the subway for his own safety at halftime. Haskins had been uncertain whether he should offer Worsley a scholarship at his height, but his local New York recruiting guru Willie Brown had said he was worth an offer. He had been MVP of an NYC championship game at Madison Square Garden. Said Worsley, "Black never came into it at all. I knew with Shed and Cager I was not going to be totally alone down there."[7]

Willie Cager had heard about Texas Western and went out on his own after dropping out of high school in New York. According to Cager, "I wanted to get away from there as far as possible."[8] (He later settled in El Paso after finishing college.) He finished high school at El Paso Technical High School while working at a gas station; he slept in one of the grease pits while he finished his high school equivalency and had enrolled at Texas Western on his own. Cager, who had a heart murmur, could not play extended minutes, which made him an ideal sixth man.

Bobby Joe Hill, a quick point guard, was from a tough neighborhood in Detroit. He was All-City as a senior, averaging twenty-three points a game, and was also an excellent defensive player, as he was to show in the NCAA championship game when he stole the ball from Louis Dampier in a game changing play. He had enrolled at Burlington Junior College in Burlington, Iowa, but quit school after his first year. Don Haskins called him up at home and asked him to come to Texas Western. He showed up out of shape, at nearly 220 pounds, but Haskins set him to work and he turned into a very good point guard. Hill was known for his amazing quickness and full-court play; he could blow by players with incredible behind-the-back dribbling. Haskins actually tried to get Hill to dribble with the ball more in front of him, but it didn't work, so Hill went back to playing as he had before and went on to dominate games from the backcourt.

Orsten Artis and Harry Flournoy grew up in Gary, Indiana, but went to different high schools. Artis, in addition to being very quick and a good defensive player (also a good rebounder for his size) was an excellent shooter at six-one. He had been recruited by a number of top schools. Haskins recruited him by challenging him to a free throw shooting contest; if Haskins won, Artis would go to Texas Western. He made nine of ten, but Haskins made all ten. "I had to keep my promise,"[9] Artis said. (Artis once hit 125 in a row in practice.) Artis was known as a clutch player who could be counted on to score when it mattered; according to Flournoy, "When he shot it, you might as well go back down the floor because he was going to make it."[10] Artis and Flournoy were good friends and roommates at Texas Western, the same age, and co-captains of the 1966 team.

Flournoy's high school had been mostly White. "All the best players on the team were Black, but there was this unspoken rule that no more than three blacks could play at once."[11] Flournoy, at six-five, although not a great shooter (he averaged only three points a game in high school), was a great leaper with a knack for positioning and grabbing rebounds (as would later be displayed on the 1966 *Sports Illustrated* Final Four cover, to Kentucky-great Pat Riley's detriment). Haskins had recruited Flournoy by following him home in his car. Flournoy was a relatively raw recruit, but by working hard, he developed into a quality player; in 1966, he led the team in rebounding with an average of nearly eleven a game—a remarkable total for a six-foot-five player.

David Lattin, from Houston, at six-seven and 245 pounds, was a very strong center. He was known to be physically intimidating on the court, famously striking fear into the heart of six-eight Jim "Bad News" Barnes—a very tough opponent. He had actually first gone to Tennessee State but was unhappy and got on the bus for twenty-four hours straight to meet Haskins and transfer to Texas Western. Lattin was very intelligent and articulate off the court, in contradiction to the prevailing stereotypes of the time; he even had his own campus jazz radio show. He had style too, wearing alligator-cut loafers and sharkskin suits and tooled around campus in a late model Buick Riviera. On the court, he was all business. He played well in the NCAA tournament in 1966 against some tough competition, including Kansas All-American Walt Wesley, out rebounding two of his opponents and scoring twenty-nine points in one of the games. He later went on to run his own successful sports apparel business.

In the regular season, Texas Western had an excellent 23-1 record. It is all the more remarkable that during the season the team faced racial discrimination by officials in many of their games. In the game that cost them an undefeated season, a two-point loss against Seattle, Bobby Joe Hill was knocked down on a cut to the basket, and it was not called (that game involved a local official who was clearly biased throughout the game). In several other games, the whistles were clearly against them; officials avoided calling obvious fouls against their opponents. It is of note that the officials in the final game were to be all White, so Texas Western was not expecting a friendly whistle (most of the questionable calls in the championship game went Kentucky's way). But their defense was almost unbeatable when they were well focused. According to Harry Flournoy, "Once they crossed the half-court line they were ours. That basket we were defending—that they're trying to score baskets on—that's our basket."[12]

They faced discrimination in other areas too. As the team began to have success during the season, they gained national notice, and death threats began surfacing, making it harder to find hotels to stay in. There was even an incident where one player was jumped in a bathroom and beaten up. After the incident, the assistant coach made the team go places in groups to try to prevent things like that from happening again. At one of the games, Nevil Shed tried to respond to someone in the stands calling him names, but Coach Haskins ordered him to ignore them. Shed tried to argue that he needed to defend his reputation. "Coach said, 'Are you those things they're calling you?' I said, 'No, I'm not.' Coach said, 'Then show them who you really are.'"[13] Later, as they were ascending in the rankings and becoming a legitimate threat to be champions, they even found blood on the walls of their dressing room and on their uniforms.

There was no question that Texas Western was a very tough team. They had to be, to get to the national championship game against top competition and biased officiating. Four of the players were from tough neighborhoods in New York and had played their way into college against top New York competition. Nevil Shed was kicked out of a game for punching an opponent, who had held his shorts coming off a screen, and Coach Haskins was so furious, he threatened to cut him from the team. He wouldn't even let him ride the bus back to the hotel after the game. "The idea of not being able to play in that game was just horrible to me, so I tried my best to avoid Coach Haskins at all costs, hoping he'd forget about everything and let me play."[14] Haskins eventually relented. But Haskins knew he had to have discipline on his team with tough players from tough neighborhoods.

Coach Haskins and Coach Rupp had done a remarkable job coaching their teams to the title game; given the obstacles both coaches faced in getting their programs to the championship, they both go down as two of the best coaching performances in history. They would, along with Duke, form the basis of what is possibly the most famous Final Four in American history. The outcome of this Final Four was likely to affect more people's lives than any other Final Four ever played—an outcome that could have been much different.

CHAPTER 4

RACE RELATIONS IN AMERICA IN 1966

At the time of this writing, it has been more than fifty years since the events in this book, and much has changed (although judging from the George Floyd era, not everything). It is hard for me to remember what racial issues were like in 1966. I remember quite a bit from my life then, but, being less than ten years old at the time, I had almost no appreciation for what was actually happening, or any understanding of the historical background of what was occurring. All I knew was what I saw on TV and some things that were happening in my own town.

In many states without Jim Crow laws, racist attitudes still permeated society at that time. In Boston in the 1950s, a supposedly progressive part of the country, the great Boston Celtics player Bill Russell endured racist insults and behavior that today would be considered unthinkable. In Chicago, Black basketball players who attended Loyola in the early 1960s couldn't dance with or date White girls and had to live in restricted areas, and many restaurants did not make them feel welcome. Neighborhoods in Chicago were rigidly segregated; when Black residents moved in, White residents often moved out. So even in states without Jim Crow laws, Black people had to endure racist bosses, judges, police, and White people in various neighborhoods.

But in the South, racism was everywhere, and it was much

worse. Having grown up in the South, it is hard to describe today just how much tobacco and racism cast a pall over almost *everything*. Throughout the tobacco growing regions and the Deep South, where low-paid Black labor was central to the economy, racial inequality was at the heart of the whole economic system. Black people typically earned far less than White people, worked at lower status jobs, went to poorly funded (typically one-fifth as much per pupil) schools, and lived in segregated, less well-off communities. Racism and segregation in the South in those days was like cigarette smoking; it was everywhere. It was so much a part of the fabric of society that racist attitudes were taken for granted.

The forces of segregation were strong and well organized throughout the South. They fought tenaciously to defend the status quo, especially in the area of athletics. Racists believed that once Blacks could get a level playing field there, they would expect it elsewhere. As the Georgia governor said in 1956, "One break in the dike, and the relentless sea will rush in and destroy us."[1] Or, as stated by a Georgia state senator in 1957, when Black players and White players meet on an equal athletic playing field, "it is only natural that this sense of equality carries into the daily living of these people."[2] The 1966 NCAA title game would be the last break in the dike that turned it into a flood.

It was many years later that I finally started having a better understanding of what actually happened back then. Prior to the mid-1950s, segregation existed pretty much everywhere in the South and border regions, including Kentucky. The Brown vs. Board of Education of Topeka case, which overturned mandated school segregation in 1954, resulting in the integration of multiple state universities in the South and border regions, including the University of North Carolina, is one of the catalysts that made the civil rights movement possible. That ruling occurred after years of litigation by NAACP lawyers and legal challenges to segregation. After that case, there was now a firm legal foundation on which to challenge segregation everywhere.

But it wasn't until a year later, when Rosa Parks refused to give up her seat on a bus in December 1955, in Montgomery, Alabama, that the civil rights movement actually began. Parks, who months prior to the incident had discussed doing something of that nature with local activists, started a boycott of the Montgomery bus system, led by Dr. Martin Luther King Jr. The boycott stretched on for more than a year, and participants carpooled or walked miles to work and schools, sometimes using a sophisticated system of carpools with volunteer drivers and dispatchers. After a year of losing most of their revenue, despite repeated harassment of King and other protest leaders, the city transit company gave in and allowed the buses to be integrated.

Thus began the decade-long struggle to end legal segregation in the South. The Montgomery bus boycott was soon followed by more protests and more action. In 1957, the year after the Montgomery protests had ended, the Little Rock Nine integrated the schools in Little Rock, Arkansas, starting the next major battle in the struggle, where federal troops were sent in by Dwight Eisenhower. There were soon more protests in other parts of the South. Then there were youth marches for integration in Washington, DC, in 1958 and 1959. Lunch counter demonstrations against segregated facilities—originating fifty miles from Duke and Durham in Greensboro—started on February 1, 1960, and quickly swept the South. Dozens of communities participated, and almost all of the protests were nonviolent.

The movement, which began the SNCC (Student Nonviolent Coordinating Committee), grew throughout the spring of 1960, from February to June; eventually more than 90 percent of the students at North Carolina A&T State University participated, marking the first time since the 1920s that Black students had demonstrated. The SNCC worked hard at maintaining non-violence, urging participants to always be polite and approachable and not to retaliate if they were bullied or cursed at: "Remember love and nonviolence."[3] In 1961, 1962, and 1963, the SNCC, whose members were often arrested, began organizing voter registration in Southern communities, in which a substantial number of the participants were White. In addition to the SNCC activities, the NAACP, began organizing boycotts of businesses that denied Black people service or employment opportunities, often organizing picket lines around targeted stores. The SNCC and NAACP activities were very successful in ending discrimination at many businesses throughout the South.

It might be difficult for people to understand today how truly courageous Blacks and civil rights workers actually were in that era, especially as they tried their hardest to maintain a nonviolent response while often being subjected to incredible abuse from both White racists and Southern authorities. Being a civil rights activist in the South was much more dangerous than just holding hands and singing "Kumbaya." Blacks lost their jobs or their farms for voting. Peaceful pickets were often attacked by White racists. Sit-in protesters were beaten and had condiments poured on them. Throughout the South, there were bombings and shootings. There were crosses burned on people's yards at night. Freedom Riders in 1961 (among them future congressional leader John Lewis, who was beaten at a bus terminal) had buses burned and were beaten by locals with pipes and baseball bats as police looked on. Peaceful demonstrators were beaten with ax handles. A number of civil rights workers in Mississippi were actually murdered.

When James Meredith attempted to register at the University of Mississippi in September 1961, there was a full-blown riot. One hundred seventy US marshals, there to help protect Meredith, were attacked by a mob which eventually grew to about twenty-five hundred. Klansman and locals had come in with shotguns, squirrel rifles, and automatic weapons. The marshals were assaulted by everything from construction materials, hunks of concrete from smashed up campus benches, gasoline bombs in soda bottles, to shotguns, handguns, and rifles.[4] Nearly twenty-seven hundred national guardsmen were mobilized in the region to quell the riot, and more than two hundred federal troops were wounded, thirty by gunfire.

But the forces of racial progress refused to be intimidated. After 1961, the protests in favor of civil rights continued to pick up intensity. By 1963, civil rights demonstrations were reaching a peak. In that year, 930 demonstrations took place in 115 cities in eleven Southern states. Over twenty thousand people were arrested that year. Ten people were killed that year in racial violence, and at least thirty-five bombings occurred. In Birmingham, in the summer of 1963, protestors, including hundreds of children, were attacked by police dogs, hit with firehoses, and taken to jail. In a show of remarkable courage and self-restraint, almost all of the protestors in the South, at King's behest, maintained a peaceful response to this incredible racist onslaught of violence and hatred, which to this day is truly remarkable.

The protests culminated in August 1963, in the famous March on Washington, attended by nearly a quarter-million people, about one-quarter White, which included a long list of distinguished speakers and entertainers—among them future Senator Mitch McConnell, there to help protest against Southern opposition to civil rights legislation—where Dr. King made his famous "I Have a Dream" speech. This march had been organized by the NAACP and other organizations who felt that the moment had come in history, after the Birmingham protests earlier in the summer, to do something effective about civil rights.

In 1963, the Kennedy administration, spurred on by the March and determined to do something about the ongoing violent opposition to civil rights, finally introduced a strong piece of civil rights legislation, shortly before Kennedy was assassinated. His vice president and successor, President Lyndon Johnson, was determined to move the bill through Congress. The time for change had come; a comprehensive civil rights bill was introduced into Congress in February of 1964.

Back in the 1960s, even though there was considerable partisanship, there was much more overlap of views between the parties, and the South had not yet become Republican as it did after the Voting Rights Act was passed. When young Mitch McConnell joined the Republican party in the late 1950s (he had earlier lived in Georgia and Alabama), at that time it was the party of civil rights, as it had been since the Civil War (the party of Lincoln); the Democrats still controlled much of the South in 1964, although its movement towards the Republicans was clearly gaining momentum. When the Civil Rights Act was introduced, Republican senators were motivated by images of violence against civil rights protests in 1963 in Birmingham and elsewhere. Republican House Minority Leader Charles Halleck, looking at a 1963 civil rights bill sponsored by President John F. Kennedy, pledged that his party would move quickly to get the bill heard by the House Judiciary Committee, stating that the Republican record on civil rights "has been unmatched for 100 years and as always our attitude on this issue is constructive."[5] Prior to the passage of the 1964 bill, nearly one hundred different civil rights bills were introduced in Congress, many of them Republican sponsored.

After Kennedy's assassination, President Lyndon Johnson picked up the civil rights bill started by Kennedy, and worked hard to get it passed in early 1964. Southern Democratic senators used filibusters extensively to block civil rights legislation, which future Senator Mitch McConnell had ample opportunity to view. They had perfected tactics that were used almost entirely to perpetuate Jim Crow laws and segregation in the South. In fact, for nearly one hundred years that was their primary purpose in the Senate. They made sure that their senators served multiple terms, thereby increasing their seniority and ability to block such bills. Between 1953 and 1963, they had successfully blocked 121 different civil rights bills, nearly one a month. Even though they disagreed with the rest of the party on many issues, they actually stayed with the Democratic Party so that they could maintain majority control of committees to block civil rights legislation (they were able to exclude Black people from much of the New Deal legislation in the 1930s). Back then, cloture (closing off debate) required a two-third vote of the Senate. Prior to 1964, it had only occurred once in thirty-five years. Sixty-seven votes were needed to move the 1964 legislation through the Senate, even more than today's sixty votes, required since 1975. But it hadn't actually been necessary before then; prior to 1964, no cloture vote since 1950 on civil rights legislation had received more than even a majority of the Senate.

By 1964, a decade of civil rights activism had brought a huge amount of progress. An earlier, relatively weak civil rights bill had passed in 1957, and another one passed in 1960. These bills, which included conditions for federal funding of universities (ultimately to affect both Duke and Kentucky) started bringing about change in the South. But the segregationists weren't giving up without a fight. As soon as the 1964 bill was introduced, they immediately resumed their old tactic of endless debate. They began debate in early April and simply talked on and on, blocking all other Senate business. But the bill had an unlikely ally. The Republican senate minority leader, Everett Dirksen, had decided to throw his weight in behind a civil rights bill. Dirksen during that time worked long and hard to ensure that the bill would pass. He carefully examined each provision and made a number of amendments to ensure that it would be successful and acceptable. Dirksen was getting older and his health was starting to fail; he had treatment for ulcers at the time of the bill and died a few years after its passage. But he persisted, aware of the historic implications of his efforts. He worked tirelessly, often fifteen-hour days, talking with each wavering senator to be certain that he could accept the bill and vote for it. There were many partisans in his party who still opposed the bill. But Dirksen understood that, in the end, fairness, decency, and common sense trumped partisan considerations. His counterpart, Senate Majority Leader Mike Mansfield, in 1964, stated Dirksen's "patriotism has always taken precedence over his partisanship."[6]

Finally, after two and a half months of debate, the bill's proponents and Dirksen were able to locate enough votes to end the filibuster. The 1964 bill filibuster, the longest in history, was the first civil rights bill on which a filibuster had ever been broken. One of the primary reasons for the bill's eventual passage was a famous fifteen-minute speech prior to the vote to end the filibuster, attended by all one hundred senators, by Dirksen on June 10, 1964. Dirksen, in his inimitable slow bass voice, (he often started statements with a sonorous "I believe," which sounded like it was coming from a half-asleep foghorn) "The time has come for equality of opportunity in sharing of government, in education, and in employment. It must not be stayed or denied."[7] Dirksen discussed the failure of attempts to block earlier reform efforts, stating that "an inexorable moral force which operates in the domain of human affairs swept these efforts aside, and today they are accepted as part of the social economic and political fabric of America." He closed by saying, "We are confronted with a moral issue. Let us not be found wanting in whatever it takes in moral and spiritual substance to face up to the issue."[8] Asked about his motivations for finally aiding the civil rights cause, Dirksen stated, "I am involved in mankind, and whatever the skin, we are all included in mankind."[9] For his efforts on behalf of the Civil Rights Act of 1964, Everett Dirksen died a hero of the civil rights movement in 1969.

In the Senate roll call immediately following his speech, Dirksen delivered twenty-three votes to break the filibuster. One of the senators who played a lead role in breaking the filibuster with Dirksen was John Sherman Cooper from Kentucky. Cooper had come out in favor of the Civil Rights Act in 1963. "The expedient argument of states' rights with respect to constitutional and human rights would 'destroy the Republican party' and do a great wrong to African Americans."[10] Young Mitch McConnell asked Senator Cooper how he could take such a strong stand on the issue, one that so many of the people who elected him opposed. To which Cooper responded, "I not only represent Kentucky, I represent the nation, and there are times when you follow and there are times when you lead."[11] According to Marlow, "The press praised him for following his conscience instead of Kentucky polls."[12] In 1966, the year of the game, Cooper was reelected with nearly two-thirds of the vote.

Sixty years later, the passage of the Civil Rights act still stands as a great legislative achievement; many people view it as the single greatest piece of legislation in American history. But it is important to recognize how different America was back then. The country was more culturally homogenous back then, being mostly married and White, with women who primarily stayed home and raised children. There was still a military draft—which people at the time (rightly) viewed as a contest between democracy and tyranny—so most senators and congressmen were veterans, many of whom had fought in WWII. People didn't have cable television either, so what they saw came primarily from three networks. There were no competing cable TV views of reality back then. And people didn't have the internet or global consciousness then either, as the lunar missions hadn't occurred yet, so people identified much more strongly with being an American. So even though the Civil Rights Act had faced strenuous opposition from Southern senators, the rest of the country was able to work from a more common set of experiences, which enabled them to work bipartisanly to effectively pass legislation in a manner not typically seen in the twenty-first century.

The passage of the Civil Rights Act of 1964 had addressed many of the legal issues of that time. However, the problem of voting rights suppression had still not been addressed. In 1965, enthusiasm for civil rights was starting to fade as the war in Vietnam was beginning, and White America turned its attention toward this more immediate issue. Realizing this, King and the NAACP decided to march in Selma, Alabama, known for both disenfranchising Blacks through the use of a very lengthy, complicated voting test and brutal local enforcement, to bring the matter squarely to the nation's attention while it was still possible to get new legislation enacted. King, Ralph Abernathy, and other leaders such as John L. Lewis, led a march for voting rights from Selma to Montgomery, at which many protesters were praying when police clubbed and gassed them (including Lewis).

As expected, millions of people saw police beating defenseless citizens attempting to exercise their constitutional rights to assemble and vote on television. (It also began the SNCC's move away from non-violence, as its members became more radicalized by the experience.) Television itself had a huge effect on the civil rights movement in the '50s and '60s. Unlike before WWII, people in the rest of the country could actually see firsthand on TV the stupefying cruelty and brutality of the Old South. The resulting national outrage from the televised beatings echoed immediately through the halls of Congress, resulted in the passage of the Voting Rights Act of 1965. The Voting Rights Act also occurred after a lengthy filibuster, defeated by a vote of seventy to thirty. John Sherman Cooper brought young Mitch McConnell along to witness the signing of the Voting Rights Act. My parents and I were also present in Congress for debate on the bill, which means it is possible that young Mitch McConnell and I ("Mom what's this all about?" "Shhh! Be quiet!") were both in the Senate Chamber at the same time. The act eliminated many legal barriers to voting by Southern Blacks, which resulted in huge changes in Southern Black voting participation. And it was very effective in the long term; aided by NAACP lawyers, between 1965 and 1989, the number of Blacks registered to vote increased from about 2.5 million to 12 million, while the number of Black officials increased by fourteen-fold, from about four hundred to seventy-two hundred, with more than three hundred mayors and four hundred state legislature members.

So the two major civil rights acts of the mid 1960s had alleviated much of the more blatant legal causes of segregation in the Old South. By 1966, much of the more obvious discrimination, especially in the South had been removed by the earlier bills, and momentum in Congress had slowed. A bill to help end housing discrimination, mentioned by President Johnson at his State of the Union address, ultimately was not passed by Congress that year. It would ultimately pass in 1968 after King was assassinated. As the situation in Vietnam continued to escalate, White America had much less energy to concentrate on civil rights issues as it had in the first half of the 1960s, as the war would occupy its attention for the better part of a decade.

However, the slowing progress of civil rights reform in 1966 was beginning to frustrate a large portion of Black America. By 1966, at the time of the Final Four, much of Black America's patience with the progress of civil rights reform and with the violent response it was receiving was finally being exhausted; racial violence began spreading in the form of race riots. Especially in the summertime, when bored, frustrated youths with no opportunities were out in the streets, the earlier non-violent protests were now becoming more violent. The first race riot of the civil rights era began in 1962, in Albany, Georgia. The SNCC had been working on a major voter registration effort, but after gaining no concessions from the local authorities after nearly a year of protests, efforts turned violent when two thousand protesters threw bricks and bottles at police. In 1963, there were two riots in Birmingham, Alabama (one of which had been triggered by a Ku Klux Klan bombing of a motel and the house of MLK's brother), and Cambridge, Maryland, where five people were injured. But the first major riot, in 1964, was the Harlem riot, which lasted several days and killed several people. There were six more riots that year, including Rochester, NY, Elizabeth, NJ, Patterson, NJ; Philadelphia, PA, and Dixmoor, IL.

But they paled in comparison to the huge Watts riot of August 1965, which began after a White police officer arrested a Black man for a traffic violation during a heat wave with temperatures approaching 100 degrees. These riots killed thirty-four people and burned down dozens of businesses. Nearly thirty thousand people participated, with more than one thousand injured and four thousand arrested. They covered forty-six square miles, with large areas burned down. Nearly sixteen thousand law enforcement personnel were involved in finally quelling the riots, which lasted more than a week.

The riot was so bad, and the fears of it spreading to other states were so strong, that the publisher of the *Lexington Herald* newspaper, a friend of Adolph Rupp's, didn't even publish accounts of it for fear of stirring up the Black community. That was typical of the response of the *Lexington Herald* back then; they printed anything Rupp said, regardless of whether it was true or not, but nothing about the riots or protests or what was going on at all. This would be of some significance after the 1966 game, where Rupp's responses to the game were given inordinate coverage, while civil rights protests were largely ignored. In the *Lexington Herald*, the civil rights movement didn't exist at all. In an apology published in 2004, the paper admitted that it had been done deliberately; they didn't want Blacks joining marches or participating in protests.

When the 1966 Final Four was played, it had only been seven months since the Watts riots. In fact, an *additional* race riot occurred in Watts only days before the 1966 Final Four. Racial tensions had already triggered violent protests in many parts of the country, and more were expected for that year. And while most riots were typically triggered by police confrontations with various Black citizens, they were caused for other reasons as well. The civil rights movement was at a crossroads: the era of peaceful protests and progress appeared to be fading, as riots became more common, especially outside of the South.

And so, in 1966, the civil rights movement and Black America were considering how best to proceed. Dr. King was starting to move north, starting the Chicago Freedom Movement in January 1966, expanding civil rights activities from the South to the North. He had had his first march in Chicago on February 23, only a few weeks before the game, which prompted Mayor Richard J. Daley to devote more resources to doing something about the more run-down parts of the Black community. The very weekend of the 1966 Final Four, King said that "the moral force of SCLC's nonviolent movement philosophy was needed to help eradicate a vicious system which seeks to further colonize thousands of Negroes within a slum environment."[13] The same weekend, Daley led a countermarch to King with seventy thousand people in it, to prove to King who really ran the show in Chicago.

So at the time of the 1966 Final Four, the struggle was changing from a Southern *legal* battle to a national *economic* battle and a battle over providing better opportunities in the schools. Black America was pondering whether to go down the integrationist path of going out and being more a part of White society or go down the Black power separationist mode. King wasn't convinced that the second path would work effectively. King was more in favor of the first path, believing that "America must be made a nation in which its multi-racial people are partners in power."[14]

However, other Black civil rights leaders were starting to believe that the second mode was the way forward, and so did many Black Americans. Stokely Carmichael, a close associate of King's in the early 1960s, who had walked with him at the front of some civil rights marches, famously said, "This is the twenty-seventh time I have been arrested and I ain't going to jail no more."[15] Prior to 1966, there had been little to no discussion of Black radicalism. The SNCC, in which Carmichael had been a prominent leader, had originated during the sit-ins of 1960, and had been instrumental in nonviolent change. It had organized demonstration, sit-ins, and voter registration drives in various locations, and had been largely bi-racial.

However, after the attacks at the Edmund Pettus Bridge in 1965, the SNCC started becoming more and more radicalized, and began kicking out moderates. After the fall of 1965, *after* the Voting Rights Act was passed, the SNCC ceased being concerned with creating any kind of bi-racial coalition. In 1966 game, the SNCC was being taken over by left wing activists and anti-Vietnam war demonstrators. That May, a couple months after the 1966 Final Four games were played, Carmichael was elected chairman, replacing John Lewis, and the organization completely changed. It withdrew from the White House conference on civil rights on May 23, effectively ending the era of bi-racial civil rights activism. The White and Black hands which represented it disappeared, and a black panther replaced it. Said Carmichael in the summer of 1966, "We been saying freedom for six years and we ain't got nothin'. What we gonna start saying now is Black Power."[16] The spiritual leader of the group was changed from Gandhi to Malcolm X. As Carmichael said in 1966, "It is a call for black people to define their own goals, to lead their own organizations."[17] It began to advocate guerilla warfare. Most of the White people were kicked out, and the SNCC began espousing violence (in direct contradiction to their actual name).

So in early 1966, at the time of the game, the civil rights movement was indeed a changing. According to Clayborne Carson, Carmichael became an emblem of Black militancy; he saw that Black people were ready to reject peace and interracial compromise because they felt the civil rights movement had not done enough to improve the lives of Black Americans. Carmichael, whose attitude had been formed during the Southern racial struggle, was attempting to formulate a political response to the post-civil rights era, and his view of things coincided with that of many urban Blacks, especially in Northern areas. "Carmichael and other outspoken militants in SNCC were no longer restrained by concern for the sensibilities of white people."[18]

Out in Oakland, inspired by the death of Malcolm X in 1965, Bobby Seale and Huey Newton were also just beginning to define a more violent approach with the Revolutionary Action Committee. They adopted black outfits and black berets and started encouraging a more confrontational attitude toward both the police and the government, which at that point was in the process of sending thousands of Black soldiers to Vietnam. The timing of the 1966 game corresponds almost *exactly* to the time that Black radicalism was starting to take hold, and the civil rights movement was changing from being mostly Southern and bi-racial to being national and Black. The new national emphasis on Black power, as opposed to integration, was starting to take hold in cities throughout the country, especially among younger Black men, just months after the 1966 game. This meant that the era of bi-racial non-violent cooperation on civil rights was ending. So in fact, the 1966 Final Four occurred at an important crossroads in Black American history, one in which Black radicalism was beginning, and millions of Black Americans were looking for direction as to how next to proceed.

And it soon became clear in the summer of 1966, that this new, more radical emphasis was partly responsible for the multiple race riots happening across the country. In 1966, there were four more significant riots, while in 1967, there were sixteen major riots (including the giant Newark and Detroit riots, which lasted for days, claimed dozens of lives, and affected tens of thousands of people), and nearly a hundred other significant racial incidents. In the summer of 1967, I remember turning the TV on and seeing them happening with some regularity.

King's earlier appeals to non-violence were no longer being heeded by much of the Black community. One of the riots occurred on March 28, 1968, in Memphis, as a march led by King himself was attacked by local police, and marchers fought back, burning or looting more than 150 stores. King, sensing that his non-violent approach was no longer being considered effective, realized that his time in history may have been coming to a close. In his last speech, he explained that he wasn't concerned about living a long life, nor was he worried or fearful about his future—all he wanted was to do God's will. "Mine eyes have seen the glory of the coming of the Lord."[19] The next day, April 4, 1968, he was assassinated. In the days directly following Dr. King's assassination, there were race riots in more than 110 cities. Folks in Boston famously remember James Brown's incredible performance the night of King's assassination, which was also broadcast live by local station WGBH, that kept the people of Boston off the street well into the night, thereby saving Boston from a disaster. Raleigh, on the other hand—about twenty-five miles from my home in Durham—dealt with violence and fires for nearly a week after the riots. King did not die in vain, however; his efforts in Northern cities the last two years of his life resulted in the passage of the last great piece of civil rights legislation a week after his death, the 1968 Civil Rights Act, which banned racial housing discrimination. King was mourned by the entire country. His death marked the end of an era of Black leadership and large scale organized civil rights activity.

On the other side of the race divide, the Ku Klux Klan, which had been around for nearly one hundred years, was very active throughout the South in the 1960s, largely in response to the civil rights movement. At the time of the 1966 game, the total membership was estimated at nearly twenty-five thousand. In fact, as civil rights activity had increased in the 1960s, and White anxiety over Black gains grew, Klan membership shot up throughout the South. The Klan participated in cross burnings, shootings, and bombings throughout the entire region. In the spring and summer of 1965, there were dozens of incidents in Alabama and Mississippi. Realizing the extent of the problem, President Lyndon Johnson sent legislation to Congress to curb their activities.

The Bob Verga Shift

In the Deep South, the Klan was clearly a significant problem. However, the place where they were strongest was the border state of North Carolina. On the surface, this was somewhat surprising; North Carolina was known to be more liberal and willing to abide by federal orders than states further south. This being the case, segregationists in North Carolina found themselves without any state and local authorities to collude with in resisting federal integration orders, something that was quite common further south. An examination of newspaper articles from the time shows that the Klan's resurgence coincided with the enactment of the Civil Rights Act of 1964 and Voting Rights Acts of 1965. In North Carolina, it was clear that the state would not be blocking the enforcement of federal law so local residents turned to the Klan to help them resist the changes going on around them.

In 1965, of the 381 "klaverns" in the South, nearly two hundred of them were in North Carolina, the state with the most members by far, with a peak membership of more than twelve thousand. This was more than half of the membership in the South—more than all other Southern states *combined*. Starting in 1963, the Klan in North Carolina, led by Grand Dragon Bob Jones, in the space of a few years grew to be a huge menace. Unlike most traditional Klan activities in previous years, which occurred at night, the North Carolina Klan often marched in broad daylight; a public rally in Raleigh in the summer of 1966 drew eighteen hundred Klansman. They had daylight street walks through the middle of towns with hoods and robes before their nighttime rallies, which often caused trouble. In Reidsville and Salisbury, fights broke out between Klan members and Black residents when they occurred.

Bob Jones, who had once been kicked out of the Navy for refusing to salute a Black officer, was known as an incredible showman with a flair for organizing rallies. He drove tirelessly around the state in his "Dragon Wagon" promoting KKK rallies. He estimated he drove more than one hundred thousand miles around the state in three years. And he knew how to get turnout;

he put out two thousand fliers for each rally. The Klan even had a booth at the state fair in 1966 with loudspeakers that blasted out hate-filled Klan music. He routinely held rallies with several thousand people, bands, concessions, and multiple speakers. The Klan burned crosses in public too. On May 28, 1965, less than ten months before the 1966 Final Four, they burned crosses publicly on the grounds of courthouses and city halls at thirteen different cities and towns, including Roxboro and Oxford less than fifty miles from the Duke campus. They knew how to tap into the fears and resentment of low-income Whites who believed their jobs were threatened by integration.

Between 1964 and 1966, there was a Klan rally almost every night somewhere in North Carolina, according to sociologist David Cunningham, author of *Klansville, U.S.A.* (When I checked that assessment with Cunningham, he said that was during the warm weather months. In the coldest time of year, the meetings were closer to weekly.) "It was sort of a skewed county fair environment."[20] Locals could purchase KKK souvenirs and refreshments and listen to live music by the Klan house band Skeeter Bob and his Country Pals, who performed songs that praised the Old South and attacked Martin Luther King Jr.

There would often be a religious speech by Klan chaplain George Dorsett (who later would be turned into an informant by the FBI, ultimately ending Jones' reign of terror). Dorsett was no fan of school integration. "I sometimes believe it is better to keep our children in the house and leave them without a spark of education, rather than throw them in the pit of integration."[21] The nights would end with the burning of a sixty-foot-tall cross. The crowds were large too; according to David Cunningham, small rallies had two hundred to three hundred attendees while large rallies had two thousand to three thousand, with the largest estimated at about eight thousand. By the time of the 1966 game, hundreds of thousands of people in North Carolina had been to Klan rallies. Even Dr. King was amazed by it: "North Carolina, the largest Ku Klux Klan state? Is this possible in 'liberal' North Carolina?"[22]

Now, when I was growing up in North Carolina, I knew there were things going on with the Klan. Occasionally, I would read about a bombing or cross burning or about people being arrested or other such activity. I knew that a lot of people were involved in Klan activities. However, when researching it now, I am *still* surprised at the full extent of what was going on back then. To discover that they were actually burning crosses about ten miles from my home back then was a truly stunning discovery.

The North Carolina Klan did not typically engage in the brutal murders and fire-bombings that occurred in the Deep South states, but they were involved in a widespread and violent terror campaign for several years. According to Cunningham, in North Carolina there were *hundreds* of acts of terror: crosses burned on people's lawns, bricks thrown through people's windows, shots fired at people's houses, and beatings. In 1965, in New Bern, Klan blasts bombed Black churches, businesses, and automobiles. In Vanceboro, the Klan burned a cross on the mayor's lawn. They stoned school buses. They staged violent attacks on civil rights marchers. They came out at night and harassed people who supported integration (my father actually stood outside guarding the house one night after receiving a Klan threat when he had signed a civil rights petition). The list of atrocities that is known is only the tip of the iceberg; a large number of incidents were never reported. And the Klan felt they could do it with virtual impunity; they even had a special operations unit devoted to terror. Prior to 1966, no Klansman in North Carolina had ever been prosecuted for a racial attack.

In January 1966, Governor Dan K. Moore appointed a committee of representatives of state agencies to do something about the Klan's violent activities. Moore stated, "We're through playing games with the Klan."[23] The committee was tasked with preventing further violence and finding those responsible for acts of violence in North Carolina to bring them to justice. Prosecution of top Klan leaders began a couple of weeks before the 1966 Final Four, and by late 1966, the Klan was starting to decline significantly from its peak in 1965, as more of its leaders were put in prison. The NC Klan chaplain George Dorsett claimed that the Black power movement in late 1966 had helped increase Klan attendance, although there isn't any indication that the Black power movement at that time was significant in NC.

So when we examine events of that era, we see that the 1966 NCAA championship game occurred at *precisely* the moment in history when the civil rights movement was starting to go in a different direction. The civil rights movement, had, up until then, been a largely Southern movement which was concerned with removal of legal barriers to Black opportunity, a large number of which the passage of the Civil Rights Act and the Voting Rights Act had helped to remove. The struggle was shifting in early 1966, first to dealing with racial issues on a national level, corresponding to King's move from south to north in 1966, and second, to dealing with economic issues (why so many Blacks throughout the country were economically disadvantaged). And it also occurred at a moment in history when many Blacks were considering abandoning King's nonviolence in favor of a more confrontational approach, as well as at a time when the KKK was still very active relative to what it had been before the civil rights era. So the 1966 game occurred at a moment in history when large numbers of Black youth were looking for some kind of positive direction as the civil rights movement was changing.

So whither the 1966 Final Four. What would have happened then? Would a Black victory over a White team provide any positive direction for Black America? Conversely, could a White team playing a Black team have triggered racial troublemaking? Could it have happened in Durham? Well, in reality it didn't happen that way. In the actual historical case, there was little reason for it to happen; race riots usually start for negative reasons, and Texas Western won the game, an event of positive significance to the Black community. It also isn't likely because most race riots in that era occurred in summer months and were usually a result of run-ins of local residents with police. However, there's no way to be completely sure. Dr. King's death, only a couple of calendar weeks after the Final Four in early April, triggered riots throughout the country. So given the fact that the Klan was still strong in 1966, we *can't* be completely sure that a close rough game *wouldn't* have provoked any kind of disturbances.

It helped that the actual game played in 1966 between Kentucky and Texas Western was not really as close as the final score; Texas Western won a clear-cut victory. There was no question about the officiating or which team won. Anyone who saw the game saw Texas Western win and a public repudiation of Adolph Rupp. There was little to argue about; no obvious close calls to dispute to start racial trouble at work or at other locations. Given the state of race relations at the time, that was indeed a favorable outcome. The game was also on late, at 10 p.m., and not nationally televised—it was only televised on tape-delay in a number of American cities. So, the actual potential for immediate troublemaking was relatively minor, limited to the cities where it was televised.

But supposing another team had played the game, say Duke? A bigger White team, with a better front line than Kentucky, maybe? A team that matched up well with Texas Western and wouldn't back down under the basket? What would have happened if the game were closer, maybe rougher, or even, where more fouls might have been called or there were issues with the officiating? How would people have responded to a game like that? Would that have been a game that gave Black America any positive direction? Or would it have been a game that only stirred up trouble, seen by every one of the one hundred cities that were to have race riots in 1967?

We'll never know for sure. But the odds are actually about fifteen to one that this *was* the game that tens of millions of people would have seen, read, or heard about in 1966 throughout the country. And in North Carolina, that meant the odds were about even that Durham would have seen an all-White team beat an all-Black team. What would have happened then?

CHAPTER 5

BOB VERGA'S ILLNESS: THE VERGA-CONLEY MATRIX

As Duke and Kentucky prepared for what was billed as the actual national championship game in the semifinals, it appears that almost none of the participants understood the significance of what was about to happen; everyone involved was almost entirely concerned with the athletic competition of the games, not the racial and social aspects, which were ultimately to impact tens of millions of people's lives. The two teams preparing for the eagerly awaited showdown between the number one (Kentucky) and number two (Duke) rated teams in College Park, Maryland, were focused on the partisan athletic aspects of what was to happen. Everyone was awaiting, what was supposed to be, a close, hard-fought game between what were believed to be the two best teams in the country. Most people believed that this game was the actual national championship game. That occurred fairly often back then, as the Final Four teams were not seeded; they were paired by region. So there was actually a one in three chance of the two best teams meeting in the semifinals.

However, the top two teams were not quite the same as they had been for most of the season. One of Kentucky's best players, Larry Conley, had not been at full strength due to the flu for several days prior to the game. But Duke's team wasn't healthy either. One of Duke's best players, All-American shooting guard Bob Verga, had come down with a serious case of strep throat the week before the game. Verga was something of a campus legend. In high school, he had been unstoppable, averaging over forty points a game, and had won the New Jersey state championship in 1963 by two points, 82–80, on a twenty-five-footer at the buzzer. His father, a wealthy New Jersey doctor, had bought him a red sports car in which he drove around the Duke campus. He was an excellent all-around athlete, later making a living as a tennis coach after his professional basketball career ended. His girlfriend was a gorgeous New York model. He was the campus runner-up in the pool tournament, and he often went to the all-Black Stallion Club in Durham on Cornwallis Road, back when it was still segregated. The same artists who appeared there sometimes played on the juke box at Card Gym, where Verga would sometimes walk through on his way to Cameron Indoor Stadium.

Kids idolized Verga back then. He was the guy who did in real life the things everyone else did in their dreams. He was the guy who really hit the buzzer-fantasy long-heave jump shot to win the state championship. Verga got the awesome chick that everyone else wanted, drove the hot car, got featured in the sporting magazines, scored bushels of points in every game, and partied with the '60s Black soul music stars. I myself, looking up to Verga as the last kid off the bench on his church league team, couldn't even imagine playing like Verga. Bob Verga looked like someone from another planet about a million light-years away from anything I could ever be.

My brother was a huge Verga fan too, often listening to the games on the radio. Other people did too. One Duke fan, who lived in Cary, North Carolina, never actually had the chance to see a game in Cameron. However, if they were close enough to Durham, the dad and two sons would sit in the car and listen to the entire game on the radio. If the station faded out, they'd find a hill or somewhere the reception was better. Especially if it was a close game, they'd drive around forever to hear how it ended. Fans didn't want to miss the ending of a Verga game; he was a great clutch player, so it was often exciting.

Duke was clearly a better team with Verga on the floor. Verga was the Steph Curry of his day. He was a great shooter from anywhere, who shot nearly 49 percent for his career (nearly six points higher than all-time Duke scoring leader J. J. Redick). Most of Verga's shots were from three-point range, in an era where they only counted for two points. He had incredible shooting range; he could score at a good percentage from almost anywhere inside thirty feet. He routinely shot from beyond twenty-five feet and did not hesitate to put it up; he had the green light to shoot almost any time he was open, which he often did. Teammate Mike Lewis said, "Sure Bob shot all the time, but that was what he was supposed to do. He did it better than anyone else in the country, so why should we put restraints on him?"[1]

Verga's jump shot looked strange; he sort of sling-shotted the ball more from behind his head than in front, but it was deadly accurate. His senior year at Duke, he averaged more than twenty-six points a game—the Duke scoring average record until J. J. Redick broke it in 2006 by only a half point (with the help of the three-point shot). If the shots Verga took which were actually from three-point range counted as threes, his average that year would have been nearly thirty-two points a game, well beyond Redick, and essentially an unbreakable Duke record. Verga went on to play about six years in the ABA, averaging over twenty points a game, playing in the ABA all-star game, and was a legend in the Jersey Shore summer basketball league (which he helped found in 1969) for years after that.

In 1966, when the Kentucky game was played, Verga was still a junior, on a team with three other main scoring options: Mike Lewis, Jack Marin, and Steve Vacendak (Bob Reidy was mostly a glue player, but did contribute a respectable nine to ten points a game). Yet he averaged about nineteen points a game, and he was voted second team All-America at the end of the year. He also affected the offense in other ways as well. A good ball handler, he spaced the floor and ensured that he be guarded at all times. Verga made it harder for the other teams to double down on Marin and Lewis and ensured that they took better shots and scored more easily, a significant factor against the shorter Kentucky team (they would not have been able to employ as many double teams on the larger Duke players). He was known as a clutch scorer; he could get baskets when the game was on the line, as it would have been down the stretch in a close game against Kentucky. In one game, when Duke was trailing against Michigan by fourteen at the half, he scored twenty points in the second half—including nine of the last eleven—to help win the game.

Verga was not known as a particularly good defensive player, but he was quick enough to acceptably guard most backcourt players his size. He was a good enough defender to play several years in the ABA, where lack of *any* defensive ability (the ABA was *not* known for defense) would have kept him out of the lineup. His presence also assured that there was sufficient backcourt depth to guard the opposing team's players throughout the game. Against Kentucky, who were a deeper team that relied extensively on their fast break, this was an important factor. His absence increased the defensive load on the remaining players and ensured that they would be more fatigued down the stretch when the game was decided (as when Larry Conley himself raced the length of the floor to score the clinching field goal with about a minute to go).

The week before the Kentucky game, Duke beat Syracuse by ten points in the East Regional final, with future longtime Syracuse coach Jim Boeheim in his last game as a college player. Boeheim was convinced that Duke would have won with Verga; Verga had been Most Outstanding Player in the East Regional, scoring twenty-one points in the championship game against Syracuse, and he noted that the Duke team was also bigger and had a better point guard in Steve Vacendak. About Verga, he said, "Verga made eight or ten shots, deep shots. They would have been three today. Verga got sick in the semifinals or they would have won."[2] Seeing Duke with a healthy Verga, his Syracuse teammate All American Dave Bing said, "Duke is the best team I've seen. I think they can go all the way."[3] It appeared to reliable independent observers that Verga's illness was indeed a difference maker.

Verga was considered doubtful for the Kentucky game the next week. As it turns out, he managed to go on the floor and play for more than half of it. However, as he was only a shell of what he was when he was healthy, he scored only four points; the illness had clearly incapacitated him. Verga had lost five pounds the week before the game. Verga's illness has gone down in Duke legend as the main reason Duke lost the Duke-Kentucky game. Teammate Bob Riedy said after the game, "That wasn't Verga. He just couldn't play that night. We were even surprised that he dressed for the game."[4] Directly after the game, Coach Bubas said, "I hope you fellas don't think that is the way Verga plays all the time. He was a sick boy."[5] As Verga himself said after the game, "My illness told in my legs. You shoot with your legs, and it told on me."[6] Duke lost by four points, 83-79.

Clearly Verga's illness had a significant effect on the Duke team, but was it decisive in changing the outcome of the Kentucky game? Duke coach Vic Bubas thought so. Bubas said "You'll never know for sure, but I think we would have won with a healthy Verga."[7] Verga himself seemed to think so too. "We went into the game, I was averaging twenty-some points and I came out with five [actually four]. We lost by four."[8] Adding only five points to the Duke total would have changed the outcome, and it seems clear that Verga's additional scoring could readily have done that. In the Kentucky game, the game was tied with four minutes to go; it was that close without him.

However, the issue was clouded by the illness of Kentucky's Larry Conley. Conley had a bug for nearly a week and received three penicillin shots that week. So he was not at his best for the Duke game either. Now, Larry Conley was a pretty good college basketball player too. He won a state championship in high school in 1961 and finished as runner up in 1962. He was, along with Riley and Dampier, first team All-SEC his senior year, at the time of the game. He was also a pretty good student, being an academic All-American in 1964 (there haven't been many in recent years), his academic success on display as he went on to become a very articulate and capable broadcaster. Conley was the best passer on the team, being the team leader in assists on the 1966 team, and actually is still number nine on the all-time assist list in Kentucky history. Adolph Rupp even compared Conley to Bob Cousy in college. According to Rupp, "We played against Cousy twice when Cousy was at Holy Cross. . . . A better passer than Cousy of Holy Cross."[9] Conley was only eligible for three years. With freshman eligibility, he might be near the top of the list. He was also a good, although not outstanding, defensive player.

But Conley's absence did not affect Kentucky as much as Verga's did Duke for three reasons. First, Verga was, overall, a better player. Verga was averaging nearly nineteen points a game versus Conley's eleven, and he had a better overall career (second team All-America in 1966). Conley was good enough to be All-SEC, but he was only the fourth leading scorer on the Kentucky team; his scoring level was almost at the same level as two of the other starters, Thad Jaracz and Tommy Kron. Secondly, Verga's production was much less replaceable than Conley's. Conley's playmaking skills were helpful to Kentucky. Dampier, Riley, and the other players were able to pick up much of what Conley did, as *all* of the Kentucky players were good passers and ball handlers; that had been the reason they had been so successful all season and was how the team had been designed. Duke's backcourt without Verga was somewhat thin; there was no one in the backcourt rotation capable of replicating Verga's shooting and ball handling.

And finally, Conley simply wasn't as sick as Verga in the actual game. Both were sick, and wound up guarding each other, as neither could guard anyone else. When Verga tried to guard Louie Dampier at the beginning of the game, Dampier had little difficulty head faking him for an easy fifteen-footer. Dampier finished with twenty-three points. Verga's illness affected Duke more than Conley's did Kentucky because he was a better player and he was sicker.

Conley managed to play a total of twenty-eight minutes in the game, and unlike the wheezing Verga, was able to contribute when he was on the floor. Verga, on the other hand, shot only two for seven and had four points; Conley scored ten points, only one less than his season's average. In the first half, when Conley sat down, Kentucky went from up seven to down five, so Conley was clearly well enough to help his team. Conley had a deep chest cold, was running a 102-degree fever, and breathing over a vaporizer. He played sparingly but still made a difference. According to the *Lexington Herald*, "The Wildcats appeared to be at their best with their playmaker operating at forward."[10]

So Conley was still able to play well enough to be a factor in the game, while Verga clearly was not; had he been in the game near the end, he would have been able to help guard Conley and also score down the stretch if the game was close, at which he excelled. The long time *Sports Illustrated* writer Curry Kirkpatrick agreed with that analysis. "The outcome turned on which significant player—Larry Conley of Kentucky or Bob Verga of Duke— could recover more completely from similarly severe cases of the flu."[11] While Verga managed only two baskets, Conley was able—near the end of the game when he had played more than twenty minutes—to somehow grab a defensive rebound, race the length of the court, and score to give Kentucky a seven-point lead with a minute left. Conley was asked where he got the energy to hit the clinching layup. "I don't know. I saw we had them three on two, and knew I had to go in."[12] At that point,

Verga was out of the game, unable to provide the late-game, backcourt defense needed to guard Conley. So yes, the Duke legend is correct; Verga's illness made more of a difference.

But was Verga's illness the deciding factor? Who replaced Verga and Conley when they sat down (which Conley did often in the game, frequently signaling to the coach to take him out when he was tired)? Kentucky also had slightly better backcourt depth, although Rupp typically did not play his bench players on that team many minutes, sticking with five or six players; their top backcourt bench player, Bob Tallent, who replaced Conley for part of the game, was closer in ability to Conley than Verga's replacement, Ron Wendelin, was to Verga. Wendelin was typically Duke's third guard in the rotation, and had started a couple of games, sometimes giving good production. Verga played for twenty-eight minutes in the game, even when sick, which shows that Wendelin's production was typically far below Verga's; even Verga's two for seven, four-point effort in the game was considered on a par with what Wendelin would produce in the same time. Wendelin actually played much of the game for both Verga and Vacendak, shot one for four and managed only two points—well below a healthy Verga's likely offensive production in the same time on the floor. Verga's absence also forced Wendelin and the other Duke backcourt players (the other starter Steve Vacendak in particular) to play more minutes, helping them tire out down the stretch when Duke lost the actual game, a significant factor against a team like Kentucky that relied extensively on it's fast break.

By contrast, Tallent scored four points in the actual game in many less minutes in the game than Wendelin. According to Pat Riley, "Tallent played a hell of a game what time he was in there."[13] Overall, the Kentucky Conley-Tallent guard combination outscored the Duke Verga-Wendelin one in the game by 14-6. By comparison, in the base case where all four players are healthy, the Verga-Wendelin duo on average that year combined for twenty-one points, versus fourteen for Conley-Tallent. That's a net change of fifteen points, well more than enough to likely change the outcome in Duke's favor if all of the players were healthy.

Now, on the surface, the fifteen-point difference is obviously misleading, since the other Duke players—Marin and Lewis especially—were going to have more chances to score against Kentucky's smaller front line to make up much of the difference. But Verga's absence also meant that the Kentucky guards were free to double down on Marin and Lewis, which they could not have done with Verga in the game. They didn't have to worry about a Duke offensive rebound and kickout to a wide-open Verga, which was a virtually automatic score. That forced Marin and Lewis to work harder to score, and made them take harder shots, and more of them; both Pat Riley, who primarily guarded Marin, and Thad Jaracz, who primarily guarded Lewis, fouled out trying to guard them in the game, so they clearly needed help with the taller Duke players. And with Verga in the game, they wouldn't have gotten it. (Kentucky still had sufficient frontcourt depth with six-foot-eight Cliff Berger and six-five Tommy Kron to guard Marin and Lewis down the stretch after Riley and Jaracz got in foul trouble.) Verga being out also allowed Kentucky to switch off their best backcourt defender from Verga to Steve Vacendak, who was not as good a shooter as Verga, but who had to shoot more with him out of the lineup. Vacendak took more shots than usual in the actual game and wound up missing more than half of them.

Verga's absence was felt primarily on offense; it assumes that there were no great differences in defensive ability between Verga and Wendelin, which the record is not quite clear about. Dampier and Conley, the players Wendelin helped guard, managed to get about their averages in the game (Dampier got twenty-nine while primarily being guarded by Steve Vacendak, Duke's best defensive player), while Wendelin committed four fouls, so it doesn't appear that he provided any significant improvement on that end. And it certainly would not appear to have been enough to compensate significantly for overall loss of defense in the latter stages of the game due to fatigue, when Kentucky was finally able to pull away and win the game (Verga out of the rotation forced both Vacendak and Wendelin to play more minutes). So the loss of Verga's offensive ability (and defensive depth) was indeed decisive.

So let us examine a Verga-Conley matrix to see what the likely outcomes would have been under various scenarios of the two players being sick. There are four scenarios of the two players being sick or well that could have determined the outcome that night: neither sick, one or the other being sick, or both being sick. The historical case is in the lower right-hand corner. Examining the matrix and examining the players at full strength and when they were sick, the outcomes become more complicated.

In the base case, both players were healthy. The above analysis shows that if the game were played with a full-strength Verga and a full-strength Conley, it appears that the edge in an original four-point game would have swung (slightly) to Duke. There is no guarantee that Duke would have won in that case; most games have a considerable swing, plus or minus ten points or so, depending on game-to-game factors such as shooting, fouls, fatigue, random bounces, injuries, and team chemistry issues. Jack Marin and Verga both liked to shoot and didn't always get along, so the Duke point guard Steve Vacendak constantly had to measure how he doled out the assists to keep both happy. With Verga out, Marin got to shoot about as much as he wanted, but it seems reasonable to conclude that the odds would have been much more in Duke's favor, and it is more than likely that they would have won.

It would have been helpful to examine the games on a statistical game simulator. However, these simulators rely on a number of advanced statistics which were not kept back then. After checking with multiple simulator services, I confirmed that it was not possible to do this without the additional statistics.

However, an examination of the closeness of the actual game and Verga's crucial role in both shooting and defending Kentucky's up-tempo offense (he was the one Duke player who would have made a difference on both ends of the court) gives little doubt that such simulations would readily have shown that Verga's presence would easily have given Duke the five more points needed to win the game.

VERGA-CONLEY MATRIX

	Verga Not Sick	**Verga Sick**
Conley Not Sick	Duke Likely Wins (sorry Pat Riley)	Kentucky Wins
Conley Sick	Duke Wins	Kentucky Likely Wins (Historical case)

So was it just a coincidence that Verga was sick? That is also interesting to speculate on. Well, in order to ensure that Duke lost, it could actually have been any of the top four Duke players. I'm including Steve Vacendak in the list to be conservative; while he didn't score as much (he averaged around thirteen points a game, still significant), he was an excellent defensive player, and was ACC player of the year in 1965.

So let's examine the odds of one of the top four Duke players being out of the game. A typical healthy person at ages eighteen to twenty is conservatively sick about four days a year. So looking at the top four Duke players, that's about sixteen days a year where one of them would be sick. If we double the number for four cold weather months between December and March, we find that maybe one of the four top players would get sick about twice a month during the winter, or about once every fifteen days. That's about a fifteen-to-one odds that one of the sick days of the top four players would fall on the game day. So the odds of the game occurring the way it did, with or without Conley being sick, were about fifteen to one. A fifteen-to-one chance that the game America saw in 1966 would have been completely different.

So was the game actually fixed? Say that someone up there—disproportionately preoccupied with American college basketball, and actually having some idea of the social significance of the 1966 Final Four, which all the participants clearly did not—having examined the possible outcomes of a Duke-Texas Western game, decided to put an all-powerful finger on the scale? Or maybe a gambler somewhere figured out how to make one of the Duke players sick to change the outcome? That's basically what would have had to have happened. And yet, when looking at the actual odds of one of the top Duke players being sick, and the way events turned out with Duke losing, maybe it isn't so far-fetched. Who knows.

CHAPTER 6

THE 1966 FINAL FOUR

When writing the story of how the 1966 Final Four games actually happened, it almost seems like something of an afterthought. Compared with the consequences of the games later on, why write much about the games when it's what happened before and after that seems so much more relevant? The Kentucky-Texas Western game has been written about very extensively and has had a movie made about it (whose accuracy has been challenged by many of the participants). But in order to understand the incredible consequences of the games, it is necessary to have a look at what it was that people actually saw or heard in the 1966 Final Four that changed their lives. The championship game itself was not carried live on national TV, and it started at 10 p.m. EST. However, a large number of people heard it on the radio, especially in Kentucky, and it was also on the news. So the game still had a large impact at the time it was played, and an even greater one in later years.

The 1966 Final Four was scheduled to be played on March 18 and 19 in Cole Field House, in College Park, Maryland, one of the largest venues existing at the time. On March 17, the four teams, Utah, Duke, Kentucky, and Texas Western, were in College Park ready to play. America eagerly awaited the upcoming games, especially the Duke-Kentucky game, which was widely perceived as being the national championship game. The Texas

Western team, being the first team to start all-Black starters, was attracting national media attention; however, even though they were ranked third and came in with only one loss (they had not beaten a top-ten opponent during the regular season and had barely gotten by two regional opponents), they were not considered serious championship contenders by the (all-White) media. So the opening tipoff of the Final Four was awaited with considerable anticipation, especially the Duke-Kentucky game.

It is important to recognize today how different the Final Four and the NCAA tournament were back then. Today's sixty-four-team March Madness of televised games, brackets, and company betting pools is a far cry from the world of 1966. In 2016, the television rights for the NCAA tournament went for $8.8 billion; in 1980, they went for less than $10 million. In 1966, the rights for the NCAA championship game cost the TVS Television Network, a syndication company, only $140,000 (maybe $3 million in today's money).

However, college basketball had already come a long way in twenty-seven years since the first NCAA tournament was played in 1939, right before WWII. It was now considered an important sport, worthy of *Sports Illustrated* covers, and the NCAA championship itself was considered a major sporting event. But in 1966, there were still only twenty-two teams in the NCAA tournament (the west and Midwest brackets had only one first-round game while the east and Mideast had two), which meant that the finals were played a couple weeks earlier in the year. The NCAA brackets were determined by the NCAA committee in matchups with various conferences, based on their perceived overall strength; higher seeds didn't have to play in the initial round. Most of the tournament games were not televised; in 1966, the Final Four was only televised regionally.

Many conferences back then only sent the conference champion to the NCAAs, even if there were other ranked deserving teams. That meant that the NIT still had some significance back then, with many nationally ranked conference runners-up participating. In the ACC, only the ACC tournament champion actually made the NCAAs; winning the regular season did not guarantee an ACC team an NCCA berth, as it did for the 1966 SEC regular season champion Kentucky (the only representative of their conference that year as well), regardless of ranking. This led University of South Carolina to eventually leave the league in 1971, as they continually had to play (and lose) the ACC tournament in the unfriendly arenas of North Carolina—their lone tournament win occurred that very year when six-three Kevin Joyce famously outjumped six-eleven Lee Dedmon for the ball on the deciding play of the game in South Carolina's last conference game as a member of the ACC.

Duke had won the ACC tournament in 1966, barely getting by University of North Carolina (UNC) in the semifinals by a score of 21–20, with Duke center Mike Lewis hitting both winning free throws with four seconds to go. This was a game that was also near the beginning of Dean Smith's sixteen-year reign of four corner offense stallball, Smith being described by author Art Chansky in *Blue Blood* as a "daring young coach and strategist."[1] Many people at the game significantly differed with that assessment, pouring forth an avalanche of boos and epithets, and throwing trash at the UNC bench, hitting the UNC coaches with several balled-up paper cups. This was a response that would be often repeated in the next sixteen years. After the game, Duke coach Vic Bubas tersely stated, "I have no comment on their style of play. It's in the rulebook and a coach can elect to use it. That's his decision."[2] Smith's response, with his usual concern for good sportsmanship was, "I didn't want a good game, I wanted to win."[3]

Despite barely getting by UNC to win the ACC tournament, Duke had played well in the first two rounds of the NCAAs. They had been ranked number one most of the season before losing a couple games in February to slip behind Kentucky to number two. They were led by sophomore guard Bob Verga and senior forward Jack Marin, both averaging more than eighteen points per game, and both eventual second team All-Americans. They had beaten St. Joseph's in a close game in the regional semifinals and Syracuse—with future Hall of Famer Dave Bing and future Syracuse coach Jim Boeheim—by ten points in the regional finals, having put on a strong stretch run in which Verga had helped significantly, as discussed in chapter five. And so, they eagerly awaited their semifinal game with Kentucky.

Kentucky was the champion of the Mideast regional. They were the SEC champions, with a record of 26-1, with their only loss in late February. Starting unranked, they had played their way up in the rankings, taking over the number one spot from Duke in February. All-Americans Pat Riley and Louie Dampier led them in scoring, averaging more than twenty-one points a game each. They had come into the game having defeated Dayton and Michigan, with the great All-American Cazzie Russell, whom Duke had played two years before, in the Mideast regional by seven points in each game.

The champions of the Midwest were the Miners of Texas Western, ranked number three. Like Kentucky, they had started the year unranked, but had played their way up the polls, being first ranked in early January. They had almost gone undefeated, losing their final game to Seattle by two points on a questionable no-call. However, despite their outstanding regular season record, they had barely gotten through their regional, beating Cincinnati in overtime and Kansas (then the number four ranked team) in double overtime on a disputed call on a last second shot by Jo Jo White, the future great Celtics player, where his foot was ruled to be out of bounds. The narrowness of their victories contributed to the perception of them being underdogs.

Utah, with All-American forward Jerry Chambers, represented the western regional. They were the only team besides UCLA to do that between 1964 and 1976 (UCLA was not in the NCAA tournament that year). They were a not particularly impressive

23-6 coming into the Final Four, having gone 7-3 in the fairly weak Western Conference, and were unranked in the final AP poll. Their starting center was out for the Final Four with a broken leg, meaning they had almost no one to guard David Lattin. Consequently, Utah was not taken seriously as a championship contender; in the movie *Glory Road*, the Utah team and the semifinal game are not even mentioned. Despite the fact that Utah ultimately finished fourth, Chambers actually set the four game NCAA tournament scoring record that year with 132 points.

The Utah-Texas Western game was not particularly eventful. Even though the tournament MOP, Utah forward Jerry Chambers (the only player on a fourth-place team to ever do that), went for thirty-eight points, Texas Western still managed to pull away and win 85-78. (The game actually did have ironic racial implications. After Harry Flournoy and David Lattin had fouled out trying to guard Chambers, Texas Western used a White player, six-four Jerry Armstrong, to control him down the stretch, saving the Texas Western season.) The game was not as close as the two games Texas Western had played directly before. Its primary significance would be to guarantee that Texas Western would be the first all-Black team to play for the national championship. If Utah had won (Texas Western had been heavily favored), the game would indeed have been considered historically significant, but that was not the case.

But the second semifinal game, between Duke and Kentucky, was the game with greater historical implications. Coming into it, this game was considered by a large number of observers, as well as most of the players on the actual teams to be the actual national championship. It is important to recognize that the Final Four teams were not seeded back then; they were matched up by region. That meant there was typically a one in three chance that the actual championship game would be played in the semifinals. John Wooden, who had just won two, and was about to win eight more, seemed to think it would be that year: "Duke is the best team I've seen all year. But I haven't seen Kentucky. Let's say the champion will be the winner of Duke-Kentucky."[4] Most other coaches at the time agreed that the winner would likely be national champions. Duke was the ACC champion, while Kentucky was the SEC champion, both Southern all-White conferences. Both of them were schools with a significant history of basketball success—Duke's being more recent with Final Fours in 1963 and 1964 under Vic Bubas, but Kentucky's with four national championships under Adolph Rupp was more illustrious. Both teams had multiple All-Americans; Pat Riley and Louis Dampier from Kentucky were All-Americans, as were Bob Verga and Jack Marin for Duke. Two of the Duke seniors, Jack Marin and Steve Vacendak, had been on the 1964 Duke team that lost to Wooden's UCLA squad in the championship game. There was immense anticipation on March 18, 1966, as the two programs prepared to meet in College Park, Maryland, even though the illnesses of Verga and Conley had clearly affected both teams as described in chapter five; due to the way the teams matched up, Duke thought they could still win without Verga contributing, as did Kentucky with Conley.

Before the game, my family and I prepared to watch the game on TV. Back then, all we had was a black-and-white, portable, nineteen-inch model, with rabbit ears antenna. Most people didn't have color TVs in 1966. There was only one family on our block who had a color TV, a big console model. We used to go down the street to their house in the summer on Tuesday nights to watch *Batman* and *The Green Hornet*. There was a choice of about three or four network channels back then, and that was it. At home, as we prepared for the opening tip, we were all huddled around our little black-and-white TV to see our beloved Blue Devils in the Final Four on TV. It was a big deal.

As tipoff time approached, the Duke players went out to play the game with one of their best players, Verga, only a shell of himself. Duke's burly six-eight center, Mike Lewis, went up and controlled the opening tip over six-four Pat Riley (Riley was famous for stealing tips with early jumps), and the game was on. The first half of the game was fairly close. Duke, knowing they had a size advantage down low, tried to keep the game at a slightly slower pace and get the ball to their larger front line, while the smaller, deeper Kentucky team pushed the ball upfloor quickly at every opportunity, even with Conley in rough shape. Kentucky got out to an early lead, but Duke, switching defenses, caught up and passed them. Both Verga and Conley played in the first half, with Conley being more effective. Since they were both sick, the coaches had to have them guard each other; they couldn't guard anyone else. Conley was feeling a little better, and ultimately managed ten points, one less than his scoring average. Verga, trying his best to help his team, could muster little, shooting fourteen points less than his average and doing almost nothing on defense, as discussed in chapter five.

As halftime approached, the game was still close. In the first half, Duke had successfully worked the ball in to its frontcourt players, Marin and Lewis, who scored effectively over Kentucky's small front line (they would finish the game with fifty points between them, well above their combined averages). Mike Lewis, the Duke center said, "We felt we could win even without Verga. Kentucky didn't have much size. I should have scored more than I did."[5] Both Kentucky and Duke started in a zone, but the well-matched shooting of each team forced them to play man to man. Marin, in particular, used his two-inch height advantage to score against Pat Riley effectively. On the other end, Kentucky used their quickness and depth to keep pace and get transition baskets. At halftime, the score was 42–41 in favor of Duke. It looked like the game would go down to the wire.

As the second half began, it was clear that Verga would not be able to do much more. Verga sat on the bench near the end of the game, his time on the floor over. Conley was able to play some in the second half but was still not at full strength, often raising his hand to come out. But as the second half wore on, Kentucky's superior depth began to show as the Duke players started tiring down the stretch, and it was clear that Duke missed Verga more than Kentucky missed (a still passably functioning) Conley. After the lead changed hands in the second half, Kentucky started leading down the stretch, behind their greater depth, and Duke couldn't quite close the gap. Marin and Lewis, who had been able to help Duke keep pace with Kentucky in the first half, started missing their shots and falling behind on defense. Without Verga's scoring and defense, Duke could not keep pace with the faster Kentucky team; they repeatedly tied the score at sixty-three, sixty-five, sixty-seven, and sixty-nine, but they couldn't take the lead, as Kentucky kept forging ahead.

After Duke tied the score for the final time at seventy-one with about four minutes to go, Kentucky went ahead for good. Duke, playing from behind and needing to score, had to foul, playing at the pace Kentucky wanted. Finally, near the end, Duke managed a last gasp comeback. They cut the margin to four points with under two minutes to go in the game, and they had the ball. Mike Lewis, tiring from having to carry more of the scoring load, missed a shot down low that would have tied the game with less than a minute to go. Kentucky rebounded (the shorter Kentucky team actually outrebounded Duke by four rebounds) and scored on a fast-break layup by Larry Conley, (who was down to his last gasp at that point) to put the lead back up to seven points and effectively end the game. At that point Duke was through; their last comeback had fallen short. Kentucky hung on to win by four points. And so, the team that earned the right to play the fateful game with Texas Western was University of Kentucky.

As Mike Lewis's potentially game-changing shot fell off the rim, I fell on the floor in tears, as Duke's defeat was now inevitable. As the game ended, my father turned off the TV and tried to console me. Our beloved Blue Devils, the greatest Duke team in the pre-Krzyzewski era, had been defeated. The 1966 team would never again be replicated at Duke; the window of championship opportunity during the rest of my life in Durham was closed forever. I would never again see Duke play in the NCAAs the entire time I was growing up in Durham. All summer in a day.

And my childhood hero, Senior Captain Steve Vacendak, playing his last game in a Duke uniform, felt the same way. Losing the chance to play for the national championship his senior year (he had also played for it as a sophomore in 1964, losing to UCLA) hurt Vacendak more than anything ever had as a basketball player. Vacendak, a very tough player, always played with heart and emotion in every game, taking charges, diving for loose balls, and leading the team. According to the *Durham Sun*, he was inconsolable after the game, sobbing on the Duke bench, feeling as if his world had come to an end. "Steve felt Duke could beat Kentucky—and it hurt deeply when the decision went the other way."[6]

As the Duke and Kentucky players walked off the court, they congratulated each other, not to meet again in the NCAAs for another twelve years, when they would play for the actual championship. What neither team knew that night, but which Rupp had actually suspected, was that history was closing in on both programs. The era of all-White basketball teams was coming to an end. It would be nearly a decade before either program reclaimed their former greatness, with mixed-race teams (and without Adolph Rupp or Vic Bubas as coaches), which Kentucky was still very slow to embrace. In the meantime, UCLA, who was about to play all-time NBA scoring champion Lew Alcindor and had actually won the two previous championships, was building a mixed-race dynasty for the ages, which would render both programs irrelevant for the next nine years. But in 1966, no one on either team knew that.

And so, the semifinals were over. The national championship matchup was, fatefully, to be Kentucky and Texas Western.

Surprisingly, the game itself was somewhat anticlimactic for two reasons. First, most observers believed beforehand that the Duke-Kentucky game was the actual national championship. As one Kentucky player said: "We beat Duke and to be honest, I was surprised we did. . . . So, we kind of felt like we had already won the championship because we beat Duke."[7] The *Washington Post* even suggested that the game would be anti-climactic in comparison to Kentucky's semifinal matchup against Duke, since many saw them as the two best teams in college basketball. Had all players been healthy on both teams, it may actually have turned out that way. But secondly, even though the actual championship game was competitive, it wasn't really that close, or even particularly dramatic. Texas Western won a convincing victory in a methodical, relatively unemotional fashion. And what we see in subsequent chapters is how different the game everyone saw would have been if Duke had played it.

At the outset, Kentucky was considered the favorite. Despite their short height, the Kentucky team was 27-1, losing only once at the end of the season. They successfully beat taller teams the whole year, many of them with good Black players such as Cazzie Russell. Even with Conley not at full strength, they still played well enough to beat a Verga-less Duke. So Kentucky was actually considered the favorite, and they were helped by the fact that Conley was recovering to close to full strength. He ultimately played thirty-five minutes in the final game and scored ten points, one less than his average. Texas Western's leading rebounder, Harry Flournoy, re-injured his knee early in the final game, and played only six minutes, so the injury situation during the game slightly favored Kentucky.

It's been stated that at the time the game occurred most of the media did not generally recognize the racial implications of the game. The Kentucky players themselves did not discuss the racial implications of the game before they played it either. As Larry Conley, noting before the game that no one in the

Kentucky locker room was considering the racial implications of the game, stated, "All we wanted to do is win the national title. That's it. And if people ever portray us any differently, it's just wrong."[8] However, prior to the game, it was clear that many White people from Kentucky definitely did. The Kentucky pep band played "Dixie" repeatedly before the game. Legend has it that the Kentucky fans also waved Confederate flags, but the game films don't actually show any. Some observers said there were, others said there weren't. Frank Fitzpatrick, the author of *And the Walls Came Tumbling Down*, claims to have found at least one in a photo of the game.[9]

So, it was actually the White fans from Kentucky who were playing up the racial aspect prior to the game. *They* seemed to understand what the implications were and were making it clear before the game that they knew it. And Rupp did during the game as well. At halftime, Rupp supposedly told his players that they would never be able to show their faces in Lexington if they let five Black players beat them. And in retrospect, it becomes clear that at least the Kentucky supporters knew it had clear cut historical significance; it was then, and still is today, the only time in history that an all-Black team and all-White team have played each other for a major sports championship.

But the teams playing the game largely did not see it that way. Not only did neither team recognize the racial implications of the game before it was played, but neither team took the other seriously either. At the shootaround before the game, the Texas Western players were acting casual and not too concerned about things. Right before the game, the players were napping. When asked about the game, they appeared nonchalant. Coach Haskins, trying to get his players motivated and getting mad when he couldn't, said, "I'm trying to tell them how good Kentucky is and they're all just looking at me like 'You've gotta be kidding me.'"[10] Haskins looked at Bobby Joe Hill (the game eventual MVP): "He was taking a damn Sunday nap just before the national championship game," Haskins recalled years later. He was so mad, he hit him with a white board eraser.[11]

On the Kentucky side, the media and coaches were virtually unanimous that Kentucky would win. Only one of the polled coaches gave Texas Western a chance. The Eastern media hadn't taken them seriously, thinking that teams from remoter parts of the West couldn't play. Even the officials hanging around before the game didn't take them seriously. The Kentucky players were also confident; they had mostly recovered from the flu and weren't too concerned about Texas Western. They hadn't scouted them very much before the game. Said Conley, "The only thing I knew about Texas Western was that they were ranked third."[12] In contrast to today, when teams have huge amounts of videos and scouting reports to examine on other teams, Rupp had almost no information about them. In a cab on the way back to his hotel from the Duke game, Rupp actually asked the cab driver if he knew anything about Texas Western; none of his coaches knew anything about them at all.

But he certainly learned something about Coach Haskins and his team the next night. According to Frank Fitzpatrick, the two coaching protagonists were perfectly cast for the drama: "Rupp, the snarling epitome of an unyielding establishment, made a compelling villain. Haskins, the laconic loner who rode in from the West, was an appealing American hero."[13] After the pre-game meal, Coach Haskins called a meeting with all the Black players in David Lattin and Bobby Joe Hill's hotel room. He informed them that Adolph Rupp had said at a press conference that five Black players couldn't beat his five White players. According to Lattin, he then said, "It's up to you."[14] Then he walked out of the room. He didn't say anything else about it. Lattin turned to Bobby and asked him if he believed Rupp had really said that. Bobby replied that he didn't know if he said it or not, but that there was no way they were going to lose. According to Harry Flournoy, "From that point on Kentucky had as much chance of winning that game as a snowball had of surviving in hell."[15] Another Texas Western player wondered why Rupp would say something that could jeopardize his own team like that.[16] According to Kentucky player Pat Riley, Haskins made the whole thing up to inspire his team. "Adolph never said one word to us. I don't ever recall him ever saying one word [about] black-white."[17]

The game began with Riley trying to steal the tip, but the refs called it and gave the ball to Texas Western, and it soon became clear that Texas Western was something Kentucky had definitely not seen before. According to another Texas Western player, "It wasn't a regular game—we were so driven to win."[18] Pat Riley, not quite understanding what was about to happen, stated, "We realized immediately that this team was different than any one we'd ever faced."[19] Haskins drew up a play for David Lattin. On the second possession of the game, the Texas Western center David Lattin drove in and slammed home a vicious dunk on Pat Riley. (Players rarely dunked then; only center Mike Lewis did it occasionally for Duke.) David Lattin recalled later, "Kentucky players knew they were in for a game. The dunk made a difference."[20] He then blocked a Riley slam attempt a few plays later, sending Riley sprawling onto the floor. "We had no idea what we were getting into," Riley said. "But these guys came out, and after they had dunked on me about three times, I knew they had a lot more to accomplish than we did."[21] The tone for the game was set; Texas Western was not backing down.

Haskins decided to surprise Kentucky by playing a three-guard team, including six-one Orsten Artis, five-nine Bobby Joe Hill, and five-six Willie Worsley (who was incredibly quick and could actually dunk), to get more speed in the game against Kentucky's smaller team. The decision worked. On two subsequent plays, Bobby Joe Hill got two steals and breakaway layups, which gave Texas Western huge momentum. Dampier was changing directions on his dribble when the ball disappeared. "I wish I could forget those two steals," Dampier said. "I wish I could say that he fouled me, but he didn't."[22] Kentucky had been able to run their offense effectively against other teams, including Duke. Duke—especially without Verga—wasn't quick enough to stop Kentucky from getting good shots. But Texas Western was. They had a combination of inside size and backcourt quickness that Kentucky hadn't seen before. Kentucky's 1-3-1 zone (Rupp actually hated zone defenses, and almost always played man to man), which they used because they were shorter than the Texas Western frontline, was not particularly effective against Texas Western's methodical passing attack and quick players (there was no shot clock back then).

On the other end of the floor, Don Haskins had emphasized tough transition defense throughout the year—that was how they had won so many games. So Kentucky had to deal with likely the best defense they had seen all year. They were able to hold Kentucky without a field goal for nearly seven minutes in the first half, effectively shutting down their fast-paced offense, which almost no one had done all year. Texas Western's quickness enabled them to pressure the Kentucky players and disrupt their offense (a number of plays Kentucky ran against other teams didn't work at all against Texas Western). In addition to Texas Western's size advantage in the front court, they were also effective in guarding the perimeter and were quick enough and had enough depth to put pressure on Kentucky's ball handlers and contest Kentucky's transition game.

As the game wore on, Kentucky simply could not score effectively against Texas Western, having to shoot mostly outside shots, and was not big enough or quick enough to keep them from scoring on the other end. In addition to Lattin scoring down low, the quick Texas Western backcourt players were able to get, and hit, enough good outside shots against the Kentucky zone defense to keep the lead. Texas Western also hit most of their free throws, which they had practiced extensively, ultimately scoring almost 40 percent of their points from the line. Rupp and the

Kentucky players started getting frustrated. Rupp called timeout with about ten minutes gone in the first half and started yelling at his players. But it was to no avail. Texas Western took the lead for good about ten minutes into the first half. Kentucky stayed close, but they were not able to catch up with Texas Western in the first half.

At halftime, the score was thirty-four to thirty-one with Texas Western in the lead. As Larry Conley recounted years later, "The thing that sticks out in my mind is the tremendous defensive ability of Texas Western. They took us completely out of our game."[23] Sportswriter Frank Deford, who was in the Kentucky dressing room at the half, claims that Rupp made several racist remarks to the Kentucky players—including calling the Texas Western players coons, which made the Kentucky players visibly duck their heads and wince—to get them fired up to beat Texas Western. "He talked that way all the time. He hated black people," Deford said. "I mean, he was a virulent racist."[24]

But in the second half, regardless of Rupp's instructions, Texas Western pulled ahead. Kentucky mounted comebacks, but each time, Texas Western responded. With their deliberate offense and excellent transition defense, Texas Western was able to control Kentucky on both ends of the floor. When Kentucky cut it to one at 39-38 and 46-45, Texas Western responded with runs of their own, keyed by clutch shot maker Orsten Artis. Finally, with the score 54-51, Texas Western went on a six-point run, and the game was essentially over. Texas Western won 72-65. After the victory, no one brought them a ladder; five-six Willie Worsley had to sit on the shoulders of six-eight Nevil Shed to cut down the nets.

So what did everyone see during that game? Well, actually, everyone besides the author. It was on too late for me to watch, and I wouldn't have watched it anyway, being too destroyed by Duke's loss in the semifinal game to watch the finals. I was actually filled with schadenfreude over Kentucky's loss. (I was sitting there at age seven saying "Ha, ha, ha, your team lost too!") I did see Duke win the consolation game against Utah, with a healthier Verga, which made me feel a little better.

What the people who *did* see it saw was a few different things. It was a clear-cut Texas Western victory; even though Texas Western shot twenty-eight free throws to Kentucky's eleven, (two Kentucky players fouled out of the game) there was no doubt about the fouls. The shorter, slower Kentucky players were forced to foul the bigger, quicker Texas Western team, who responded by shooting twenty-eight of thirty-four from the free throw line. According to Rupp, "There was not a single boy on our team as strong as any on Texas Western."[25] So even though they made five more shots and outrebounded Texas Western, Kentucky's inability to stop them without fouling made the difference. (After the game, Rupp made sure to remind the press that his team got five more field goals than Texas Western.[26]) No one complained that the officiating was biased against Kentucky. In fact, an examination of the game film shows that almost all of the questionable calls appear to have gone against Texas Western, further proving the legitimacy of their victory.

What they also saw was that the Texas Western team was clearly physically better. They were taller, stronger, and quicker. Kentucky did not have the size or the quickness to either guard them or score effectively against them. And Texas Western's defense clearly had the Kentucky players stymied. Kentucky took twenty-one more shots than Texas Western, but still lost because they missed most of them. Kentucky shot 38 percent for the game, the lowest percentage they shot all season (their two All-Americans, Pat Riley and Louie Dampier, were a combined fifteen for forty in the game) and well below their average. Texas Western's defense had them completely frustrated.

So what people saw was a clear-cut Kentucky victory, in which Texas Western physically dominated and also effectively controlled the game, playing a disciplined, well-coached team basketball game; on one possession they actually passed the ball twenty times before feeding David Lattin for a dunk. The all-Black team won a convincing victory and did so in a manner which completely refuted the stereotypes of racist observers. The message to Black America was clear: you can go off to college, play, and win. As Duke center Mike Lewis said, noting how this game was actually viewed as a historical turning point, even though he and the other players on the floor didn't see it that way at the time, "It accelerated the change. If they hadn't won, I don't know what would've happened. But it did happen, and it was positive."[27] Inspired by the game, an entire generation of young, Black Americans realized that they could step forward to claim the life that their abilities rightfully gave them.

What is also surprising about the game is that at the time it was played almost no one involved, the players or the media, recognized the full implications of the game. David Lattin, virtually alone, did have some understanding of the racial significance (as we shall see later), but almost all of the rest of the Kentucky and Texas Western players said that at the time of the game, they were motivated by a simple desire to win the game. Said Texas Western's Harry Flournoy, "It was just simply an opportunity to show the nation what we had. We didn't say, 'We're going to go out there and whip those white players' butts.'"[28] According to Louie Dampier, they weren't even aware that Texas Western had five Black starters, "I had calls from L.A., Detroit, all over the country asking me that very question and it was like they were disappointed when I said, 'No we weren't thinking about the black-white thing.'"[29] According to Larry Conley, considering the game more than thirty years later, "All the racial overtones developed much later. We were kids, nineteen, twenty, twenty-one, trying to play a game."[30]

All the players on both teams had played extensively against players of the opposite race, some of them with teams that were predominantly of the other color. There had been Black players in basketball for nearly ten years, so most of the players didn't think about it much anymore. And the media, while obviously recognizing the difference, did not seem to believe that what was happening was particularly historic either. After the game, neither *Sports Illustrated* nor most newspapers discussed the racial aspect of it; they were sitting at the press table stunned after the game not knowing what to write. According to David Lattin, "It wasn't until the following year that people started to write about it. They didn't talk about it all that much after the game. . . . Nobody came to talk to us in our locker room."[31] As it became clear how it had affected millions of people who were not in the world of college basketball, the significance became clear.

So what would people have seen if Duke had played the game? The question of what might have been is always hard to answer. Would Haskins have played all-Black players against Duke, or would he have played one or two White players to defuse racial tensions? Haskins had a number of White players, and some of them were at an acceptable level; he had used one of them, Jerry Armstrong, as a defensive specialist in the Final Four game against Utah.

The answer appears to be that Haskins was determined to go all-Black against either team. When he saw the Duke-Kentucky game and saw that both were all-White Southern schools, he decided to go all-Black in the title game, before he knew which team had won. He had gone with all-Black starters throughout the year, and his top seven rotation players were Black. He likely realized that he could use the racial implications of the game to motivate his players. He had done so against all-White Kentucky; so it's very likely Haskins would have done the same thing with Duke.

In addition, the only really significant difference between Duke and Kentucky that might have resulted in a lineup change was six-eight center Mike Lewis, but he would clearly have been guarded by David Lattin, who was Black. Lewis himself wasn't considering the racial implications of the Final Four at the time.

The Bob Verga Shift

"We didn't care anything about that stuff. It didn't matter to us if Texas Western had five Martians starting."[32] But a lot of other people did.

Don Haskins was interested in winning. The national championship was at stake. Haskins had almost always started his Black players, or whoever he thought was playing the best. So even though Haskins might have realized that a Black against White game might have caused national racial troublemaking, he was not going to give up the national championship to promote racial harmony, especially when most of the players on his team would have been only too glad to beat an all-White Duke team. Texas Western's best White reserve, the previously mentioned Jerry Armstrong, was too slow to guard Duke's backcourt players and too short to guard their frontcourt ones. According to Armstrong, race was secondary in the original game. "Everything was all about the game, and everybody conducted themselves in that way."[33] So it appears almost certain that the team Duke played in the finals would indeed have been all-Black, since the seven best players on the Texas Western team all were.

What the Texas Western team saw when they stepped out on the floor that night was going to be essentially the same, regardless of if the team was Duke or Kentucky: an all-White Southern team who deserved to get their comeuppance. Before the game, Haskins brought the seven Black players into the locker room to discuss the game. David Lattin remembers thinking it was odd that only the Black players were there, not quite yet understanding the full significance of the situation. "We never thought we'd be the only guys who were going to be playing in that game. That hadn't happened all season."[34]

It's hard to say exactly how much Haskins racial appeals to his players mattered, but the Texas Western players were clearly motivated by Rupp's alleged statement that no five Black players could beat his team. Vic Bubas, the 1966 Duke coach, would never have said anything like that, and it would have been very hard for Haskins to convince his players that Bubas would have; he simply didn't have Rupp's reputation. But it seems very likely Haskins would have used the obvious racial implications of the game to motivate his players against Duke. Unlike University of Kentucky, which was in a border state, Duke was segregated until a few years before the game and was located in a former Confederate state with a long racist past. Duke itself, despite the liberalism of much of its faculty and student body at the time, had historically *not* been a leader on racial issues, as was well known by Black America; desegregation at Duke had come late, in 1963, several years after the University of Kentucky (which as a public school had been required to do so by the Brown ruling), and had been resisted by Duke's board of trustees for more than a decade, as described in chapter one.

When Loyola, with four Black starters, had beaten an all-White Duke team (coached by Vic Bubas) by twenty points in the 1963 Final Four, they had clearly been racially motivated, knowing that Duke's undergraduate program was still segregated. Black Loyola player Les Hunter, who had led his team with twenty-nine points and eighteen rebounds in the 1963 Duke game, stated years afterwards, "We weren't just playing a team, we were playing an ideology."[35] Duke was a team he viewed as representing a racist system. The papers noted that Hunter "took personal charge of Loyola's thrust to its final margin,"[36] indicating that it was clear to independent observers that he was deliberately running up the score on Duke (Loyola won the game by twenty points after leading by only two well into the second half).

So it wasn't going to matter to Haskins or his players that one program was trying to integrate their program while the other wasn't. As Duke's Mike Lewis said about Rupp, "He wasn't exactly going to head down to Birmingham and join the marchers. But our coach [Vic Bubas] was a forward-thinking guy. He knew [integration] was coming and wanted it to get started."[37] Bubas knew that the rest of the ACC was starting to integrate. He knew recruiting quality Black players was going to be essential if Duke was going to compete, as became painfully clear a couple of years later when UNC started playing Charlie Scott, who Duke at the time of the 1966 game was also recruiting—a battle Duke would ultimately lose with major repercussions. But if Duke had played the championship game, everyone else around it, like Haskins, would have seen the same thing as Kentucky: White players from Southern schools who represented a tradition of racism.

And it wasn't just Texas Western that was going to see it that way. A large number of other people, who were not familiar with the programs, were going to see it that way too. The *Louisville Courier* writer Karl Ruby noted before the Duke-Kentucky game that the finals would be Black against White regardless of which team won. Frank Deford, in previewing the games, wrote, "All seven of the Texas Western regulars are Negroes, hardly a startling fact nowadays but one that becomes noteworthy because of the likely meeting with Kentucky or Duke."[38] Deford also noted before the game that it was clear that some groups were already referring to the game as a contest for racial honors. And Duke didn't do much to help dampen that perception. In 1966, Duke, as a Southern school in a state which had fought for the Confederacy (one of Duke's founders had been in the Confederate Army at Appomattox), still displayed Confederate battle flags at games and played "Dixie" at sporting events. So, regardless of the opponent, Kentucky or Duke, the national public perception, regardless of the actual (and significant) differences between the two schools, would clearly have been almost identical.

What Black America—who had cheered for Texas Western in the original game and would be cheering for them against Duke in the alternative game—saw in the two schools that night would have been racially pretty much the same either way. Knowing that the two schools were both mostly-White Southern schools and seeing only White players on either team, Black America would have most likely interpreted the game as a racial battle, *regardless* of which team played. It probably wouldn't have mattered that Duke was in the process of actively trying to recruit quality Black players while Kentucky was not.

So since what a number of significant groups—the Texas Western team, Black America, the media, and racist extremists—would have seen would have been almost identical, would they also have seen a similar game? Well, the original game was not that close, but against Duke, it appears likely that things would have been different. In the actual game, Texas Western won the game at the foul line because the shorter Kentucky players could not stop the Texas Western players without fouling and also had to foul down the stretch. With Duke's larger front line, that would not have been the case; Lewis, Reidy, and Marin were as tall as the Texas Western front line. Also, unlike Kentucky, who had trouble guarding Duke's front line, Texas Western had players who could guard the Duke frontcourt players effectively and likely would have played more of them (including six-eight Nevil Shed) instead of the shorter, quicker team they used against Kentucky.

In particular, Duke's Mike Lewis, at six-eight and 235 pounds, was known for being a very tough player who did not back down; he was the leading rebounder in the ACC that season. He clearly could match up with David Lattin, a player for whom Kentucky had no answer. Lewis wishes he could have had the opportunity. "I'm not sure we could have beaten Texas Western the next night but I would have liked a chance to try."[39] When they met a few years later playing on the same team in the ABA, Lewis introduced himself, thinking Lattin wouldn't remember him. According to Lewis, "Lattin said, 'I remember your big ass, and if we'd played, I'd have kicked yours too.'"[40] But we can't be sure of that; Lattin tended to play down to the competition, especially when it was White. Don Haskins hated playing against a White center because Lattin didn't consider them legitimate competition for him. Lattin would come by his office the night before games and ask if the center was Black or White. "I'd tell him white guy. And he'd say, 'Aw, man.'"⁴¹ However, Mike Lewis, future All-American and leading rebounder in the ACC—who also wrestled steers in Montana—would likely quickly have awakened Mr. Lattin about the situation, very likely on his first dunk attempt, which Lewis might have put into the third row, with an unprintable remark. Both players seem to think it would have been a competitive (and probably pretty rough) game.

Texas Western was not known for being an up-tempo team; they liked to run a methodical half-court offense. However, their backcourt quickness would have allowed them to effectively capitalize on Duke's weakness, lack of team speed (although Duke liked to play up-tempo when Verga was healthy, which they likely would have done against Texas Western), as Kentucky did in the actual semifinal game. According to Haskins, when he saw the Duke-Kentucky matchup at the beginning of the Final Four he thought his team would play better against Duke. "We'd much rather come up against a taller team that's a little bit slower than we are."⁴² Many of their players were quicker than the Duke players, especially in the backcourt (although ACC player of the year Steve Vacendak was a pretty good defensive player, who played very tough, hard-nosed defense), meaning they could have used that to get by the slower Duke players for better shots. Then again, Jim Boeheim, who played Duke the week before, thinks that Verga and Vacendak were good enough ball handlers that they could have handled the Texas Western pressure defense better. And, while some of their guards were good shooters (they had been good enough to shoot over the Kentucky zone), they did not have shooters at the same level as the best Duke players, Marin and Verga.

Kentucky's short team had a hard time getting rebounds to start their running game and scoring in the half court against Texas Western's bigger, quick defensive players. Duke clearly had some low post offense and inside offensive rebounding with Mike Lewis, which Kentucky did not. In addition, they had two

All-America level shooters in Jack Marin and Bob Verga, who had shown an ability to score effectively against similar players, and did so as professionals, and also had Mike Lewis to deliver punishing screens to get them open. While there is no doubt that Texas Western's superior inside defense and overall quickness would have made it harder for all of them to score, it seems reasonable that they would have done well enough to compete, as they had against other teams all year.

So in the end, what a Duke-Texas Western game probably would have looked like is as follows: It is almost certain that the game would have been all-White against all-Black. It is likely that Haskins would have tried to motivate his team with a racial appeal. The two teams were evenly matched in height. The Duke team had better shooters, but Texas Western was quicker, a better rebounding team, and played better defense. Texas Western also had a slightly better bench; most of Duke's scoring came from their starters (the bench scored little), while Texas Western's bench often contributed substantially. It would have been a close, evenly matched game, one that likely would have gone down to the wire, between all-White and all-Black teams, with some tough inside players who didn't back down and with some pretty tough defense being played. *Just the kind of close game that would have a lot of fouls and cause controversy and racial troublemaking.* So the game that America saw that night would indeed have been substantially different—in a way that would very likely not have had a positive impact on all the people who saw it.

In the case of the actual game, it was only in hindsight over a period of months or years that the racial implications of the game became clear. If Bob Verga's illness hadn't occurred *and* Duke had played the game, it seems reasonable to believe that the game would have had a similar lasting long-term impact. The question then becomes of what kind and how much?

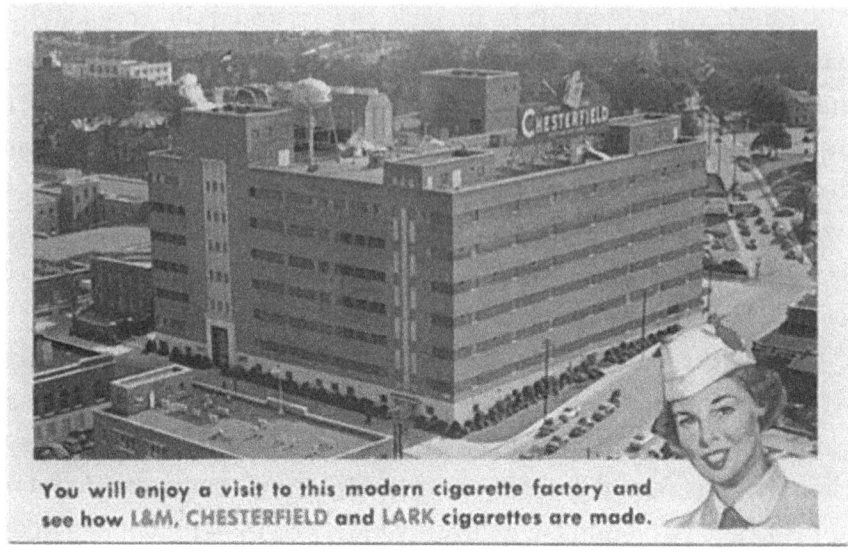

Durham cigarette factory, *Flickr/Creative Commons*

1965-66 Duke Blue-Devils basketball team, © *Duke Athletics*

Vic Bubas, 1966 Duke Basketball coach, © *Duke Athletics*

Adolph Rupp, 1966 Kentucky Basketball coach, © *UK Libraries Special Collections Research Center*

Don Haskins, 1966 Texas Western Basketball coach, © *UTEP Athletics*

1966 Texas Western Basketball team, National Champions, © *UTEP Athletics*

Martin Luther King speaks at the 1963 March on Washington, *AP Photo/File (Associated Press)*

Duke All-American guard, Bob Verga, © *Duke Athletics*

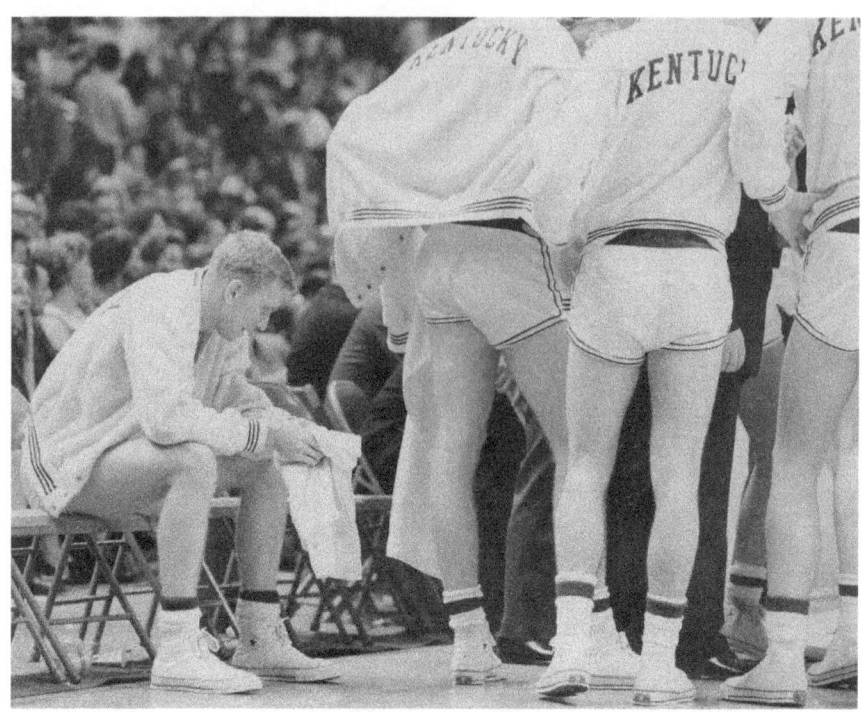
Larry Conley after fouling out against Texas Western, © *UK Libraries Special Collections Research Center*

1966 Duke Kentucky game, © *UK Libraries Special Collections Research Center*

1966 Kentucky Texas Western game, © *UK Libraries Special Collections Research Center*

Duke center, Mike Lewis, © *Duke Athletics*

Texas Western center David Lattin, © *UTEP Athletics*

Downtown Durham Duke pep rally, © 1966 *Durham Herald Sun*

Durham Morning Herald 10-3-66

Carnival-Like Atmosphere Pervades Ku Klux Klan Meet

National Rally Draws Staunchest Supporters As Robert Shelton Makes Surprise Appearance

(Staff Photo by Moore)

Estimated 2,500 Hear KKK Speakers

Gathering Attracts Klansmen From Nine States

By JIM CARR
Herald Staff Writer

Grand Dragon Robert Jones wouldn't make a crowd estimate at Sunday's Ku Klux Klan rally, but it was obvious that he was pleased with the turnout.

"I'm tickled to death with it," Jones told newsmen as he looked out over the sea of faces that swarmed over what is normally a Durham County pasture.

Members of the press estimated the gathering at about 2,500. Jones chuckled when he heard the figure.

"I'll just look in the newspapers tomorrow morning," he said. "Whatever they say, I'll multiply by four and come up with a pretty accurate figure."

Billed as a "national rally," the event attracted Klansmen from nine states, although Jones admitted that "Most of us here are North Carolinians."

Imperial Wizard Robert Shelton, making a surprise appearance, represented Alabama. Georgia sent a sizable delegation, via chartered bus, which constituted the "degree team" for a special Klan ritual which preceded the actual rally.

A Klansman named Ernest Gilbert, from somewhere in Mississippi, brought greetings from his home state. Jones said there were also small delegations from Pennsylvania, New Jersey, Florida, South Carolina, and Tennessee.

"I haven't seen anybody yet from Virginia or Maryland, though," he said as the speechmaking ended and preparations for the cross-burning ceremony began. "I was expecting some people from there, too."

A carnival-like atmosphere prevailed throughout the afternoon and on into the evening, with the exceptions of Klan rituals and a disturbance involving several college students, which interrupted the imperial wizard's address.

A glance at license plates in the huge parking area confirmed that practically all sections of North Carolina were well represented. Many robed Klansmen brought along their entire families. A Durham County unit served fried chicken and soft drinks, and more than a few picnic dinners were spread along the rolling hillside.

Grand Dragon Calvin Craig of Georgia evoked the greatest response from the crowd when he predicted victory for arch-segregationist Lester Maddox in the Georgia governor's race.

"Lester Maddox will stand up as tall as any man in the United States," Craig told the gathering. "I honestly believe Washington would rather   Luther King be governor   see Lester Maddox be the

Craig said Maddox would "stand up for the people of Georgia as George Wallace does for the state of Alabama."

Although not actually present, the name George Wallace was much in evidence at the rally. Automobile tags backing "Wallace for President" were displayed on many of the cars around the area, and were on sale at the rally site.

Connoisseurs of Klan literature had a field day. There were posters, leaflets, folders, bumper tags and practically any other type of handout imaginable being circulated around the area.

Other groups tried briefly to get into the act, including the National States' Rights Party and a group opposing Durham's proposed hospital bond issue, but Jones quickly scotched their efforts.

"This is a Klan gathering, and only Klan literature may be handed out," he told the gathering. "We are paying for the use of this property, and I'm not going to let any other group use it this afternoon."

A heavy chill set in as the two hours of speechmaking ended at sunset and the red, white, green and black-robed men and women slowly formed a circle in the middle of the field.

The 50-foot cross was still smoldering as hundreds of cars began winding their way back toward the highway.

National meeting of the KKK in East Durham, © 1966 *Durham Herald Sun*

Gene Banks, Duke's first top Black recruit, © *Duke Athletics*

Adolph Rupp signing Tom Payne, his first black recruit, © *UK Libraries Special Collections Research Center*

Christian Laettner's shot in 1992, © *Raleigh News & Observer*

Duke National Champions 1992, © *Duke Athletics*

Rupp's Runts, America's 1966 Basketball Heroes, © *UK Libraries Special Collections Research Center*

CHAPTER 7

WHAT IF FOR DUKE AND DURHAM

So what would have happened if Duke had played the game instead of Kentucky? Well, it depends on which group you are examining. Overall, there were three main groups affected by Bob Verga's illness and the outcome of the 1966 Final Four; Black America and the states of North Carolina and Kentucky, as represented by each of the three main teams in the Final Four (as for the impact in El Paso, it would not have changed substantially if Texas Western had beaten Duke, due to El Paso's relatively low Black population). The degree of difficulty in assessing the impact on each group varies. In the case of Kentucky, the impact of the switch is easy to determine; simply take the known effects of the 1966 game and subtract them to get the outcome of the changed game using the 1992 Duke Kentucky game discussed in chapter eleven to see how the Kentucky folks would have responded if Duke had won. In the case of Black America, the effect is more complicated; take the known effects of the game and subtract out the ones that might have been changed by the switch—which, when examining the matchups, is fairly straightforward to determine. But the case of Duke and Durham is much harder; determining the impact of what would have happened without any actual original impact to examine. Therefore, drawing on a number of different sources—what is known about the actual original game in Durham, knowledge of how the historical game affected people in Kentucky, the 1963 Duke-Loyola game, and the 1968 King assassination—will help determine with some level of accuracy what the likely impact of a Duke-Texas Western game would have been on Durham.

The actual question of what would have happened in Durham is complicated because Durham was and is a complicated town. Durham in 1966 was divided into several neighborhoods, differing by race and occupation. The White community then was actually fairly diverse, divided into a variety of different neighborhoods. On the west side of town was the Duke community, consisting of Duke University and the regions nearby associated with it (Duke Forest, the faculty ghetto) and staff associated with the school. That was where I lived. On the southwest side of town, in Hope Valley (in 1966 the Hope Valley Country Club was still segregated, and Duke's first Black player, C. B. Claiborne, could not attend the team banquet there the same year Duke played in the Final Four) and in Forest Hills were the fairly well-to-do White merchants and businessmen (in a neighborhood deliberately designed with no streets leading to the nearby Black community). They primarily worked in local businesses and for various large companies. On the north side of Durham, centered around Northgate shopping center, was a White community, mostly middle to lower-middle class, who tended to work in various businesses in the downtown area. On the east side of town was East Durham, which consisted of various lower to middle income Whites, often associated with the tobacco industry and farming.

In the southeast and east central side of Durham was most of the Black community, which comprised about 40 percent of Durham's population. The Black middle and upper classes, which often worked at NC Mutual, North Carolina College (now NC Central University), and Mechanics and Farmers Bank were fairly well educated and fairly well off; they lived around the Hillside Park area near North Carolina College. The Black lower classes were in various areas around town, including some around Fayetteville Street, Hayti (a large portion of which was destroyed a few years later to build the Durham freeway), Lyon Park, the East End neighborhood, and some in different areas such as the Crest Street Community, where my mother sometimes helped in community activities.

So when looking at how the game would have affected the various communities in Durham in 1966, it is likely each of them would have responded differently. And, that response would have been conditioned by race and by existing opinions of Duke University. Duke and Durham have always had an ambivalent relationship. On the one hand, the local community has always been proud to have a nationally prominent university nearby. Duke has given Durham a prestige that, especially back in 1966 when it was still mainly a tobacco town, it would not have had otherwise. In addition, Duke has also been a significant local employer, adding a large number of jobs to the region, giving work to many people locally that would not be obtainable elsewhere.

On the other hand, Duke and Duke basketball have historically *not* been particularly popular with the local population. As an elite, expensive private school with high admission standards, the attendees have largely been from out of state. Most local residents in the Durham community were graduates of the nearby state universities, North Carolina College, NC State, and the University of North Carolina. The fact that NC State and UNC had nationally prominent basketball programs back then (NC States' program had been the top one in the region through most of the 1950s under Everett Case) meant that they commanded far more loyalty from the local population in the ACC than did Duke, even though the Duke teams of the mid-1960s were actually at or near their historical peak in local popularity. In particular, during the early to mid-1960s the Duke-UNC basketball rivalry was at an all-time high. UNC already had a tradition of basketball excellence and had won a national championship in 1957 under Frank McGuire—the first for a school in that region—and the year after the 1966 game was about to embark on a very successful era under Dean Smith. Consequently, there were far more UNC and NC State fans than Duke fans in Durham.

At the time of the 1966 game, tensions between Duke and the local White population were approaching their all-time high, a peak that would be reached few years later near the height of the war in Vietnam, when Duke students were subject to being drafted. Conversely, Duke's relatively slow decision to integrate, after nearly a half century of racial exclusion, several years after the state schools had been forced to do so, and its poor treatment of Black students and workers, had meant that Duke had not particularly endeared itself to the Black population of Durham and North Carolina either, despite it's more recent liberal activities on their behalf in the years before the game. So at the time of the 1966 game, there were relatively few locals of *either* race actively cheering for Duke in Durham regardless of whom they played, although the team was good enough to sometimes sell out the indoor stadium.

It should be remembered that an all-White Duke team had already played a Loyola of Chicago team with four Black starters in the NCAA semifinal game in 1963, as discussed at the end of chapter six; Loyola had a White starter and at least one White bench player had participated to some degree as well, unlike Texas Western. The White Loyola starter, John Egan, had been recruited by Duke. Had he gone to Duke, his replacement, Pablo Robertson, was Black, so it is possible that if a suitable White starter could not have been found (it was the custom at the time to start at least one or two White players), the 1963 Loyola team Duke played would have been all-Black, giving the game more racial significance. Loyola had already played a game that year with much greater racial significance in the Mideast regional semifinal against an all-White Mississippi State team from the Deep South, the so called "Game of Change," discussed in chapter two. That game had enough significance that John Feinstein, the former *Duke Chronicle* sports editor and author of several book about college basketball (he was actually there between 1973-77 when the Duke team was at the bottom of the ACC), considered writing a book about it (at least two books have been written about the 1963 Loyola team).

The game Loyola played against Duke actually had less racial significance than the Mississippi State and 1966 championship games; the Loyola team was not unlike other mixed race teams Duke had already played that year, as the ACC and border states were much more willing to play Black competition at that time than the Deep South states. (The Dixie Classic in the 1950s, which was played in nearby NC State in Raleigh, had done much to bring quality Black players to the ACC area.) It was not the championship game and Duke had lost it, meaning there was no possible championship parade to stir up trouble, and the Black side of town was obviously not unhappy with the result either (Loyola had won in a rout, deliberately running up the score against the all-White Duke team). There was almost no mention of the racial aspects of the game by the media before or after it was played, except by the *Charlotte Observer* who coyly stated in the headline of their column concerning the matchup with the high-paced Loyola team before the game: "Duke Has No Fear of 'Race'"[1] and future Maryland coach Lefty Driesell, who noted before the game that Loyola "started four colored players. And colored players can just naturally jump higher than white boys."[2] (That's how many people said things back then.)

In addition, the overall racial situation in 1963 in Durham was much more positive; thousands of Duke students and local Black residents protested together to end segregation at Howard Johnson's only two months after the game, where my family and I had been present. On a state and national level, the 1963 game's racial situation also predated almost all of the later race riots. Race relations were not at the level of instability they would reach a few years later at the time of the 1966 game, which occurred a few months after the Watts riots and near the peak of resurgent

KKK activity in North Carolina, which had not yet begun in the spring of 1963 before the passage of the Civil Rights Act.

As the team prepared to go to College Park in 1966, no one on the White side of town appeared to consider how the Black side of town saw things, as people were actually more focused on the game against number one team Kentucky (Duke was ranked number two at the time). As Duke was preparing to head off to play Kentucky, the team had a pep rally downtown, headed by the 1966 team, the mayor of Durham Wense Grabarek, the city council, and the Duke president Douglas Knight. According to the mayor, who proclaimed the weekend of the Final Four "Blue Devil Weekend," "The *entire* city is proud and pleased to honor this team which has compiled a magnificent record, and to praise Coach Bubas,"[3] after which a special hand-sewn Duke flag was raised on the Five Points flagpole. The chamber of commerce had requested that the city council name the period in which the team would be in competition—including when they presumably would have played Texas Western—as Blue Devil days, and asked Durham residents (which would presumably have included the Black community) to wear clothing with blue and white fabrics while the team was in contention (also presumably including the finals against Texas Western). However, looking at photos of the downtown Durham pep rally, it is not possible to reliably identify one Black resident of Durham who had felt "pleased to honor this team" with their presence, including *any* of the nearly one thousand Black residents who worked at or attended Duke; Duke's poor treatment of their Black workers and students had left them with almost *no* support in the Black Durham community.

Coach Bubas seemed almost completely unaware of how the Black community saw things; after the team returned, he publicly stated he wished his team had been able to play Texas Western, not in any way considering how the Black population of Durham would have seen it. And when the team returned to Duke at the Raleigh-Durham airport after losing to Kentucky,

Bubas stated, "We really appreciate this welcome . . . I think it is wonderful that you should come out to welcome us home."[4] However, examining the photograph of the team at the airport, there is not *one* Black person in the picture of approximately one thousand who came out to welcome them home. It appears that almost *none* of the approximately thirty thousand Black residents of Durham who comprised about 40 percent of the city's population seemed to care enough about the 1966 Duke team to show any visible support, before or after the game. And they made it clear in the *Carolina Times*, the local Black paper, prior to the Duke-Kentucky semifinal game, that they were not all that interested in what Duke was doing. When Duke made the Final Four, the upcoming Duke-Kentucky game was given second billing on the cover of the sports page to the defeat of the local Black high school team (Hillside, the author's high school) in the state tournament. Apparently, no one on the Black side of town was giving any thought to a potential Duke-Texas Western game either.

In the original Final Four, when Duke played Kentucky but not Texas Western, the team appears to have had little to no support from the Black community in Durham. It therefore seems very unlikely that they would have gotten any if the opponent had been Texas Western. When looking at the actual championship game, even Black people in Kentucky were cheering for Texas Western against their own team. "A lot of people won't like to hear this, but we were rooting for Texas Western," said Porter G. Peeples, longtime president of Lexington's Urban League. "African Americans all across Kentucky identified with Texas Western."[5] Even Black students at the University of Kentucky were rooting for Texas Western. Chester Grundy, then one of about fifty Black students at UK, said he and about eight friends gathered to watch the game, stuffing towels under the door to keep people outside from hearing them cheering for Texas Western. "It was clear we needed to be for them."[6]

It is reasonable to assume that if the Black community of Kentucky in 1966, which had lived in Big Blue Nation for more than thirty years, was cheering for Texas Western, that the Black community of Durham, which had shown almost no support for Duke, and which had a much stronger and more recent experience with racial discrimination by Duke, would have done likewise in the event that Duke had played the game. Even when Whites played for a school that was not disliked by the Black side of town, people on the Black side of town were always going to pull for whoever was Black, regardless of who the White guys were. Racism was still that strong in Durham.

It should also be remembered that in addition to still having largely segregated neighborhoods, Durham in 1966 still had segregated schools, one of which I attended. This was less than two years after the Civil Rights Act. Race still trumped everything in education. An examination of the Durham High School yearbook for 1969 shows that almost all of the students were still White, even though Black students from the East End neighborhood nearby were twice as close to Durham High as they were to the Black school Hillside which they actually attended. An examination of the 1967 Durham Hillside High School yearbook shows that almost all of the students were Black, even though students from a largely White neighborhood in Forest Hills less than a mile away attended Durham High (they later attended Hillside with me), which was much further away and even in a worse neighborhood. Durham High was located in an industrial area directly shaded in the early morning by a number of tobacco warehouses, while Hillside was located in a nice, sunny residential area nearby. How all of this was actually resolved in 1971 is shown in the movie *Best of Enemies* about how a local Klan leader actually decided to work with a local Black leader to help integrate the schools. (I was at some of the meetings shown in the movie.) But in 1966, that was all still years away.

So what *would* have happened then in 1966? Would there have been racial unrest in Durham if Duke had won a close game in the Final Four? As previously mentioned, most racial disturbances of that era typically occurred in summer, in locations with extreme racial income inequality, and were usually instigated by run ins with local police. Durham, with the stabilizing influence of the Duke and North Carolina College communities, and with a tradition of peaceful protest, actually appears unlikely to have had a serious racial disturbance after the 1966 game, which occurred in the cold month of March.

In fact, after Dr. King's assassination in 1968, the Durham community responded with nonviolence, in sharp contrast to what was happening in the rest of the country. There was a march by Duke students on the Duke president's house (about a block and a half from my home at the time) where more than four hundred Duke students protested conditions for Black workers at Duke. Fourteen hundred Duke students then famously held a week-long "silent" vigil in King's honor, in which students demonstrated for better pay for Duke employees, who had historically been underpaid, as discussed in chapter one.

The Duke Black community largely agreed with Dr. King's non-violent approach to the situation. Some of the protesters who had marched to the president's house were viewing with concern what was happening in the rest of the country. One protester said, "We were all sitting there with the TV on watching buildings burning in Washington and rioting in cities and there was a real feeling that this was an apocalyptic age."[7] Another saw riots on TV and saw how people were saying "How could they do that? I thought how could they not."[8]

On the Black side of town, local civil rights leader Dr. Howard Fuller played a crucial role in keeping things in Durham quiet the night of King's assassination (aided by a heavy rainstorm) by convincing the marchers to postpone the march until the next day. At the North Carolina College student union that evening, the furious crowd catcalled him "Uncle Tom." But Fuller wanted to make sure the response was nonviolent. "I didn't think it was the way to respond to King's death given who he was."[9] The Ku Klux Klan, although well in decline (the state membership had shrunk from a peak of about twelve thousand in 1965 to less than a thousand in the spring of 1968), was also still around. When I talked with Fuller about it, Fuller said he was convinced someone would have been killed if people went out at night.

At a memorial service the next day, speakers stressed restraint from violence in King's memory. In the actual march the next day, according to the local paper, "With their heads held high, organized into a single file line, the poised youth marched in silence."[10] The march started at Fayetteville Street and ended in front of City Hall where a prayer service was held and eulogies given for Dr. King. Fuller helped lead the march. A famous picture shows him looking up at a nearby rooftop during the procession. "I remember exactly what I was thinking," Fuller said. "I had just spotted some white men with rifles on top of the building. I was wondering if that was the Klan."[11]

So at a moment in history where violence was erupting throughout the country, Duke and Durham put forth a peaceful and positive response on both sides of town. Although there were some reported cases of arson in Durham the next day, the response in Durham was much more peaceful than in nearby Raleigh—a city of similar size, twenty-five miles away, where rioting and arson raged for nearly a week after the assassination. Durham, in contrast to much of the South, had changed peacefully during the civil rights era. The only significant racial disturbance that occurred in Durham in the 1960s happened in 1967, when two Blacks were injured by shots fired from a car, resulting in windows being broken and one person being hurt. But even that was followed by a largely peaceful protest. It doesn't appear that a Duke-Texas Western game would have triggered racial violence in Durham; Durham was simply too well educated and traditionally non-violent for that.

I had the privilege of speaking with Howard Fuller about the situation in 1966 after the Texas Western game. His opinion of the matter is that a Duke-Texas Western game would not have likely had anywhere near the impact that King's assassination did on the Black side of Durham. Fuller doesn't believe that the game would likely have caused any violence because the NCAAs were not as big of a sporting event back then, and the emotional impact of the game did not equal that of King's death. It didn't have enough of a broad appeal to all segments of the Black population to create that level of emotion.

Still, it almost certainly would not have contributed to racial harmony in Durham. What is surprising about the situation was how little understanding the local authorities seem to have had about how the town actually felt about things. It was known at the time of the pre-game pep rally that Texas Western was the likely finals opponent; they were nationally ranked third, and unranked Utah was known to be a weak semifinal team. In addition, the local authorities had seen firsthand at the rally how little support the 40 percent of Durham comprising the Black community had for the Duke team. Yet at the time of the pregame pep rally, when Vic Bubas stated, "We're going to come back as number one this time,"[12] it was widely believed that the Duke-Kentucky semifinal was the actual championship game because it was presumed that Duke would then beat Texas Western if they won. No one on the stage, including the Duke president and the local government, seemed to have any grasp of what that would actually have meant.

So, what would it have meant? If Duke were to play the game, it is likely that Duke's recently better relationship with Black Durham was going to be damaged. When people went to work in Durham the next day or saw each other on the streets, it probably would have led to racial tensions. People from Duke who participated in civil rights activities might have received a less friendly welcome than in years before.

The Bob Verga Shift

And what would have been the response of the White side of town? Obviously the Duke community would have been cheering for Duke, but what about the people in the rest of the town or the rest of the state? Well it's hard to find anyone outside of Duke that would have seen it very positively. The folks in Forest Hills and Hope Valley—home of the previously stated still segregated Hope Valley Country Club, a large number of whom were all UNC alumni and fans—would not have been particularly thrilled about it, nor would the neighborhoods with NC State fans in them either. But that was to be expected; they simply wanted to have their teams win, not Duke. That would have been true regardless of who Duke played in the finals.

With regard to the less well-educated folk in East Durham and in the surrounding area, it seems likely that even if they did not particularly like Duke, which many did not as the Duke students were mostly Northerners, they would not have been cheering for Texas Western. And racist extremists on either side were going to see the game the same way, regardless of if the team was Duke or Kentucky. And in fact, there was a significant difference between the events of 1966 and in 1963 or 1968: the presence of a large local Ku Klux Klan. It's almost a certainty that every one of the nearly two hundred KKK klaverns in North Carolina would have been cheering for Duke.

The Klan had already solicited Duke All-American Art Heyman the year of the 1963 Loyola game and would have likely been waiting to embrace Duke again in 1966. Heyman, who was Jewish (the Klan even then often railed against Jewish financiers at rallies), often received encouraging letters from the local chapter of the KKK, which encouraged him to keep winning in the name of Christian White supremacy. According to Heyman, he was actually written by the Grand Dragon of the KKK in Tuscaloosa, Alabama, himself. "Each year, before the start of the season, he'd send a telegram from Tuscaloosa telling me to uphold white supremacy."[13] He was even offered a membership in the Klan!

At the time of the Heyman letters, the North Carolina Klan, which had not yet been restarted by Bob Jones, was actually not a significant factor as it then was further south. Three years later, at the time of the 1966 games, after nearly two and a half years of Jones' tireless efforts, the Klan was close to its all-time peak in membership, and marched publicly in North Carolina, including Durham. The Klan would obviously have been very likely to embrace a Duke basketball championship in the spring of 1966. Durham had one of the largest Ku Klux offices in the state in 1965, with a meeting hall big enough for five hundred people and a parking lot capable of holding two hundred cars. The estimated total Klan membership in Durham at the time was roughly two hundred to five hundred people. Klan members typically lived in East Durham or in the rural areas surrounding Durham; I knew of almost no Klan members in the northern, western, and southwestern parts of Durham near my home near the Duke campus at the time of the game. The Klan marched publicly and held sizable rallies a few miles northeast of Durham off of Red Mill Road on April 24 and September 17 in 1965, at which a total of about thirty-seven hundred people attended. My mother later saw a Klan rally downtown; the Durham Klansmen at the time wore green robes instead of the traditional white ones.

Despite the Klan's sizeable presence in Durham, it's hard to say what kind of response would actually have come from the local Klan if Duke had won the championship. By the time of the 1966 game, the state enforcement campaign, spearheaded by Malcolm Seawell, was clearly having an effect on the Klan. A couple of weeks before the game, seven top grand dragons from around the South had already been indicted, including the North Carolina Grand Dragon, Robert Jones. The weekend of the game, a Klan rally in Robeson County scheduled for later in the month was stopped via a court order. The Klan had been quiet right before the game due to cold weather, but according to the Durham paper, their activity would pick up "just as soon as it warms up enough for them to get back in the cornfields."[14] Thus, it seems unlikely that the Klan would have mounted any significant organized response to the game at that particular moment.

On the other hand, Jones had little difficulty in turning out nearly two thousand when Dr. King showed up in Raleigh in August 1966. And the Klan also held their national meeting seven miles east of Durham in October, with more than twenty-five hundred participants, and from which five Duke students had been removed for protesting. Another Klan rally with a sizable attendance was held in Durham on November 2. So the Klan had well-attended rallies near Durham before *and* after the 1966 game: they were clearly a significant presence in Durham at the time.

It is therefore possible that local Klan leaders acting more independently of Jones could have done something in Durham at the time of the game. Although with little advance notice it may not have been particularly large or well organized, since Klan rallies were typically planned well in advance. (David Cunningham isn't sure they could have done it either.) But given the number of Klansmen in Durham and Wake County at the time, where there were many small klaverns, and the number of people who actually attended the Durham rallies, it wasn't out of the question. But any noticeable Klan turnout connected with the game would have surely caused trouble locally and possibly attracted negative media attention, which would have had lasting implications for Duke basketball program recruiting.

A Duke victory over Texas Western would have also likely antagonized the Black population of the entire state of North Carolina, almost all of whom, much like the Black population of Kentucky, were going to be cheering for Texas Western. In addition, it may have engendered a negative response from some of the White population, many of whom were UNC fans. It would also have been considered an encouragement to the Klan and other White supremacists in the state, potentially stirring up trouble elsewhere in the state, especially in the eastern tobacco growing regions where the Klan was much stronger. So essentially, a Duke victory would have likely stirred up trouble and resentment throughout the state, leaving Duke isolated on the west side of Durham as much of the rest of North Carolina turned away from them.

When Texas Western won the championship that year, their team was greeted joyously by the city of El Paso with a huge victory celebration at the airport. The Texas Western team was put on a flatbed truck which served as a stage where each player could make a statement. The players then got into convertibles for the twelve-mile ride to the campus, escorted by motorcycle policemen. Along the route, they were happily greeted by hundreds of fans raising their index fingers in the number one salute.

According to Ray Sanchez, the assistant sports editor at the *El Paso Herald Post* during the 1966 season, the whole city went into a crazy reverie, including students starting bonfires on campus and people out in the streets celebrating and honking their car horns. "It changed everything. It put us on the map, made us proud, made us happy and we're still celebrating even now."[15] Eddie Mullens, who was the school's sports information director for the '66 team, said, "To many, many citizens, this is one of the greatest things ever in the city's history."[16]

But for Duke and Durham, it would probably have been quite different. If Duke had paraded through Durham, they would have been saluted by half the city with raised *middle* fingers instead of raised *index* fingers; they may have even had to jump below the convertible seats to avoid being hit by rocks and bottles. They also would have had to choose their route carefully because the direct route to Durham from the airport up route 55 went through the Black community. Having alienated much of the Black side of town and the rest of the state with the victory, and faced with some possibility of a KKK presence at a victory parade, would the Durham police department have even allowed a Duke rally or a parade in downtown Durham? Given the display of ignorance of the implications of the game by the local White leadership before the game, it actually isn't out of the question. However, they likely would have been clearly reminded by the Black community as to how they felt about a Duke victory over Texas Western—and would likely have had to cancel any postgame downtown motorcade.

After the King assassination two years later, Duke students deliberately avoided marching outside the Duke community for fear of inciting racial unrest. It seems possible that a similar situation would have prevailed in 1966. For Duke, the joy of winning a championship in 1966 would probably not have been shared with the Durham community. My beloved Duke basketball team, forlornly clutching their national championship trophy, would likely have been obliged to sit on the west side of town to celebrate on campus alone, denying my family the thrill of watching them parade downtown.

And how would Duke University have been perceived nationally after the game? The game was going to be nationally famous, which meant that everyone who saw or read about the game throughout the country was going to see the exact same thing: an all-White team from a rich, (almost) all-White Southern school playing an all-Black team with players from relatively poor neighborhoods. Win or lose, Duke was destined to be cast as the racist villains in someone else's movie. They might even have been considered the champions of Southern racists if they won. If they won, it was a victory for tobacco and racism. If they lost, they got what they deserved. No matter what the outcome would be, Duke would go down in infamy.

The game being nationally famous also meant that hundreds, possibly thousands, of prospective students were going to see the game and possibly change their mind about applying to Duke. If Duke won the game, it appears that all of Black America, including any potential future Black students, would see Duke as the team that beat Texas Western. Bill White, a former high school football coach in Louisville, said about the actual game,

"I'm a black person. I'd imagine every black person in America was rooting for Texas Western."[17]

At the time of the game, there were still only about two dozen Black students at Duke. They were already having issues with the Duke administration—including the use of the Confederate flag and the playing of "Dixie" (which the Duke pep band did until 1968). In fact, in 1968, students occupied the Allen Building at Duke (Duke's first Black player, C. B. Claiborne, was in attendance) because they wanted the university to pay them more attention. They rallied for changes in the curriculum, more Black faculty, courses in African American studies, and less harassment by the campus police, as well as ensuring that the university would no longer use segregated private local facilities. It's not a stretch to imagine that Duke playing Texas Western would have added an additional factor that would have further alienated the Black community at Duke.

The final irony of this is that what everyone would have seen on national television, and the way they would have perceived the game, was the exact *opposite* of the way things had actually happened in Durham in the years preceding the game. A considerable portion of the Duke community, which for nearly a decade had actually been trying to change and was working to fight racism in North Carolina, would likely have been typecast by the national media as racist villains. Prior to the game, racists were viewing the game as a racial battle regardless of which team played, Duke or Kentucky. Duke would have been nationally embraced by White racist extremists that much of the Duke community had spent the past ten years trying to discredit. The efforts of hundreds of decent and well-intentioned people in Durham might have been discredited by one basketball game: a tragedy of classic Greek proportions.

As for the Duke players, they were very isolated on West Campus, and knew little about how we kids or anyone else in Durham felt about the racial situation surrounding them. For

The Bob Verga Shift

Steve Vacendak, the Duke captain and starting senior point guard on the 1966 Duke team, the Kentucky game was his last in a Duke uniform; he was known for being an intense competitor and was incredibly disappointed that he did not get to play for the national championship. But he had, at the time, little understanding of how the Durham Black community would have seen the game. He stated that neither he nor *any* of the other players on the Duke team understood the racial situation in Durham or the rest of North Carolina at the time, nor how the actual Kentucky-Texas Western game would actually affect Black America. According to Vacendak, they were consumed with their classes and with winning basketball games. None of them were thinking about how a Duke victory would have likely antagonized the Black population of North Carolina and cast the Duke team as the heroes of the North Carolina Ku Klux Klan.

On a personal note, it is worth ending this chapter with a quick discussion of how all of us kids in Durham in the 1960s would have seen the game. Back in those days, basketball was the game that all of us played in Durham, White or Black. It didn't matter which neighborhood you lived in; everybody played. And all the kids on both sides of town worshipped our basketball heroes. Guys like Bob Verga, Steve Vacendak, Jack Marin, Larry Miller, Bobby Lewis, Billy Cunningham, Bill Russell, Oscar Robertson, Elgin Baylor (there were no Black stars yet in the ACC in 1966), and later on, players like Charlie Scott, Phil Ford, David Thompson, Dr. J, John Lucas, and Walter Davis: those guys were GODS in North Carolina. Every kid in Durham was at Pistol Pete's basketball camp in 1969, and the two best players there were Black future Hillside High School guards John Harrell and Barry Stanback. John Harrell later played for NC Central and Duke, playing for Duke as the starting point guard in the NCAA championship game against Kentucky in 1978.

So what good would it have done for kids in Durham for Duke to have played Texas Western? If Duke had won the game, would all the Black kids have said that they fixed the game so the White boys across town would win it? Would their parents, who had endured a lifetime of Jim Crow prior to the Civil Rights Act, have cursed our Duke team as the White team that took away the first ever Black national NCAA basketball championship? My childhood heroes might have become the villains of the entire Black community of Durham, including most of my future high school classmates—a personal tragedy that would have changed my entire childhood. We White boys would then have seen our beloved Duke basketball team be turned into the champions of all the racists in the state, including the local KKK. What kind of a role model for us would that have been?

If Texas Western had won the game, we Durham White kids probably would have resented the Black players for taking away our national championship, as our heroes suffered an emotionally devastating defeat worse than the Kentucky loss. We might have spent the next decade during the UCLA era thinking about that, as Duke's only chance for a national championship would have been taken away by an all-Black team; during that era, I personally never forgot the 1966 Kentucky loss. In the end, it wasn't going to matter which team won. The entire city of Durham—and all of us kids in it who still went to segregated schools in the late 1960s—were going to lose.

So, after a careful examination of the situation, Duke University and the city of Durham could not be expected to have derived any benefit from Duke playing Texas Western. The game would have very likely stirred up trouble, divided the city along racial lines, discredited hundreds of decent people in Durham, discouraged applicants from going to Duke (especially Black ones), and forever cast our Duke heroes as racist villains in front of the state of North Carolina and a large national television audience. It's hard to imagine the damage to Duke and Durham being much greater than that.

CHAPTER 8

WHAT IF FOR DUKE BASKETBALL

Duke. Now there's a proud and well-known name. It stands for the words "excellence in college basketball," and it has for almost the entirety of the past forty years. Coach Mike Krzyzewski built a program of enduring excellence which has survived and prospered over four decades of continual changes in college basketball. Regardless of the changes in the times—three-point shot, shot clock, one-and-done players, changes in the ACC)—Coach K always found a way to respond with a great program that continually rose to the occasion with high quality basketball.

The five championship banners hanging in the rafters won over a space of nearly twenty-five years—one more than Adolph Rupp at Kentucky—are testimony to K's enduring greatness as a coach, a greatness over time rivaled only by John Wooden, Dean Smith (yeah, yeah, I had to mention him), and Adolph Rupp himself. Accompanying the banners in the rafters are a number of retired jerseys, most of them from the Krzyzewski era. If you are old enough, you can remember many of them when they played: Christian Laettner. Grant Hill. Shane Battier. Bobby Hurley. Jason Williams. Danny Ferry. Shelden William. Johnny Dawkins. J. J. Redick. All All-Americans. Several of them were National Player of the Year (NPOY).

Of the Krzyzewski players whose jerseys were retired, about half were Black, half were White. Krzyzewski was able to successfully recruit great players of both races. Looking at how his teams have played over the years, most of his championship teams were like that. They played ball usually associated with White players, (passing, jump shooting, patterned offense) *and* they played ball usually associated with Black players (driving to the basket, isolation play, full court run and gun). Duke has excelled at both styles of play simultaneously. Krzyzewski knew that winning was about using his players' full abilities. If they were great streetball players, like Johnny Dawkins or Bobby Hurley, he let them play full court run and gun. If they were great three-point shooters, like Shane Battier or J. J. Redick, he let them put it up from the outside. If they were good low post players, like Elton Brand or Christian Laettner, he let them play down low. Coach K's teams excelled either way, and that's why they won so many games.

Would all of this have occurred if Duke had played the 1966 game against Texas Western? How many of these great players would have come to Duke if Duke had played that game? Well, it's hard to say that one game could have impacted Duke recruiting over a long time period, but in 1966, college basketball was changing. What had once been a segregated game dominated by White players was in the process of becoming more and more Black (today, more than half of all college players are Black). Black players outside the South were already starting to dominate. The 1966 game opened up the South for them to play in too.

As it was becoming clear that many of the Black players had superior athletic skills, the pressure to compete was forcing the other programs of that era to integrate. The other ACC schools were in the difficult process of integrating back then. UNC recruited their first top Black player in 1966, the legendary Charlie Scott, who would revolutionize Carolina and ACC basketball, and the other conference schools were trying to do likewise, with varying levels of success. However, it hadn't been easy for them. The Black players knew of the long tradition of racist exclusion of the ACC schools, which had been all-White until the mid-1960s. UNC's first Black player, Willie Cooper, was on the varsity team in 1965-1966, and was the first North Carolina Black player to play in the ACC as a freshman in 1964. The actual first Black ACC player, Billy Jones, started playing for Maryland during the 1965-1966 season, in Cole Field House, the site of the 1966 Final Four. Jones said that his Black friends and he received plenty of letters from college recruiters, but he was the only one who attended a major school. "The minute they found out you were black, the communication stopped."[1]

Up until that point, Duke had been unable to recruit Black players to come play there. The Duke staff, with Vic Bubas, Bucky Waters, and Chuck Daly, were making a good faith attempt to recruit Black players to play at Duke. But the going was not easy for two reasons: First, Duke was a school with Ivy league level academic standards. It was difficult to find players of either race who could make the grade at Duke. And second, Duke, like almost all of the elite White Southern schools, had a tradition of segregation that automatically placed them at a disadvantage against schools outside the South. In addition, the lingering racism of the South, where until a couple of years before the 1966 game players could not use public facilities, itself tended to influence the better Black players to want to play elsewhere. And finally, Duke, being an expensive private school, relied heavily on its national reputation to recruit—unlike state schools like Kentucky, who by default were going to attract in-state applicants for financial and social reasons (many great Black North Carolina players from that era, such as Michael Jordan, Bob McAdoo, and Phil Ford, all came from within the state and went to UNC because it was the state flagship school with a national winning reputation). Duke had to recruit nationally to compete. Any damage to Duke's national reputation would have taken away its ability to compete with other similar schools—all competing against each other for the same top players—to get quality Black players to enroll.

The other issue recruiters faced in North Carolina in the 1960s was the activity of the Ku Klux Klan. Many Black players simply did not feel safe traveling in the South and going to away games, even after the Civil Rights Act was passed. According to NBA great Earl Monroe, who played at Winston-Salem State University between 1963 and 1967 (about seventy miles away from Duke), when later discussing the presence of the Klan in Indiana during his pro career, stated that he had already dealt with the Klan in Virginia and at Winston-Salem. "I wasn't about to put myself in that situation again."[2] Wake Forest University's (also in Winston-Salem) first Black recruit, Charlie Davis, saw a Klan rally and a cross burning when he was in Laurinburg in early 1967. So if Duke had won the 1966 championship against Texas Western, there is a good chance the media would have seen the Klan celebrating a Duke victory in North Carolina. Klan activities were often reported in the media at that time, and a Klan celebration of a Duke victory would have likely been reported in the media. Since Duke often recruited out of state players, such press coverage, similar to the extensive coverage of the Klan's public response to Dr. King speaking in Durham a few months later, could readily have been used by recruiters from rival schools to deter Black athletes from attending Duke.

Until 1966, Duke had little success recruiting quality Black players. The staff tried their hardest, but continually came up short. Many Black players were not particularly interested in attending schools where they would be in a very small minority and not necessarily feel welcome. Duke's first Black player, C. B. Claiborne (who was actually not recruited specifically for basketball), finally matriculated at Duke in 1966 and was on the freshman team. Bucky Waters, who recruited Claiborne, said, "The package of C. B. Claiborne, the kid he was, you can't say it was a Jackie Robinson, but clearly the first kid at Duke would be under a microscope just because he was different, and he was the first."[3]

Claiborne said it was an opportunity he couldn't walk away from but that he never set out to be a pioneer in ACC basketball. He viewed it as something that needed to be done at the time. "I was in a position to do it, and it was appropriate, and the experiences at Duke were just what you would have expected them to be, given that place, given the time."[4] Reflecting on it more recently, Claiborne said, "Deep down, I still probably would have preferred to play at [North Carolina] A&T. But that would have been a selfish decision on my part."[5] Claiborne actually spent much of his time at Duke at nearby North Carolina College, the local Black school across town where he even had a cafeteria card, as there were only a few other Black students at Duke then. Claiborne had his issues with white hecklers then too. "I can remember hearing racial slurs and seeing confederate flags when we played against Alabama in Tuscaloosa. When I went to the foul line, I gritted my teeth and told myself 'If I never make another free throw, I'm going to make this one.'"[6] This was, in fact similar to what Rupp would have had to deal with had he put Black players on his team in the early 1960s.

After Claiborne went to Duke, other Black players were finally beginning to take note and give Duke a look. It appeared that Duke might be able to start bringing in quality Black players and keep up with the changes occurring in the other programs. But so-called progressive Durham was still not a very friendly place for Black athletes. Claiborne got the sense that some students at Duke were not too thrilled with his inclusion. "They would never say anything to my face. But you can read some things from body language, like a certain kind of expression or when somebody turns their back on you."[7] Claiborne remembers not being invited to the team awards ceremony at Hope Valley Country Club because it was still segregated in 1966, a matter which the Black community at Duke found particularly offensive.

Something else was happening in 1966, which would prove to be an even greater obstacle to the Duke program. The Vietnam War, which had begun in 1965, was in the process of being escalated with no end in sight. Protests were breaking out at college campuses throughout the country. The Duke campus, like so many other schools, was becoming a hotbed of opposition to the war.

The upshot was that the attitudes of the college players were starting to change. In the early 1960s, old-style militarist coaches like Adolph Rupp were able to rule their programs in a very strict disciplinary style. But by the late 1960s, that was under pressure to change. As the general process of questioning authority was happening everywhere in the country, so it was happening with Duke basketball.

Vic Bubas, the Duke coach at the time, sensed the change. Bubas, while not known to be as militarist as Adolph Rupp, was also a disciplinary coach, and he could see that his way of doing things was not likely to succeed in the environment of the late 1960s. The Duke program was already starting to fade. The 1966 team was the last under Bubas that would play in the NCAAs. After the 1966 game, Duke never again in that era put forth a program that would be a legitimate championship contender (and at that point John Wooden and UCLA were making everyone else's attempts at doing so futile).

Even in the ACC, Duke was fading. In the early and mid-60s, Duke had won multiple ACC championships. But now, with Black players at NC State and UNC starting to dominate, Duke was becoming an afterthought; a good program but not one that was a championship contender. Meanwhile, UNC played UCLA for the national championship in 1969, being duly destroyed by Lew Alcindor, who also easily dispatched Duke twice the year before, scoring a combined fifty-seven points and thirty-eight rebounds in the two games they played. Without the ability to recruit quality Black players, the Duke program could no longer compete at the highest level.

It was clear even as soon as the first year after the 1966 game what the difference was for Duke. North Carolina's first great

Black player, Charlie Scott, was a game changer against Duke. Bubas had tried to recruit Scott, who was a good enough student to get into Duke, but Scott was turned off by Duke's tiny Black student enrollment. Being the first great Black player in the ACC, Scott knew what it would be like to play ball in the South. Said Scott, "Make no mistake, I was scared about what I was doing."[8] It is humorous to see the films of Duke playing UNC in 1969. Charlie Scott is jumping over the earthbound Duke players, who flail away helplessly as Scott essentially plays HORSE, scoring at will from almost anywhere on the floor. As Coach Bubas said when Duke played UNC in 1969, "When a guy hits thirty-foot jump shots going to his left falling into the crowd and makes forty points, the only thing you can do is say, 'Nice going man, you just did a great job.'"[9]

Meanwhile, by 1969, the protests against the war were starting to consume the college campuses everywhere. Sit-ins, riots, and demonstrations were occurring throughout the country. Vic Bubas, seeing what was going on, seeing the combined effects of the racial changes in the ACC and the war in Vietnam, realized that there was little to no likelihood of him being able to return Duke to its former greatness. In 1969, Vic Bubas resigned as coach of Duke University at age forty-two.

Bubas' replacement was an assistant named Bucky Waters, who was the head coach at the University of West Virginia and had been an assistant under Bubas prior to the 1966 game. In the beginning, the Waters regime appeared to have some promise. The 1969 Duke freshman team was rated the best in the country. And the 1969-70 Duke team, led by a third team All-American center from Raleigh named Randy Denton and a top point guard name Dick Divenzio, actually went on to win twenty games in 1970, the first time that had happened at Duke in a few years, and the last time it would happen until 1978.

Duke was able to recruit a couple of decent—though not great—Black players to play on the team. That had not been easy for Duke, due to its high academic standards. Waters noted how hard it was for these athletes to make the grade at Duke. They were being asked at a difficult age to make a significant jump academically. Even though the Duke players were the best and brightest in New Jersey and New York, Waters had to explain to them how hard Duke's curriculum was when recruiting. Many were afraid they would show up their Black communities by flunking out at Duke. As Waters said, "The black athlete was more afraid of Duke than Duke was of the black athlete."[10] With considerable difficulty, Duke finally managed to recruit its first quality Black player in 1968: six-foot-six New York native Don Blackman (recruited by Bubas before Waters' arrival). In 1969-70, Blackman, as a sophomore, had averaged about six points a game on a good team and was showing promise of doing more. Duke also picked up a couple more pretty good Black players, Sam May and Edgar Burch, around the same time.

But Waters was an old-style militarist coach. And in the atmosphere of the late 1960s and early 1970s, where authority was continually being challenged, his approach was starting to turn off both the White and Black players. At the height of both the protests against the war in Vietnam and the era of racial unrest, Waters militaristic approach was simply not going to work. One by one, what had been a promising freshman class in 1969 started leaving Duke. They simply didn't want to play for Bucky Waters. As player after player left, the Duke program began its fall into the 1970s ACC basement. And, of further damage, the Black players, including Blackman, were leaving too. Sam May and Edgar Burch did not stay beyond their freshman years. Their departure spelled almost the complete end of Duke's attempts to recruit quality Black players in the early 1970s.

And so, the program plunged into 1970s oblivion. The program fell from 20-10 in 1970 to 14-13 in 1973 and 10-16 the following year. Protests against Waters began at the games, as the students chanted "Bye Bye Bucky, we're glad to see you go," "Fire Bucky" signs began to proliferate in the stands, and petitions were handed out at games asking for Waters' removal. As players left the program and quality recruits failed to replace them at Duke, the program collapsed. More and more students and faculty were determined that Bucky had to go. And so, in September 1973, facing a revolt by almost the entire campus, Waters finally resigned as head coach. He remained at Duke as a remarkably effective fund raiser for the medical school, which he did for many years after losing his head coaching job.

Upon Waters' resignation, Duke offered their coaching job to none other than Adolph Rupp, who actually accepted the job but changed his mind and decided to stay in Kentucky and work on his farm. The job was given to assistant Neil McGeachy, who did his best to resurrect the program in his one year as head coach. However, at that point the damage had been done. Duke was in last place in the ACC, and would be there for the next four years, which also happened to correspond with my last four years in Durham, during which time they had only one winning record, by one game, in 1977. What had been a quality program, which could have produced good, if not great teams, had been effectively reduced to a shell of its former greatness. And Duke's attempts to recruit quality Black players had, at least for the time being, effectively come to an end.

McGeachy lasted only one year, even though the students liked him. It was determined that a new approach was needed, and the search began for a top-quality coach to come to Duke. The replacement for Neil McGeachy was Coach Bill Foster, formerly from University of Utah. Foster was charged with the long and arduous task of rebuilding the program. He had succeeded in building quality programs at Utah and Rutgers. And so, it was hoped that Foster could do so at Duke.

By that point, however, Duke was no longer considered worthy opposition even in the ACC. Duke went nearly six years without winning a road game in the ACC in the 1970s. Duke's basketball players in that era included such luminaries as handsome Terry Chili (whose campus nickname Herm the Sperm indicated that he was known for being better at scoring off the court than on it) and Mark Crow, known as "Crow Bar," which aptly summed up his reputation for partying, who, amazingly enough, was a respectable starter his senior year on the nationally ranked 1976-77 team, and even played some in the NBA for the then-New Jersey Nets. One of Duke's players (who will mercifully not be named here) became famous for losing one game by dribbling the ball off the side of his foot out of bounds (witnessed by the author), and another game for throwing the ball in against the rim on his own backboard.

By the mid-1970s, Duke basketball had essentially become a joke, the laughingstock of the ACC. NC State and UNC no longer paid any attention to Duke, concentrating on playing each other. UNC had a top-ten team, and NC State, with the great David Thompson (for whom Duke was actually placed on probation due to recruiting violations), was in the process of dethroning Bill Walton and the UCLA dynasty and winning the national championship. Duke by then had become simply an irritant, an annoying gnat to be flicked aside twice a year on the way to other games that really mattered.

Prior to Gene Banks' arrival in 1977, Cameron Indoor Stadium rarely sold out. You could walk up to the box office back then and buy a ticket right before the games at a reasonable price. I used to attend games in the mid-1970s as a boy scout usher when the stadium was typically about half full. I was even able to purchase season tickets for the 1976-77 season for a reasonable price (the team poster with the season schedule had a Tuborg beer logo on it, which I posted in my room). Duke basketball had become a shell of what it had been in the Bubas era; very few people in the Durham area outside of the Duke community cared about the program any longer or bothered to attend games. But my friends and I kept our faith in our beloved

Blue Devils, watching Foster trying to build up the team, hoping for better days ahead.

The talent base Foster had at the time he started in 1974 was essentially threadbare; he had almost no good players to speak of. So Foster set forth to recruit quality players and rebuild the program from scratch. He almost got future All-America and national champion Butch Lee (who was Black) his first year, but Lee went to Marquette. (Lee's national championship was largely due to 1966 UNC stall-ball wizard Smith's decision to run the four corners in the second half in a game which Carolina probably would have won going away otherwise.) Duke actually did recruit a number of Black players onto the team back then (the 1976 team had four) but players such as Willie Hodge, George Moses, Harold Morrison, and Kenny Young were not of the caliber of Walter Davis or Kenny Carr at UNC or NC State. Hodge in particular was famous for being a good athlete with bad hands. Watching him fumble away rebounds, drop readily catchable passes, or be stripped on shots was particularly frustrating, as it typified the level of play Duke displayed in that era.

And part of the reason was that racism was still going strong in North Carolina in the 1970s, especially for in-state Black players, a substantial number of whom went out of state to go to college. Michael Jordan grew up in Wilmington, an area with a historically strong Klan presence. Jordan had been suspended from school in 1977 after throwing a soda at a girl in ninth grade who called him the N word. According to Jordan, "I considered myself a racist at the time. Basically, I was against all white people."[11] Many Black players in North Carolina had similar feelings, for obvious reasons. Bill Foster was indeed facing a tough situation in recruiting quality Black players to come to a mostly White school with a poor racial reputation.

People who are not familiar with the world of college basketball recruiting cannot comprehend how competitive it is. Top recruits are identified years in advance, many of them in middle school when some of them start growing beyond the size of their peers and begin displaying significant athletic ability. The top players attend All-Star camps where they are besieged by recruiters; most top players have known and played against each other for years prior to playing each other in college. Top quality players are typically contacted by well over one hundred schools, most of whom know that they have no chance of successfully landing them. Recruits have to find ways of winnowing down the number of schools to consider, so any particular school that has known deficiencies will immediately be removed from the list. Thus, being famous for losing to or defeating Texas Western in 1966 would have immediately removed Duke from consideration for a very large number of quality Black athletes.

Once a school identifies a top player they have a reasonable chance of landing, recruiting them is a lengthy and time-consuming process lasting most of the way through high school. Schools typically send multiple letters to their recruits, contacting them as many times as they are allowed, often by alumni and existing athletes. Competition between schools that think they have a chance is fierce; schools use any possible legal means (and some not so legal ones too, for which many schools have been on probation, including both Duke and Kentucky) to land top recruits. Often, random factors can weigh into a recruit's decision: a relative or friend may have attended a certain school, a certain recruiter may or may not have been considered likable in their visit, or a player and a particular coach may or may not have hit it off.

And the situation forty or fifty years ago wasn't all that different. Top high school players went to All-Star camps back then too—typically Howard Garfinkel's Five-Star camps. The recruitment process didn't begin quite as early, but by the time they were sophomores, quality players were being contacted by dozens of recruiters. Recruiters would bombard players with letters; in the early 1980s, NC State coach Jim Valvano famously sent more than one hundred letters to future recruit (and NBA washout) Chris Washburn over a two-year period, although it is debatable as to how many of them Washburn could actually read because he was also famous for scoring 470 on his SATs, 70 points above random guessing. (He stated that he was told to take the test for administrative purposes and did not read the questions before answering.) His scores did not deter NC State; he was admitted anyway. So as Bill Foster set out to recruit quality Black players to attend Duke, where somewhat higher SAT scores were required, he was indeed faced with a daunting task.

But Foster was not discouraged. He had a talent for recognizing quality players who were slightly overlooked by other programs, which rarely happens these days. Foster recruited two quality White players, Jim Spanarkel and Mike Gminski, in his first two years (who was smart enough to graduate a year early from high school; he went on to be an academic All-American), both of whom would go on to be All-Americans. By the spring of 1977, with a mostly White team, Duke was on the verge of a return to relevance. The 1976-77 team, with four White starters and future NBA players led by All-American Tate Armstrong (the only starting Black player, Morrison was not a primary scorer), had started at 12-3, and for the first time in nearly a decade, they were nationally ranked. That team would probably have won twenty games and played in the NCAAs for the first time in more than a decade if Armstrong, a twenty-seven point a game shooter of Verga's caliber, who once hit eleven shots in a row from beyond twenty feet, had not broken his shooting wrist in a game against Virginia midway through the season.

However, the mostly White Duke team was not at a level to actually compete for a national championship or even win an ACC title that year. The 1976-77 team, along with the post-1966 Vic Bubas teams (which at that point played against many teams with Black players), show how good Duke could have been with only White players; a decent, maybe 18-20 win program capable of competing effectively regionally, occasionally ranked, and maybe sometimes playing in the NCAAs (which had been considerably broadened from twenty-two to thirty-two teams since 1966, when only the team that won the ACC tournament was allowed to go), but not being good enough to really challenge for either an ACC or NCAA championship. That was their ceiling; good but not great. Without quality Black players, Duke was not capable of taking the next step up.

So when we look at the situation even *without* the effects of the 1966 Final Four, ten years after the 1966 season and Duke was still having trouble recruiting quality Black players. According to Jim Sumner, even without the effects of the 1966 game, "I think it's fair to state that Duke was widely viewed as a school not overly sympathetic to African Americans at that time."[12] The program had finally recovered from the Vietnam-induced collapse of the Waters era to recruit quality White players, which Waters couldn't do either. But they had still not been able to recruit the kind of national-level Black players, such as Butch Lee.

Well, in 1977, Duke was finally able to do it. The Duke program that year had been working very hard to recruit a top-notch Black player from Philadelphia named Gene Banks. In 1977, Banks, along with Albert King and Magic Johnson (the future all-time NBA great), was considered one of the top three players in the country. Duke had never recruited a Black player even close to Banks' level before then. He had the kind of athletic skills that NC State and UNC Black players had had. The staff had spent more than a year doing everything they possibly could to get him, but they were by no means sure that he would go to Duke. The recruiting competition was fierce; dozens of other schools were after him, and the local school, Penn, was considered to have a good chance of getting him.

Banks had been steered to Duke by his high school English teacher William H. Deadwyler Jr. According to Banks, "Deadwyler kept hammering me about the academics and the beautiful

The Bob Verga Shift

buildings. To get him off my back, I chose to go there [for a visit]."[13] In the end, strangely enough, it was not external reasons but internal ones that sent Banks to Duke. Banks, listening to his mom, had prayed in his room as to what to do. In a dream, he saw himself wearing a Duke blue-and-white uniform. Finally, in February of 1977, Banks made his decision. He was going to Duke. The Duke staff was ecstatic when they heard; they actually had a staffer camped outside Banks' house to watch him put his letter to Duke in the mailbox who went out and got the letter from the box before it was mailed! After enduring the years of Duke's 1970s irrelevance, my Duke-faithful friends and I had been suspensefully following Banks' recruitment for most of the previous year. At the time, I was delivering newspapers in Durham in my old Volkswagen. I remember the headline that day in the *Durham Sun*: "Duke Nets Cage Ace." I beeped my horn in happy anticipation of Banks' arrival—Duke's long awaited, first top-quality basketball recruit since the days of Art Heyman and Bob Verga, long ago before the 1966 season.

And so, in the fall of 1977, Duke University welcomed its first top Black recruit since Don Blackman, nine years earlier. The impact Banks made on the team was immediate and incredible. According to Jim Sumner, "It's hard for today's fan to understand the impact of Banks' commitment. Duke immediately went from old news to trending-on-twitter status."[14] In his freshman year, Banks, along with Jim Spanarkel and Mike Gminski, who were on their way to becoming All-Americans, and new White recruit Kenny Dennard (a pretty good player himself), played Kentucky (this time coached by 1966 Rupp assistant Joe B. Hall) for the national championship, losing 94–88. I remember the game well: I was in Tijuana, Mexico, on spring break when I realized that the bus would get to Ensenada too late to see the game, so I ditched my backpack, went back across the border, and ran two miles up the road to find a bar to watch the game, getting there about two minutes before the opening tip.

Banks revolutionized the Duke basketball program. Throughout his first three years at Duke, he turned Duke back into a national power, to a status they had not held since the 1966 game. They were ranked number one repeatedly in that time, and for the first time since the 1966 game, they were considered a top national program. In his senior year at Duke (Mike Krzyzewski's first year at Duke), Banks delivered an incredible last second catch and shoot shot in his last game against UNC, which sent the game into overtime, where Banks eventually won it. Duke fans (including my brother and father) in Cameron Indoor Stadium remember the shot being the most emotionally intense moment in Duke basketball history. Banks has described the unbelievable outpouring from the crowd after the shot went in as virtually a religious experience. I had the game on the phone mic'd up to play through my stereo in college so I could listen to it with a Duke alum. The shot can be readily seen on the internet by searching for it under "Gene Banks shot." Whenever I am in a bad mood, I often take a look at it to cheer up.

Banks' recruitment helped Duke recruit the kind of quality Black players who could make the program nationally prominent once more. Banks had broken the Black recruiting color barrier and put Duke on national television where other Black recruits could see Duke basketball. Nearly ten years' worth of future Duke Black recruits, players such as Johnny Dawkins, Tommy Amaker, David Henderson, Phil Henderson, Robert Brickey, Grant Hill, Thomas Hill, and Kevin Strickland, all got to see Banks play on television. According to Duke's next Black recruit, Vince Taylor, who Banks recruited personally, "I went to Duke because of Tink. ... He was the first. There wouldn't be any others if it weren't for him. He was the one that started it all."[15]

Gene Banks was still at Duke when Mike Krzyzewski arrived, and he laid the foundation for Krzyzewski's program, with some help from Vince Taylor. Banks' presence at Duke had somehow magically restored the Duke program to its 1960s Bubas-era prominence, galvanizing everyone at Duke. Johnny Dawkins, who followed Banks a few years later, said, "I followed his career. I saw his pioneering spirit to make a decision like that [to go to Duke]. He went there when a lot of guys would've gone somewhere else."[16] According to Dawkins, Banks had shown him that a man from the inner city could thrive athletically and academically at Duke University. According to Krzyzewski, "In Johnny's case, obviously, he was the start of us developing our program at Duke,"[17] Dawkins was probably the second most important recruit in Duke history after Banks. When Duke was signing Dawkins in 1982, the headline in the *Duke Chronicle* read, "Welcome to Duke, Johnny D." He went on to be a two-time All-American, Duke's second all-time leading scorer, and a Naismith award winner his senior year, where he led Duke to a thirty-seven-win season and a berth in the 1986 national championship game against the Louisville Cardinals—which Duke ultimately lost on a Pervis Ellison put back of an airball.

Krzyzewski has stated that Dawkins' recruitment very likely saved his job at Duke; many rich alumni were looking to get rid of him a year later if his recruiting class did not produce results. Duke went only 11–17 Dawkins' first year, famously losing a game in the first round of the ACC tournament to University of Virginia by more than forty points, where seven-four Ralph Sampson slammed in the face of future ESPN commentator Jay Bilas and laughed at him. Dawkins was the most important player in it. Without Banks, it is very likely Dawkins would have gone elsewhere and Krzyzewski would have been fired. The 1982 Duke recruiting class actually holds the all-time NCAA college record for scoring by one college class with 7450 points by six recruits. A documentary was made about it: *The Class That Saved Coach K.*

But even after Duke had finally been able to bring in good Black recruits nationally, nearly ten years after the 1966 game, in the years after Banks' arrival Duke still had difficulty recruiting quality Black players in-state because most of the ones they wanted typically went to UNC. When looking at the situation of Duke recruiting in-state applicants against UNC, there are two significant non-racial reasons why UNC usually won most of the in-state recruiting battles. As the state flagship school, UNC is the place most players would like to attend; potential North Carolina applicants are surrounded by UNC alumni, they continually see UNC on TV, and they are inculcated from birth with the culture of UNC basketball. UNC basketball has a place in the hearts of a large portion of the state of North Carolina, at about the same level as University of Kentucky does to the people in Kentucky, and with six NCAA championships, has a winning tradition as strong as Kentucky's. Their hold on the allegiance of the state was even stronger fifty years ago when there were no pro sports teams to follow and the UNC basketball team was in the top ten year after year, under the guidance of 1966 Duke "friend" Dean Smith.

In addition, Duke's high academic standards precluded a large number of athletes from attending; players with NBA-level aspirations considered Duke's high academic standards more of a hindrance than an opportunity. This is why Duke recruited so few quality White players from North Carolina; most of them went to UNC also. So even if Duke and UNC were located in a state without racial issues, UNC would win most of the in-state recruiting battles anyway. Those are the main reasons Duke recruited nationally, even in the Bubas era in the 1960s; it was hard to find recruits who could play at the highest level *and* meet Duke's academic standards, and it was also difficult to break the obvious pre-existing allegiance of in-state players to UNC. Duke did recruit a few back then: Banks' classmate Kenny Dennard (North Carolina 1977 high school player of the year) and Randy Denton from Raleigh both had good careers at Duke and played in the NBA. (Dennard's NBA career was cut short due to testicular cancer, and Denton had an impressive afro when he was in the ABA in the mid 70s.) Durham natives Stu Yarbrough and Parade All-American Brad Evans also played for Duke and were quality rotation players, but most of the other White North Carolina players who might have gone to Duke went to UNC.

So what we see is that Duke recruited few quality players from North Carolina at all, and when we add in Duke's existing poor racial record, it was virtually impossible for them to recruit quality Black players, even *without* the effects of the 1966 final four. So Duke recruited all its Black players from out of state back then, typically from the Northeast. Michael Jordan, from Wilmington, was a good enough student to attend Duke, but he never seriously considered going there even when Banks was already there. A significant reason for that, as well as for the reasons stated above, was that Krzyzewski did not arrive at Duke until the spring of Jordan's junior year, at which point Smith and UNC were already well ahead in the recruiting race, causing Krzyzewski to make only a token attempt to recruit him.

In fact, Duke was not able to successfully recruit *any* quality Black high school player in state until 1982, when six-foot-five clutch scorer David Henderson was recruited from rural Drewry, making him a prominent member of Duke's all-time-greatest recruiting class with Dawkins. Henderson, the second ranked high school player in the state, had a fine career at Duke, scoring more than fifteen hundred points, starting on three nationally ranked teams. At six-five and 195 pounds, he was slightly undersized for a college forward, but he was one of the toughest players ever to put on a Duke uniform. He effectively guarded players three and four inches taller, such as St. John's National Player of the Year, 6-8 Walter Berry, playing hard-nose defense while on the floor, and rarely wearing down during games. His endurance showed through especially at the end of close games, where he scored consistently in the clutch. He brought an element of North Carolina farm-country toughness to a team of suburban White boys who clearly benefited from it, much as Mike Lewis had done for the '66 team. Henderson's senior year, he helped lead his team to a then-NCAA-record thirty-seven games and played for the national championship as Gene Banks had done. When Henderson left the arena in his final game in a Duke uniform at the end of the championship game in Dallas, Texas, my brother noted that he could barely walk; Duke's first ever quality Black recruit from North Carolina had left everything on the floor that day for Duke University.

But Henderson's overall talent wasn't quite at an All-American or NBA level, due to his clear physical limitations; he was only a fringe pro player, playing part of one season in the NBA for Philadelphia. And Duke actually recruited him because the top-ranked in-state Black player that year, Durham Southern's own Parade All-American Curtis Hunter, the best player to come out of Durham in several years, had turned Duke down to attend UNC, as so many great in-state Black players had before him. Both Hunter and Henderson were six-five and played the same position, so if Henderson went to UNC, he would have been competing directly against Hunter for playing time for the next four years (as well as a sophomore guard named Michael Jordan, who played a similar position). If he attended Duke, he knew he would play right away. In 1982, Mike Krzyzewski was quite desperate to bring quality recruits in with Dawkins, as he had brought in four lower level recruits the year before. A few years later, Duke had returned to national prominence, with Henderson's considerable assistance, especially in Duke's incredible 1984 upset of Jordan's number-one ranked UNC team, which not only probably saved Krzyzewski's job, but is also, in my estimation, the greatest victory in the history of Duke basketball. It is possible that Henderson would not have been offered a scholarship at that point, as Duke was again recruiting All-American level players.

So it took Duke nearly sixteen years after the 1966 game to finally recruit a quality in-state Black player, and the only reason *that* happened was because the player Duke had actually wanted,

Hunter, had committed to UNC, effectively blocking Henderson from going there. In fact, in the time between the 1966 game and Henderson's arrival in 1982, of the twenty quality Black NBA players (multiple years in the league, scoring average around ten points or more) produced by North Carolina—a significant number of whom were also college All-Americans—five went to UNC, *none* to Duke. And there were also a few dozen other fringe NBA players such as Henderson who came out of North Carolina during that era, and none of them went to Duke either.

So if Bob Verga had not been sick and Duke had won the 1966 Kentucky game, would Banks, Dawkins, or Henderson have ever gone to Duke? One way to assess that effect is to see how the 1966 game affected recruiting in Kentucky. The actual effect the game had on Kentucky recruiting is difficult to determine exactly. It's hard to separate the specific effects of the game from Rupp and the SEC's overall reputation for racism. It is an issue that Kentucky has faced ever since that game. Tony Kornheiser of the *Washington Post* stated, "Rupp never recovered from that. And for many black Americans, neither did Kentucky."[18] Former Kentucky coach Rick Pitino claimed 1993 Kentucky Mr. Basketball Jason Osbourne—who he tried to recruit more than twenty-five years after the game—said his grandfather, who saw the game, told him no *grandchild* of his would ever set foot on the campus of Rupp's university.

And that attitude was shared by many. According to Jerry Tipton, "Beginning with Wes Unseld in 1964, eight black high-school stars from Louisville gained the title of Mr. Basketball and looked elsewhere for a college."[19] That five of them went to in-state rival Louisville shows the effects of Rupp's legacy; given the choice between the two large in-state schools, these players chose Louisville by five-to-one—although Louisville being their hometown school was also a factor, and two of them were recruited when Kentucky was on probation in 1989 and 1990 for recruiting violations, as discussed in chapter eleven, which also likely affected their decision.

In the years directly after the 1966 game, Kentucky recruited no Black players at all, mostly because the primary determinant in Kentucky's success in recruiting quality Black players was not the overall environment or the 1966 game, it was simply the coach. Under Rupp, even after the 1966 game and up to his death in 1972, Kentucky had recruited only *one* Black player, Tom Payne, who left after one year. Once Rupp retired and his assistant Joe B. Hall (an excellent recruiter) took over, Kentucky was able to recruit quality Black players such as Reggie Warford, Larry Johnson, Jack Givens, and James Lee, and by 1975, with a mixed-race team, Kentucky was back in the Final Four for the first time since 1966.

Even for Kentucky, a state school with a winning tradition, the going was not easy. Joe B. Hall was a younger coach who had coached integrated teams before and still found it to be a challenge. When recruiting Jack Givens, who actually grew up in Lexington, Kentucky, only a few miles from the university, according to Charles Martin in *Benching Jim Crow*, "Givens had never identified with Kentucky because of the school's lack of black players, and many of his neighbors actively discouraged him from signing with the university."[20] Duke never forgot Givens, by the way; he scored forty-one points against Duke in the 1978 national championship game. (It made for a very disappointing trip back to Tijuana after the game for the author!)

It was not easy to overcome Rupp's history of racism. But as the state school in a relatively less-racist border area with an incredible winning tradition, Kentucky was always going to be a top destination for talent of any type. Even though individual Black recruits may have turned down Kentucky because of the 1966 game, the overall national talent pool Kentucky had to draw on due to its lower academic standards and its built-in attraction as a premier state program allowed it to eventually overcome this obstacle and reclaim its former greatness after Rupp left.

As for Texas Western, the game didn't make it any easier for them to recruit back then either. Winning the national championship had forced Don Haskins and his team to fight a significant amount of negative press. A very negative piece was surprisingly written in *Sports Illustrated* about Texas Western's 1966 team, which made a number of inaccurate claims, but which was widely believed anyway. According to Don Haskins, other recruiters would take a copy of that article with them on the road. "They'd go to a home visit with someone we were recruiting and pull it out."[21]

But supposing Duke had played the game instead of Kentucky and opposing coaches had been able to pull out an article showing the KKK celebrating a Duke victory over Texas Western in 1966? What would have happened to Duke recruiting then? Duke might have gone down in history as the team of racial troublemaking, possibly even the heroes of the Ku Klux Klan. Every time Duke knocked on a Black recruit's door, that game would have been remembered. Would William H. Deadwyler Jr. have recommended Duke to Gene Banks if he had remembered Klansmen cheering for Duke after beating Texas Western? Would Banks have dreamed of wearing a Duke uniform then?

And that, coupled with the other obstacles that Duke faced in that era, would likely have prevented the program from achieving national greatness in the '70s. In 1977, Duke had spent more than a decade trying to recruit quality Black players with relatively little success. The multiple factors of Duke and the state of North Carolina's racist legacy, the general Waters-induced collapse of the team (no one wants to play for a loser), and Duke's high academic standards had stymied all previous Duke attempts at recruiting top Black players. Had they played and beaten Texas Western for the championship in 1966, it is very likely that would have been the final dealbreaker; the doors to Black America would have slammed shut on Duke, for maybe a generation, or maybe forever, and Duke basketball would never again have reclaimed its 1960s place of prominence.

Having grown up in Durham and followed Duke basketball and Duke recruiting for nearly fifty years, I believe if Duke had won the 1966 championship, the program Mike Krzyzewski built would likely never have happened. The effect of the Bob Verga illness on Duke Basketball would still be felt today. The five national championship banners hanging from the rafters of Cameron Indoor Stadium—every one of which was won with quality Black players performing an essential role—would all have disappeared. In the original scenario, where Verga was sick and Duke didn't play the 1966 game, Mike Krzyzewski went on to become the winningest coach in the history of college basketball. Under the alternative scenario where Verga was not sick, Duke would have likely dismissed Mike Krzyzewski in 1983 because he wouldn't have been able to successfully recruit quality Black players. The winningest coach of all time would never have won anything of significance at Duke because the 1966 game had closed the doors of all Black America to Duke University.

CHAPTER 9

WHAT IF FOR KENTUCKY

Seeing that a Duke win would not necessarily have had a very positive effect on events in North Carolina, how did Bob Verga's illness transform events in Kentucky? To understand how Kentucky's loss in the 1966 game affected the way people in Kentucky saw things, we need to examine the aftermath of the original loss. Unlike the situation in North Carolina where Duke did not play the game, we have the actual case in which the Kentucky team *did* play the game for comparison.

Pat Riley, who played for Kentucky, found the loss of the game to be very hard to take. He said it was the worst day of his life. When the game ended, Riley sobbed on the bench. The headline on the *Louisville Courier* the next day read, "Can't Stand to See Kids Cry." (Like I did when Duke lost in the semifinals.) Said Riley, noting how painful losing was and how few chances one gets in a lifetime to play for a championship, "There are so many good teams and they all want to win the championship and you get there and you've got to do it. We didn't do it. They were better than we were, more aggressive than we were."[1]

Immediately after the game, Riley and Dampier, the Kentucky All-Americans, were gracious to the Texas Western players. Both took the unusual step of going to the Texas Western locker room to offer their congratulations. "It was just joy," Riley recalled.

"Their players were in there; their families were in there. I just went immediately, quickly through there, said what I had to say and left them to have their moment."[2] Dampier admitted it was something he had never done before., but something possessed him to enter their locker room. "I wasn't happy and hand-slapping and all that. I just congratulated them. And Coach Haskins said thank you."[3] So in the period immediately after the game, to their eternal credit, the Kentucky players showed good sportsmanship.

In the long run, however, it's hard to determine exactly what the response of other people would have been. I did not grow up in Kentucky and have never lived there. It's very difficult to describe to people who don't live in North Carolina and Kentucky how people felt about college basketball back then (and still largely do today, by the way). Unlike states like Texas and Alabama, North Carolina and Kentucky do not have a tradition of great football teams. The great Bear Bryant coached at Kentucky alongside Rupp for many years, and finally left Kentucky when he realized that no matter how much he won—famously claiming that he was once given a cigarette lighter when Rupp was given a Cadillac—he could never eclipse Rupp.

College basketball was pretty much the only game in Lexington at the time of the 1966 Final Four, as neither state had any pro teams until a few years later—the Kentucky Colonels and Carolina Cougars did not start playing until 1967 and 1969 respectively. Great college basketball players in North Carolina and Kentucky were larger than life. Players like David Thompson, Dan Issel, Kyle Macy, Pat Riley, Michael Jordan, and Christian Laettner are idolized by the people around their schools in a way that seems hard to understand elsewhere. David Thompson, more than forty years after leading NC State to the 1974 national championship, is still a hero there.

University of Kentucky (along with Louisville, to some extent) has a fan base that extends across the entire state. Kentucky basketball is still the one thing that unites everyone in the state of Kentucky more than fifty years after the 1966 game, and it was even more so during the Rupp era, when it was practically a state religion. According to Dan Issel, who played there, "The Wildcats are the greatest common denominator in our state—the one thing about which one can strike up a conversation almost anywhere or anytime there is nothing like Kentucky Basketball."[4] Kentucky basketball rose to a position of prominence in Kentucky under Adolph Rupp; it joins North Carolina as the state where college basketball has had its greatest prominence. According to James Bolin, Kentucky was a state separated within by complex political, social, economic, and geographical divisions: "For Kentucky, Rupp and the success of the Kentucky Wildcats united the commonwealth. . . . Kentuckians from Pikeville to Paducah rooted for the Wildcats victory after victory, championship after championship"[5] When Cawood Ledford broadcast UK games between 1953 and 1992, with his trademark sign-in, "The Wildcats will be moving from left to right on your radio dial," everyone in Kentucky tuned in to listen. UK players—nearly 80 percent of whom were recruited by Adolph Rupp in state—were considered to be state heroes who the entire state basically worshipped. When the University of Kentucky lost, the whole state lost.

Over the years, UK teams that have been successful have been given special nicknames. There was The Fabulous Five in 1948, and The Fiddlin' Five in 1958—two of Rupp's national championship teams. There were The Unforgettables for the 1992 team, and The Untouchables for the 1996 championship team. Each of these teams endeared themselves to the fans of Kentucky through their play and their accomplishments. The 1966 team, Rupp's Runts was especially beloved by the people of Kentucky. And why shouldn't it have been? People found it easy to root for them. Unlike most college basketball teams, they were relatively short, which made it easy for averaged sized fans to identify with them. They hustled on defense. They passed the ball well. They ran the floor and played exciting up-tempo basketball that was fun to watch. And they won.

The fact that they won as much as they did that year was unexpected; they simply weren't supposed to be that good a team. "We weren't even picked to win our conference," said Larry Conley.[6] But as the year went on and they started winning more, the people of Kentucky found themselves caught up in a true fairy-tale season. They weren't just winning, they were blowing teams out, winning by wide margins. The season was turning into a joy ride. Expectations for the team grew over the course of the season. People were swept along in the emotions of winning. At the end of the season in Lexington, the crowd in their home arena had chanted, "We're number one!" so loudly they couldn't hear the final buzzer. After that, the team had a special party with a Number One cake, with each of the player's names on it. They were congratulated by the university president, and Rupp was introduced as national coach of the year. As the team moved through the NCAAs and made the championship game, the people in Kentucky were expecting a fairy-tale, championship ending.

So when their magic carpet collided with Texas Western's and crashed in a mid-prayer collision at the NCAA finals in College Park, the people of Kentucky were devastated. During the Rupp era, Kentucky had never before lost a national championship game. They were the favorite when they lost the Texas Western game. So when they lost, Rupp and Kentucky were truly shocked. "Adolph Rupp developed a superiority complex that exists to this day," said Harry Reid. "Kentucky fans are just very resentful of anybody that would challenge what they consider their birthright of superiority."[7] It was almost as if Lexington had been hit by an atomic bomb. Or, as *Denver Post* writer Woody Paige, known years later as more of a cartoon character on ESPN with his humorous chalkboards, wrote after the Denver Broncos lost a similar football game in 1997, "If Mount Vesuvius had erupted

The Bob Verga Shift

and covered the entire [front range] in molten lava, it could not exceed the catastrophe which occurred."[8]

That about sums up how the folks in Kentucky felt about losing the Texas Western game. The entire state was essentially in mourning. And this was not a fluke occurrence. According to Billy Reed, a sports editor for the *Courier-Journal*, "I remember in 1955 when Kentucky's home court win-streak of 129 straight games was snapped by Georgia Tech. The flag over the state Capitol was lowered to half-mast."[9]

At a rally in Lexington after the 1966 game, nearly five thousand people gathered for what had been planned as a victory celebration. The mood was somber. Rupp himself commended Conley's heroic play during the final four at the rally, especially against Duke. Larry Conley, still slightly ill, apologized to the crowd, "I'm sorry. We did the best we could."[10] The rally is remembered as one that no one wanted to leave. Rupp was heartbroken; he admitted this squad had captured his heart more than any other in his thirty-six years of coaching at Kentucky.

Young Mitch McConnell was at the University of Kentucky as a law student and got to see the effects of the game firsthand. At that point, he was more concerned with his legal and political career, where he was to run for and win election to be president of the student bar association. What McConnell saw around him was something that affected the people around him much more significantly. The game triggered a tsunami of racist resentment on the campus of the University of Kentucky. It washed over the entire campus and the entire state. McConnell had a chance to see how everyone at the University of Kentucky was affected by it. Even if McConnell, who had given speeches in favor of civil rights before as an undergraduate at Louisville, was not a racist before the game he was surrounded on all sides by people who obviously were. There was no way he couldn't have been affected by it.

So what we see then is that Bob Verga's illness had a clear effect on the social environment surrounding Mitch McConnell.

Instead of seeing Kentucky lose a semifinal game against Duke, which would not have had long term racial implications, he got to see them lose to Texas Western, which clearly did. Bob Verga's illness had an undeniable effect on reshaping the culture around McConnell, and not in a positive way. Verga's illness had essentially diverted all of the racial troublemaking that the game would have created from Durham and North Carolina into Kentucky. And there was no way McConnell could have escaped it, then, or years later. It surrounded him everywhere. McConnell certainly had an excellent opportunity to learn something from the game and its aftermath. So what did he learn from it? Anything of value? Maybe he learned something that he found useful in his political career years later. We can't say for sure; only he knows the answer to that. Maybe someday before he retires, we will know the answer.

For Larry Conley the game was hard to get over; he would have given anything to have won it. "It bothered me for many weeks after that game was over, but after that period I was ready to get on with my life. You can't live in the past. You just have to go on."[11] Tommy Kron had similar thoughts after the game. He had heard many people try to justify losing by claiming that Kentucky would beat Texas Western nine times out of ten, being poor losers. He stated that they played the game once and lost: "You get over it. You start thinking about getting married, graduate school. We did try. We just came up short and got beat by a good team."[12] For Pat Riley, it took until 1972, when he helped win a championship with the Lakers, which he remembers as being a very special moment, to finally start feeling better. "That changed that hole in my stomach forever," Riley said.[13]

And so, by and large, that's what the Kentucky players did. They got over it, but they didn't forget it. They were young and had their lives to live and careers to move onto. For Pat Riley, Louis Dampier, and Tommy Kron that meant playing professional basketball. Riley and Dampier played for nearly ten years after the game: Riley in the NBA, and Dampier in the ABA, while Tommy Kron played four years total in both. Riley and Dampier were on championship teams in that time, although Dampier's role on the Kentucky Colonels was somewhat greater. By 1976, when Dampier won his title, the talent level in the ABA was about the same as the NBA, although the league was somewhat smaller. Dampier also went on to set the all-time ABA scoring record, scoring more than thirteen thousand points during his career, *and* the all-time ABA assist record against some top-notch competition. Thad Jaracz went on to be an All-American at Kentucky his senior year, although he did not play professionally; after college, he joined the military.

After Riley's playing career was through—he was mostly a journeyman NBA player, averaging about seven points a game)—he went on to much greater fame as a very well-dressed coach and executive. He won five NBA championships as a coach, four with the Los Angeles Lakers and one with the Miami Heat, and two as the general manager of the Miami Heat. His 1980s Lakers Showtime teams were among some of the best to ever play in the NBA.

Not only did the game serve as inspiration for Riley, but it also helped his professional career. For Riley, it meant that during his playing career that he likely avoided getting dunked on as much as if he had won the game, when he would have had a target on his back for playing it. When he became an NBA coach in the 1980s, he got to coach players (and against players) who had seen the game when they were growing up. Many of them remembered the game and thanked him for helping change their lives. It gave him credibility that he wouldn't have had otherwise and goodwill from being the player who helped them go off to college and get a better life.

Larry Conley, in addition to being a pretty good college player, was also intelligent and articulate; he went on to become a top broadcaster. Conley performed on nearly eighteen hundred games as a broadcaster, working for nearly every major sports network. He was known for his knowledge of the game and his genial, friendly on-air personality. Watching Conley work a college basketball game meant seeing a total professional in every sense of the word.

So, at least for a few of the Kentucky players, namely All-Americans Pat Riley and Louis Dampier, the game helped motivate them to succeed professionally at a level which neither one of them may have attained if they had won the 1966 game. Rather than being bitter about it, they managed to get on with their lives, using the game and what they learned from it to help motivate them in their careers.

For the rest of the state of Kentucky, however, getting over the game was not easy. The local media were ready with racist excuses for the loss after the game. The *Lexington Herald* wrote, "There is no disgrace in losing to a team such as was assembled by Texas Western after a nationwide search for talent that somehow escaped the recruiters for the globetrotters."[14]—implying that the Texas Western players were not real students. At Kentucky's 1966 end-of-season banquet, a local sportswriter stood up and said that people could be proud of having the best White team in the nation (which Duke with a healthy Verga might readily have disputed). No one protested, including Adolph Rupp or John Oswald, the university president.

Rupp was a very intense coach under any circumstances; he constantly berated players and challenged calls in the games. Bill Spivey, a Kentucky star in the 1950s, said, "He wanted everybody to hate him and he succeeded. He called us names some of us had never heard before."[15] Rupp once said, "Defeat and failure to me are enemies. Without victory, basketball has little meaning. I would not give one iota to make the trip from the cradle to the grave unless I could live in a competitive world."[16] He was a notoriously poor loser: "A good loss. That's when the other guy loses, not Kentucky."[17] And in this case, the fact that he had been proven wrong about the sensitive issue of race was particularly galling.

Rupp also failed to shake hands with the Texas Western players after the game, although he did shake hands with Coach Haskins.

Most of the residents of Kentucky went the same route. In the months and years after the game, when the racial implications of the game started to become clear, the Kentucky faithful were faced with the reality of having Rupp, who at that point was a state icon, go down in history as a racist villain. "Every morality play calls for a villain," wrote Pat Forde in 1996. "Although Rupp wasn't that so much as an old man anchored in the past, he would do splendidly."[18] Rupp did not help his case by repeatedly blaming other factors for the loss. He claimed that whenever the referees called a foul on them, Texas Western responded by accusing them of discrimination. At the rally in Lexington after the game, Rupp, stating that his teams (mostly outside) shots didn't drop, didn't have anything nice to say about the winning team: "All those ineligible players. . . . They were a bunch of crooks."[19] And he was blatantly racist about why his team lost: "They had some n----- on their team and we didn't."[20] And thus began the more than fifty-year obsession of the *entire state of Kentucky* with defending their state icon coach from accusations of racism, and only because of Bob Verga's chance illness.

From the point of view of the Kentucky faithful, the racial aspects of the game made the loss doubly hard to deal with. Over time, the cultural implications of the game grew even greater, as it became clear how the game affected so many people who saw it outside of Kentucky. The people in Kentucky were disparaged by Black America as the "Bluegrass Bigots." So rather than having the game be remembered as a game where Kentucky lost the national championship, the game reached legendary proportions instead. And Kentucky's role as racist villains in the game never went away either.

The legend that somehow Kentucky was cheated also lingered for decades. Rupp continued to make excuses that they lost because the Texas Western players were thugs, or ineligible, or they got too many calls their way, or that Kentucky just had a bad game. He was actually officially on record at one point as stating that Kentucky lost fair and square, but that was a rare instance. Kentucky's assistant coach Joe B. Hall had no doubts about Texas Western's legitimate win. "The Miners won that night because they played much better than we did."[21] But that statement was in the minority compared to all the others made by Rupp about the game. The Kentucky fans simply could not accept the fact that their team had lost to a Black team that just happened to be better than them.

And what made it worse for them is that Kentucky didn't make the Final Four again until 1975 and didn't win a championship again until 1978—twenty years since the last Kentucky championship, a very long time for a program that prided itself on championships. The extended time period between championships, more than twelve years after the 1966 game, during most of which the Kentucky program was not prominent, gave the loss time to sink in, much as it did for me in Durham; the Kentucky people had a long time during the UCLA era to think back on it with regret. The effects were *not* soon erased by subsequent championships, so they did *not* go away; just as they didn't in Durham as the Duke program faded in the same era; the loss resonated for more than a decade afterwards. The pressure on Coach Joe B. Hall to win in 1978 was so great that he called it a season without celebration. He wasn't happy that they won the NCAA championship, he was simply relieved.

For an entire generation of Kentucky basketball fans, the game lived forever in infamy; the pain of the loss never went away. Larry Conley said he thought his team was more famous for losing than they would have been if they had won: "That attention has endured through the years."[22] If the game had been played by any other coach in any other state, the game's significance might have faded over time. But Kentucky basketball occupies a central position in the state culture even now. Rupp is still an icon in Kentucky (his legacy towers over that of any subsequent Kentucky coach), and the game is the one thing Rupp is most famous for.

An examination of Kentucky newspaper discussions over the years shows how persistent the effect of the game has been; it has become a literally never-ending statewide obsession. An analysis of the Louisville and Lexington papers found the game mentioned nearly fifty times between 1985 and 2017. The game has forced Kentuckians, many of whom still revere Rupp, into the position of having to *perpetually* defend his racial record. In Rupp's obituaries, in 1977, the game was not even mentioned. But in 1985, an article about Rupp's son Herky included an extensive discussion of the game. In 1991, the 1966 team was written up, and the loss of the game was still considered his major legacy (that was after a *Sports Illustrated* article that year revived interest in it). The next year, Rick Pitino's team was having special scrimmages in Louisville to help combat the team's legacy of racism under Rupp. In 1997, after Dean Smith passed Rupp's all-time coaching record, the game was mentioned prominently in discussions of the two coaches, leading Billy Reed, the Kentucky sportswriter to state, "To read and hear the most irresponsible rhetoric, you would have thought that Rupp conducted his practices not in starched khaki shirt and pants but in a white hood and a sheet."[23] In 1999, the game was mentioned by Larry Conley, who still defended Rupp's racial record. "I'm on the record as saying this many times: He never made a racially derogatory comment in my presence. I know other people have said they did hear him say that, I can't speak to that."[24]

And the game's effect has persisted beyond the turn of the millennium. According to James Bolin, "The issue of race increasingly has defined Rupp's legacy in the twenty-first century, indicating the lingering importance of the racial divide in the postmodern world."[25] In a 2001 *Lexington-Herald Leader* series, framed around the question "What is the Legacy of Adolph

Rupp?" almost *every* contribution from the newspaper's readers contained some defense of the coach's stand on the race issue. In 2006 when the movie *Glory Road* came out, the game was discussed extensively in the Kentucky papers; remarkably enough, this was only a couple of years before Barack Obama became president, so by then, Senator Mitch McConnell was clearly reminded of it then. One article in 2006 described it like this: "Revered by some, reviled by others, the game owns a peculiar place in Kentucky history, reflecting a Rashomon-like dichotomy where events and their consequences vary starkly in people's memories."[26] Kentuckian David Brock, who was not old enough to remember Rupp, wrote, "I grew up idolizing black UK players. I must admit an urge towards righteous indignation when Kentucky is vilified. It is particularly convenient to mention that darling Duke was just as white in 1966."[27] In 2006, Billy Reed wrote, "This ugly and unfair misconception is the work of revisionist historians who have taken the 1966 NCAA championship game between Kentucky and Texas Western and twisted into something it wasn't."[28] At the fiftieth anniversary in 2016, the game was the subject of many articles and interviews, most of which discussed Rupp and the racial aspects of the game. In 2019, Mark Story ranked the loss, along with the one to Duke in 1992 (remarkable how Duke impacted both games, eh?) discussed later in chapter eleven, as one of the two worst Kentucky losses of all time. In 2020, when Rupp Arena was undergoing renovations, the African American and Africana studies department petitioned to have the stadium name changed, stating, "The Adolph Rupp name has come to stand for racism and exclusion in UK athletics and alienates Black students, fans and attendees."[29] That year the Kentucky basketball team shot a video about racism that was posted on the internet, knowing how their program had once been famous for it.

Rupp's outsized stature in Kentucky has guaranteed that the game has never been forgotten. And it was never forgotten even by him for the rest of his life; Rupp's bitterness over the game lingered even until his death. In 1977, Rupp was dying of spinal cancer. He was terminally hospitalized on November 9, the day after Mitch McConnell won his first election, to be judge executive of Jefferson County. (McConnell did *not* meet him then, by the way.) Basketball had been Rupp's entire life's passion: "If they don't let me coach, they may as well take me to the Lexington cemetery."[30] And the 1966 game obsessed him more than anything else in his coaching career. Rupp's friends noted that even as he was dying with cancer in a Lexington hospital, he lamented to visitors about the loss of the 1966 game. According to Russell Rice, the long-time Kentucky sports information director, "Rupp carried the memory of that game to his grave."[31]

When Rupp was dying, Rice asked him to summarize his life. Rupp said, "Just say he did the best he could. That's enough."[32] The verdict on Rupp's life will always be mixed, depending on which side of the race debate you are on. From Rice's point of view, the legacy given to him outside of Kentucky based on the outcome of the 1966 game, ignoring his lifetime of winning and four national championships, was disproportionately damning, noting how much pride and prestige he had given to a state commonly viewed as being rural and backward; it was "unfair to a former Kansas farm boy who rolled with the flow in a region that was segregated beyond the realization of persons born into today's society."[33] But years later, William Turner compared Rupp's legacy to that of people like Jesse Helms and George Wallace, as one of the last highly visible segregationists at a moment in history when America was trying somehow to deal effectively with racial issues. According to William Turner, Rupp's legacy as a winner does not change his record for denying opportunity to Blacks. "Perhaps Mr. Rupp, like many, was a creature of his times; but, while time changes all things, it does not change the truth."[34] In the end, it appears that history will agree with both verdicts.

Rupp died on the very cold night of December 10, 1977, with the voice of Cawood Ledford on the radio in the background. Incredibly, it was Ledford's broadcast of a Kentucky-Kansas game on "Adolph Rupp Night" from Rupp's home state at his alma mater of Kansas, where his number-one ranked Kentucky Wildcats won the game. This was the same Kentucky team that would beat Duke for the national championship at the end of the season and bring Kentucky their first championship since Rupp's last in 1958. Like Kennedy's assassination, everyone in Kentucky remembers what they were doing when they heard the news of Rupp's death. Flags were flown at half-staff around Kentucky after his death.

So, if Bob Verga hadn't been sick, an entire generation of Kentucky fans would not have been affected by it in the way they actually were. They would never have sat stunned as their teams lost the game. There would have been little racial bitterness from Adolph Rupp, no recriminations. There would have been little for them to stew about for more than a decade before they won another national championship. When Rupp was discussed, it would be in terms of his four national championships, with racial issues being considered secondary. There would have been little discussion of the game decades later, and perhaps no continual necessity to defend Rupp's racial record. It might not have gone on to become a permanent part of Kentucky culture. And young Mitch McConnell would never have seen an all-White team lose to an all-Black team either. Since he won his first election in 1977 in part by specifically calling for a constitutional amendment to ban "forced busing," the initiative that allowed minority students to be bused to previously all-White public schools in Louisville[35], perhaps former civil rights activist McConnell *did* learn something from the 1966 game after all! Did he forget it thirty years later in the senate, after "Glory Road" came out?

Instead, Kentucky would almost certainly have lost the game to Duke. So how would they have responded to that? Look no further than the 1992 game discussed in chapter eleven, when Duke beat the second most beloved team in Kentucky history, The Unforgettables, in the East Regional finals. Kentucky fans have spent the last thirty years hating Duke for taking away the chance for one of their most beloved teams to play for the national championship. So, if Duke had won the 1966 game with Verga, it seems almost certain they would have seen it the same way in that instance too. They wouldn't have realized that Duke actually would have saved their beloved state icon coach from going down in history as a racist villain because no one at Duke understood that Kentucky had saved their program from all-time infamy either. And they would never have thanked Duke for it either. After, all since it never occurred to anyone from Duke to ever thank Kentucky for saving their program from infamy, why should it have occurred to anyone from Kentucky to thank Duke for the same thing? Of course not!

CHAPTER 10

WHAT IF FOR BLACK ATHLETES AND BLACK AMERICA

In examining the impact of how altering the 1966 game opponents would have affected Black America overall, it's necessary to look at the historical context of how much things had already changed by 1966. All across the South, universities and schools were integrating and Black people were finally getting to step forward into a better life. When we examine the history of the civil rights movement in 1966, we see that early 1966 was a crossroads for black America; many barriers had finally been removed, and black America was now considering new options. At the time of the 1966 Final Four, millions of Black Americans were looking for some positive direction on how to proceed next. But would the 1966 Final Four give them any?

By 1966, there had already been huge progress made throughout the South. Before the 1950s, Black players couldn't play basketball against Whites anywhere in the South. Don Barksdale, a great player in the 1940s, was the first Black player to play against Kentucky in a scrimmage game in Lexington, Kentucky, with his US Olympic teammates in 1948. He later became a close friend of Adolph Rupp, who acted as assistant coach for the Olympic team and actually helped Don deal with discrimination during the games, something that Rupp's defenders never fail to bring up. Barksdale praised Rupp as a great coach, in contradiction to the people who claimed he was an unabashed racist. In the pre-civil rights era, you could be put in jail for drinking from a White fountain or killed for going out with a White girl; Black men were often killed for nothing back then, and their murderers often were not prosecuted. Barksdale wouldn't even drink from the same water bottle as his White teammates when he was playing a game for fear of some attack. According to Barksdale, "No, I wasn't scared s going to prison. I was scared I'd get killed. I was scared to death."[1] And in the pre-civil rights era, when Adolph Rupp was taking teams to the South for more than thirty years, the statistics clearly show that Barksdale was right: between 1877 and 1950, more than thirty-four hundred Black people were lynched in the Old South, an average of nearly fifty a year, or almost *one a week,* including in the 1930s, when Adolph Rupp started traveling in the South.

By 1966, with the enactment of the Civil Rights Act, that had all started to change. But people didn't necessarily believe that things had changed permanently. Many Black people knew what had happened after the Civil War when slavery had ended. They had about ten years to do something during reconstruction, after which the old slavery barrier walls had been substantially re-erected through segregation. Black America and Black athletes in the mid-1960s, especially in the South, were like prisoners who had been locked up for a long time, only to find that someone had blown up the walls of their prison and were now staring through the smoke and dust into the sunlight for the first time in nearly a hundred years. They were unsure whether it was safe to finally step outside into the sunlight.

When Black America and Southern Black athletes headed out into the world, they were still met with considerable resistance. In 1966, the Ku Klux Klan was still active in much of the South. For Black people, travelling in the South was still dangerous. There were Klansmen, racist police, and unfriendly White people wherever they went. Even though segregation in public facilities had been outlawed in 1964, they were still often confronted with hostility wherever they went. They still did not have the confidence that they could go out and embrace opportunity like White people could. As a Black friend at my church, who lived in the South in the 50s, was told back then, "N-----, don't let the sun go down on you." A sentiment shamelessly advertised on the edges of towns particularly hostile to Black folks, known as Sundown Towns.

However, in the time between when Barksdale had played in Lexington and the 1966 game, sports themselves had changed enormously. Starting in 1947 with Jackie Robinson, and continuing with other players such as Willie Mays, Major League Baseball had been integrated for nearly twenty years. The first Black professional basketball player started in 1950. There had been professional Black football players since 1920. There had been Black players in college basketball since the 1950s, especially up north. As Lane Demas, historian of Black football, pointed out, football was historically the sport of greater interest to White America, so integrating football had a greater impact on White America than did integrating basketball. Conversely, in 1966 basketball was starting to have a greater emotional impact on Black America, who at that point were already starting to view basketball as "their" game. And unlike football, which is played in a similar manner whether the teams are Black or White (although faster Black players did change the game some), basketball is a sport with a clear racial difference in playing style.

From the point of view of most of the players in the 1966 championship game, the race issue didn't actually seem to be all that big a deal; most of them had played in a mixed-race environment for a long time and were familiar with both styles of play. The Kentucky team that played Texas Western consistently played nearby Big Ten teams with Black players; this is one reason why most of the Kentucky players didn't think seriously about the racial implications of the finals game in 1966, as they had played integrated teams for a long time. In fact, the 1966 game is significant in terms of sports integration because it signaled the *end* of the last racial barriers. Once the SEC and the other Southern leagues desegregated the next year, that was the end of segregated sports. And Kentucky had been the SEC standard bearer.

Pat Riley on the Kentucky team did not appreciate the racial implications of the 1966 finals game. He was from Schenectady, New York, had played Black teams for years, had many Black friends, and hadn't really thought about it during the game. He had even played Kareem Abdul Jabbar in high school in 1961, being one of only two teams to beat him; he had been playing Black competition for so long that he didn't even think about the racial implications of the 1966 game before he played it. Before and during the game, he was more concerned with simply winning it. Within a year or so, however, he discovered that the game had opened doors for an entire generation of Black youth to step forward and claim what had been denied to them for generations. Once he realized the significance of what had happened and the way it had affected Black athletes throughout the South, he became proud of the game. According to Riley, he didn't recognize it as a watershed moment at the time it occurred. He now realized that it was an event that actually changed the direction of the culture. He didn't view it as a proud moment when he lost, but fifty years later, he's actually proud to have been a part of it. As Riley said, "That win by Texas Western mattered to a lot of players who were afraid to go to school in the South, and they went after that game. It opened up the door for a lot of opportunity."[2] He now calls the game the "Emancipation Proclamation of 1966."[3]

Kentucky assistant Joe B. Hall heartily agreed with Riley that the right team won that championship: "The Miners' victory carved the way for integration and create much needed changes and opportunities for many young people."[4] Larry Conley saw how much it meant to the Black population, and how they used it as motivation to improve their lives. As Conley said "There was so much going on back in that era. You had the Voting Rights Act and a lot of legislation trying to assist minorities back then, and I can look at it now and fully understand it."[5]

Prior to the game, only David Lattin seemed to understand the racial implications of the game when he went out on the floor that night. He realized that the game was part of a greater struggle to get Black America a better life, and that his team simply could not afford to lose, as Kentucky was carrying the banner for White racists further south. Grasping what defeat would have meant, he said he could not have gone home if they had lost the game. "My teammates and I had a part to play in the epic struggle on the streets that until this night had always seemed so distant. Our part for the Cause was here, this night, amidst this sea of white racism. We couldn't lose."[6]

Besides Lattin, the Black players on the Texas Western team were not really aware of what the effect of it was going to be on the rest of Black America. As Willie Worsley pointed out, he had his own set of priorities. According to Worsley, "There's no way we went into that game thinking this would be great for blacks. Why should we? Who knows when they're going to make history."[7]

From the opening tipoff, after which David Lattin slammed on Pat Riley, it was clear that Texas Western was the better team. They played better defense, shot a considerably better percentage, hit their free throws, and handled Kentucky's defensive pressure better. Texas Western led throughout the game. The final score, a seven-point Texas Western win, shows about how close the game was. It wasn't a blowout or a close game, but it was clear cut; Texas Western was clearly the better team, and there was no doubt about the officiating deciding the game, as it appears to have in previous Texas Western games.

Future Vanderbilt player Perry Wallace, who would become the first Black player in the SEC the next year, had just finished leading an all-Black team to the state championship in Tennessee against an all-White team in Nashville when the 1966 finals game started. He saw people in the gym watching the beginning of the Kentucky-Texas Western game on portable black-and-white TVs. He saw how Rupp was acting during the game (he later turned down Kentucky because he thought Rupp didn't show much understanding for him). He saw how the people in his neighborhood watching the game were reacting to it, and how overjoyed they were that Texas Western was winning.

Future Kentucky coach Tubby Smith (the first Black coach in Kentucky history)—who was their coach from 1997 through 2007, winning a national title—remembers watching the Kentucky-Texas Western game on television, rooting for the Miners. Remembering every detail of that day, he said it was just like rooting for Joe Lewis or Jackie Robinson. As Durham civil rights activist Howard Fuller stated, "So that was really a watershed moment, a special time for me watching it because that very next year I was going to be playing at Great Mills High School with white classmates and white teammates."[8]

In Fort Worth, future Harvard business school dean James Cash was finishing his first semester at TCU at the time of the game. According to Cash, the game had great significance because Kentucky basketball, along with Alabama football, were viewed as longtime symbols of White athletic superiority, a status which Duke basketball at the time had not quite achieved. "The level of celebration equaled those associated with a Joe Louis victory over a 'Great White Hope!' or passage of the Voting Rights Act of 1965."[9] Cash said several families had a party in Greenway Park to celebrate the victory. Many similar celebrations took place in nearby Como Park. "Without a doubt, it lifted the spirits of the black community in Fort Worth, and encouraged many to embrace and accelerate the social changes that were happening."[10] Overall, the response of Black America to the first (and last) ever victory of an all-Black championship team over an all-White team was overwhelming; the game was celebrated throughout Black America as a huge victory, one which proved that Black student-athletes could compete and win at the highest level.

William Turner, an early leader of the Black Student Union at UK in the mid-1960s had a view of the game as being more righteous vindication. He had confronted Rupp about integrating the program before the game. When he talked with Rupp about it, Rupp had not indicated any desire to have Blacks on his team. Said Turner, "Anyone who says that game wasn't all about race is in denial. The game was about nothing but race. And everybody knew that then, too."[11]

The game had an impact on a generation of Black athletes that was truly remarkable. Sociologist Randy Roberts called it the most important NCAA championship ever played. Two months after the game, Perry Wallace became the first Black SEC player by signing with Vanderbilt. In the space of one year, racial barriers in the South tumbled down as one school after another rushed to recruit quality Black players. By the 1966-67 season, every White conference in the South had become integrated. *Ebony* magazine called it "the thundering hooves of a cattle stampede."[12] Within a few years, all of the Southern schools had some level of Black participation—except Kentucky, which was not integrated until 1970.

The pace of change was not as rapid as hoped, however. In 1969 there were still only twenty-three Black athletes in SEC colleges. It wasn't until the mid-1970s that participation in the SEC reached equitable levels. But the last barrier had finally come down. All of the schools realized the obvious; if they wanted to win, they had to have Black players. As Frank Deford had prophesized in 1965, "The pressure on those that are holding out for sporting segregation is likely to become irresistible as soon as they are regularly whupped by their integrated neighbors."[13] None of them wanted to endure the public humiliation suffered by Kentucky—as Duke was about to endure by Carolina over the next few years.

And so, having seen a decisive Texas Western victory, an entire generation of Black athletes were inspired to go out and play. John Thompson and Nolan Richardson, the great Black coaches, remember how the game inspired them. John Thompson has said he was obviously pulling for Texas Western. Nolan Richardson, the first player Don Haskins met at Texas Western several years before the game, claimed that, by beating Rupp, Haskins had been responsible for Black players receiving thousands of scholarships. Richardson said that Black people believed that Rupp stood for racism: "I know the Preamble to the Constitution says all men are created equal. Rupp, he called guys 'coons.' That's what he stood for."[14]

It wasn't until the following year that the implications of the game started becoming clear. Don Haskins himself didn't quite understand the implications of the game, but eventually began to realize the significance of what his team had done. Wherever Haskins went, people came up to him and thanked him for winning the game. Black athletes and men everywhere would come up to him and thank him for inspiring them to go out and get a scholarship or go to college. The game clearly had a huge effect on sports integration, so whatever positive effects that had on Black America may have been the overall effect of the game. According to Dr. Wilford S. Bailey, the former president of the NCAA, "I am of the opinion that sports integration has been the single greatest contributor to racial progress and development in the South."[15]

It is clear that the game had a significant short-term emotional impact on Black America. But in terms of how much the game inspired Black students to do anything positive in areas other than athletics, it is hard to say how much long-term effect it had. Both Charles Martin, who wrote *Benching Jim Crow*, and Howard Fuller, the Durham civil rights activist, are not quite sure about the overall impact of the game. Fuller seemed to agree that in the short term there were many other significant events happening around the same time that the impact of the game itself was somewhat reduced; it simply wasn't as important as things like the Selma march or King's marches in Chicago. Martin showed that the impact on Black athletes was immediate and incredible; however, the impact on non-athlete Black students wasn't quite as clear.

The outcome of the 1966 Final Four game inspired Black athletes and non-athletes to go to college, often in quality integrated universities. The Black football historian Lane Demas pointed out that athletes are typically viewed as leaders; non-athlete Black students were encouraged to follow them off to quality, previously inaccessible White universities. As stated by Barbara Ward, the great twentieth-century thinker, it is prestige education in the liberal arts and in the professions in unsegregated institutions which has provided the greatest liberation from class and race. According to Ward, "The common denominator of the sense of equality, where it has appeared, has been education."[16] And Black students began using it realize their ambitions. During the 1960s, as opportunities improved, the percentage of Black students graduating from high school increased from 38 percent to 56 percent, and Black college enrollment nearly doubled between 1964 and 1970, with most of the increase occurring at previously White institutions. By the early 1970s, nearly two-thirds of Black students attended predominantly White schools. They were less than 6 percent of the total college population, meaning that the Black college attendance rate was about half the White rate, but that was a huge improvement from ten years earlier.

The economic plight of Black America also improved enormously. A study by Reynolds Farley in 1972 showed that Black America had made significant economic gains relative to White America due to the changes in the 1960s in educational achievement and income level. The 1966 game was just one of many positive factors, so it will never be determined exactly how much of an effect it, or the overall effect of athletic integration actually had. Determining the impact of the game on other segments of Black America is also hard to measure with so many other civil rights activities occurring during that era (demonstrations, riots), which at the time appeared to be more significant, but which were ultimately shown to have less actual positive impact on the Black community. The obvious implications that Black athletes could now go out and play and win did not always carry over into other areas of life, where social and economic considerations predominated, as opposed to the situation in athletics where physical prowess alone could determine the outcome.

Black athletes and Black students heading off to traditionally White schools also opened up a huge new debate within the Black community; should they join White schools and culture, where they would always be a minority, or should they stay in their own communities and schools where they have control and are more at home culturally? Howard Fuller, an expert in Black education and former head of the Milwaukee school system, has come to the conclusion that Black students may achieve at a higher level in mostly Black schools where they are in a majority, have Black teachers and principals as role models, and where the students can more readily be in leadership positions.

As Black schools were closing throughout the South under integration, the number of Black principals and administrators shrank significantly. The loss of historically Black institutions and leadership was, and has been, a significant issue. As Black scholar Alvis Adair stated in 1984, "For over a century, black public schools have provided these opportunities in a supportive and wholesome environment, free of the racial biases of peers, teachers, coaches and principals."[17] Many students who went off to White schools found that some opportunities were actually taken away from them. According to Joy Williamson, "In many instances black students encountered racially hostile campus environments where white students, professors, and administrators, openly challenged both their right to attend college and their intellectual abilities."[18] I attended a mostly Black school, where I was a distinct minority and where Black students clearly had the opportunity to be student leaders—which I did not—and I'm not sure if there's a clear answer either. It is a situation Black America is *still* debating. What the 1966 game did was help create two possible paths for Black America, where before there had essentially only been one.

One of the other long-term effects of the game was that it also established athletics as a primary avenue of success for Black youth. So was the net effect positive or negative? Black athletes clearly led the way for much of Black America back in that era. But their success had the effect of encouraging many Black students to concentrate on athletics to the detriment of other areas. According to Black writer Harry Edwards, one of the effects of the game was to produce a situation where Black students and their families relied on sports as *the* path to self-realization and economic advancement, which has created significant problems for Black society. Many Black families have pushed their children towards sports goals that the overwhelming majority could not achieve; there are only so many spots on collegiate sports teams, and the same is true at the professional level. This emphasis on sports has often been to the detriment of development in other areas; it has led to large numbers of black youth to be culturally and emotionally underdeveloped as they obsessively pursue sports careers. According to Edwards, this lack of development is partially a "consequence of the drain in talent potential toward sports and away from other vital areas of occupational and career emphasis, such as medicine, law, economics, politics, education and technical fields."[19]

William Turner, who was a Black student in Kentucky at the time of the 1966 game, and who later went on to be a college professor, agrees. His feelings about the game have been decidedly mixed. According to Turner, "Far too many young black men have sacrificed lives that may have been much more rewarding potentially if this society had not impressed on them that the avenue of success was paved on the basketball."[20] He believes the beginning of that mindset may have been the Texas Western game. If this is the overall legacy of the 1966 game, then it is indeed a tragic and unforeseen one, one not envisioned at the time, and one which Black America is struggling to deal with to this very day.

All this occurred because Texas Western had played Kentucky. So what would have happened if it had been Duke that played the game? How would people have responded to a game like that? As we have shown earlier, the game against Duke would have been closer, rougher, and may well have been decided by close calls by an all-White officiating crew, as the Duke team was bigger and matched up better with Texas Western. In the actual game, David Lattin gets the opening tipoff, and in the second play of the game, he slams on Pat Riley's head while shouting, "Take that you white honky!"[21] Incredibly, no foul was called on him. When the Kentucky center saw Lattin coming down the lane, he ran out of the paint. After that, Texas Western clearly owned the middle. The dunk became the most famous part of the game. As John Thompson said, "I remember being at the Boys Club to play ball the next day, and what we were talking about was Big Daddy Lattin dunking."[22]

Now, suppose the player on the other side had been six-foot-eight, 235-pound Duke center Mike Lewis, the ACCs leading rebounder and future ABA all-star. Haskins had had trouble getting Lattin to play hard against White centers because he didn't consider them a challenge. But David Lattin would have quickly found out that Mike Lewis was not a typical White center. Mike Lewis's response to Lattin's slam attempt and racist statement would have been something unprintable as he swatted the ball into the third row. And that would have set the tone for the evening. A close, hard-fought game with a lot of fouls called—

maybe even on the very first play. A game with all-White officials. A game that had people of different races cheering for different teams. A game that could hardly have been more divisive.

In the actual 1966 game, most of the close calls went Kentucky's way. The fact that Texas Western won the game convincingly effectively removed most concerns about biased officiating changing the outcome in the original game. The game was a clear-cut victory for Texas Western which was not as close as the final score and was a repudiation of Adolph Rupp with no obvious calls to dispute. In the event of a close Duke-Texas Western game that Duke won, it appears likely that there would have been enough disputed calls to lead a large percentage of Black America to believe that the game had been fixed by White officials.

That being the case, although the game was not significant enough an event to likely have caused riots by itself, as most riots occurred during the hotter summer months, typically due to run ins with the police, it would simply have gone down as one more contributor to an already unstable national racial situation. And when we examine riots in that era, it was, in fact, an *accumulation* of offenses—some of national origin, such as affronts to Dr. Martin Luther King Jr., which caused many of them (which the 1966 game would simply have added to). It would have been remembered the following summers in the more than one hundred cities that saw race riots in 1967 and 1968, as a large fraction of Northern urban youths played basketball, along with all the other racial provocations of that era.

In the time immediately after the game, it would have been in the papers and on the news, and with their usual penchant for exaggeration and inaccuracy, it is possible they would have distorted the racial aspects of the game. If the game were close and decided by disputed calls, it would have likely generated racial controversy. *Sports Illustrated* wrote a particularly inaccurate piece on the Texas Western team a while after the game, that claimed, among other false things, that the team exploited Black players, that they weren't real students, that the player's wives couldn't get jobs (they weren't even married!), and that the town was unfriendly to minorities. Across the country, similar things were being written about the Texas Western team; they were pariahs and villains for winning.

So, in the case of a close Duke game, it is likely that similar troublemaking nonsense would have been written about that game too. If Texas Western had won, there probably still would have been biased racist coverage of it, defaming the players and team. They did not get the same media treatment as a White championship team would have. "One thing I still feel a little bad about," said Nevil Shed, "was that we never got asked to be on the Ed Sullivan Show."[23] All the previous White champions had been invited on the show. (Sullivan's "Rilly big shew," which my family watched on Sunday nights, was considered the premier variety show at the time). If Duke had won, the media would likely have lauded them as winners, and they would have been invited on the show—giving Black America little to cheer about. The clearly racially biased media of the time might even have tried to cast Duke as racial heroes and Texas Western as racial villains if Duke had won, further inflaming Black resentment about the outcome of the game.

Over time, as the game became a legend, the racial troublemaking aspect would not have gone away. People would have argued endlessly about the game and the officiating in bars, at work, and in their neighborhoods Both teams might have gotten threats or hate mail. Haskins' players received death threats before games, so it is likely that Texas Western would have received the same treatment if they had managed to beat Duke. Haskins received nearly forty thousand pieces of hate mail for winning. "White people were saying I used them to win games. Black people said I had exploited the players. If I could have changed things, I would hope we'd come in second place."[24] According to Nelson George, winning put the players in the national spotlight, revealing that many of them were failing academically. "The question of the intellectual cost of athletic integration was being raised. Yes, a basketball scholarship got these brothers into college. But what good did it do them if they made no progress to a degree?"[25] Eventually, ten of the twelve players on the team would graduate. But immediately after the game the program received an incredible amount of negative publicity that it wouldn't have otherwise.

So unlike the real 1966 game, if Duke had played, it clearly would have been close, and would likely have caused even greater troublemaking. However, there would have been two other significant differences. First, the magnitude of Texas Western's victory was increased by Rupp's stature as a known racist coach and Kentucky status as the top national program. At the time of the game, Rupp was not only considered the top coach in the country, he was even considered the greatest college basketball coach of all time, and Kentucky was considered the greatest program in history. His teams had never lost a championship game prior to that in four separate games. When Texas Western upset Rupp, it was not only considered a huge racial victory but also a huge basketball victory against a proven champion.

It wasn't just that Kentucky was nationally and historically a better program than Duke; they carried a much greater weight in the South as well. Duke was the ACC champion and had won their conference championship several times in the previous ten years. The ACC was also a Southern and mid-Atlantic conference with a racist past. The Southern end of the ACC was as racist as any of the SEC schools: South Carolina did not suit up their first Black player until 1969, the same year as Kentucky. The very first Black player in the ACC at University of Maryland (the northern end of the ACC) had just started in 1965, and Duke had also just gotten their first Black player. So beating ACC champion Duke would have still meant something from a racial standpoint.

But Rupp and Kentucky had been the SEC champion nearly 75 percent of the time for the previous thirty-five years. Kentucky was the basketball team that all the other Deep South schools followed because Kentucky almost always beat them. A victory over Kentucky was a victory over the standard bearers of the still-segregated conference of Deep South die-hard racists, many of whom before the 1960s refused to allow their programs to even play teams with Black players at all. Not only that, but Kentucky's success in winning the SEC title most of the time had allowed them for to act as a shield for the Deep South schools. Kentucky was the northern end of the SEC and did play against teams with Black players, so by continually winning the SEC or being runner-up, they spared the schools further south from doing so in the NCAA tournament. Given the choice of one program for Texas Western to have beaten to give the victory maximum impact, it would have been Kentucky, no question. As Pat Forde wrote, "The script for this tidy little morality play called for a colossus of a coach, a legend who had hung four NCAA title banners in his gym, a stubborn man who showed little inclination to change with the times."[26] According to Perry Wallace, the first Black player in the SEC, "Coach Rupp is made to symbolize the demon, and the demon was much bigger than he was."[27] Beating Kentucky meant more to Black America in 1966 than beating any other program would have.

Howard Fuller, the 1960s Durham civil rights leader who was at the Kentucky-Texas Western game in Fayetteville, NC, agrees with that assessment. He likened the impact of the game to the Joe Louis fight or to Jackie Robinson playing in the major leagues. In particular, he cited Bobby Joe Hill's repeated theft of the ball from Louis Dampier as the most significant event of the game. Fuller believes that it was Rupp and his known racism, as well as the stature of the Kentucky program at the time, that made the difference; a victory over Duke and Coach Bubas, who had never won a national championship, would not have carried the same weight. Larry Conley said, "I wonder if the focus on an all-White team would have been as strong if we'd lost to Duke which was also all White."[28]

In addition, Duke coach Vic Bubas was clearly making a good faith effort to recruit Black players and already had one on his freshman team at the time of the game. According to Charles Martin, the author of *Benching Jim Crow*, the fact that Duke had already recruited Cassius Claiborne would significantly have lessened the impact of a Texas Western victory over Duke, as it showed that Duke was already moving in the right direction. Rupp's performance afterwards, when he didn't shake hands with the Texas Western players (although he did shake hands with Don Haskins) and refused to accept the reality of Kentucky's loss, made it relatively easy for the media to cast him as a racist villain. Rupp's post-game behavior caused them to play up the racial angle considerably more than they had before the game.

Rupp had always been known to be irascible, and at the time of the 1966 game, Rupp was becoming a cranky old man who hated to lose and made no bones about it. He was also dealing with a number of significant health issues, which made him irritable when dealing with the media. According to 1966 Kentucky assistant Joe B. Hall, Rupp was singled out in a conference that had no African Americans on the roster. "Coach Rupp was the one who got blistered for it, no doubt because of his mouthy, egotistical, arrogant manner, plus his astonishingly long string of successes made him fodder for the media and an easy target."[29] And he didn't make it easier for them to forget it years later, when his own obsession with the game and unwillingness to stop discussing it publicly kept the matter alive well after someone else might have let it go. Unlike Duke, which had lost four national championship games before finally winning one, Rupp could not get over losing one after winning four.

According to Kentucky writer Earl Cox, "If lily white Duke had beaten UK in the semifinals and gone on to play Texas Western would its coach Vic Bubas have been considered a racist?"[30] Vic Bubas, a younger, even-tempered man who, despite being an intense competitor, knew how to handle losing gracefully, would have been very difficult for the media to cast as a poor loser and a racist. Billy Reed, the veteran Kentucky writer, wrote that if Duke had played Texas Western in the last game of the 1966 Final Four, "revisionist historians never would have blown the game into an epic racial struggle, mainly because Duke coach Vic Bubas wasn't nearly as easy to stereotype and caricature as Rupp."[31] Bubas was only thirty-nine years old in 1966, had grown up in Gary, Indiana, and had played with and against Black players for years. Bubas was actually eager to integrate the Duke program and upgrade Duke's roster, as he saw how quality Black players could help his team in the very competitive ACC. Consequently, the emotional intensity and ensuing motivation occurring from Texas Western defeating a clear-cut villain would not likely have occurred for Black America either if Duke had played the game. There would have been, at best, lukewarm satisfaction at defeating a very good, but not yet all-time great, program that was already trying hard to move in the right direction.

So how would the game have been remembered years later? If it had been close and all-White against all-Black, it clearly would have been a legend that was not forgotten. To see what the long-term effects of the game on the rest of the country likely would have been, we can examine the 1972 USA-USSR Olympic basketball game as a reasonable standard of comparison. Don Haskins was actually an assistant on that team, coached by none other than his own personal mentor as a player, Hank Iba. That game—in which the ending of the game was replayed three times—at the end of which the Russians finally scored a game winning basket to beat America, has gone down in infamy. At the time it happened, in the cold war era, it was the subject of incredible anger for the US squad. To this day, the US team, led by Doug Collins, has refused to accept that they lost the game, and has never claimed their silver medals; they still believe that the officials acted improperly in giving the Russians extra chances to win the game. The emotional impact of the loss has persisted for decades. In 2004, watching the US Olympic team settle for a bronze medal, Collins, as an NBC television commentator, famously stated, "The worst part about it [the 1972 loss] was not hearing the national anthem be played."[32]

I have read a detailed account of what happened in that game. It appears that the officials may not have acted improperly on at least the original ending of the game. But the point is that the controversy surrounding the game never went away. Decades afterwards, the game was still a source of international troublemaking and resentment. And so, as the Duke-Texas Western game became a legend, it's potential for racial troublemaking might have persisted for years or even decades after the game, especially if it were close and there were questions about the officiating, as there were for the USA-USSR game. Much in the same manner that the original game became a watershed for Black America, the Duke-Texas Western game would never have been forgotten for racial troublemaking either.

The butterfly effect of Bob Verga's illness prevented a game from being played where the troublemaking potential and lack of either a clear-cut victor or moral predicament would likely have offered little positive motivation to Black athletes or Black America. America was spared seeing a game that have would have polarized the country and left one side bitterly disappointed. Without Bob Verga's chance illness, a game that occurred at a crucial moment in history, which inspired an entire generation of Black youth to go off to college, would very likely never have happened.

CHAPTER 11

THE REMATCH: DUKE-KENTUCKY 1992

When the Duke and Kentucky programs met in the Final Four in 1966, it was a good game, but not one that is considered to be very notable. Without Bob Verga, Kentucky clearly had the better team, and managed to pull ahead and win the game. The game itself has only become famous in the context of deciding which team would play Texas Western. However, until the writing of this book, the actual historical significance of the game has never quite been fully recognized outside the Duke community, where it has been a legend for more than fifty years.

Years later, the programs had a couple of memorable NCAA tournament run-ins. In particular, they played for the national championship in 1978, with Duke's Gene Banks (who revolutionized Duke basketball recruiting in chapter eight) playing against 1966 Kentucky coaching assistant Joe B. Hall in a fairly good game. In this game Kentucky clearly had the better team, comprised mostly of seniors, (including Jack Givens discussed in chapter eight) and won by a score of 94-88. They also met in 1980 (also with Banks and Hall) when Duke defeated Kentucky in the NCAAs in Lexington in a fairly close game.

However, none of the games after the 1966 game has had remotely the level of fame as the game played in the NCAA Eastern Regional Final in 1992, a game that has come to be considered possibly the greatest college basketball game of all time. That significance may be magnified even more by this book as it is placed in historical context with the 1966 game. The 1992 game, ending with Christian Laettner's incredible shot off Grant Hill's length of the court throw—so famous that it has actually been dubbed "The Shot"—which has been replayed countless times on TV, has gone down in many accounts as the greatest NCAA game ever played. The ending of the 1992 game is actually probably the most famous play in the history of college basketball.

In the 1992 game, Duke and Kentucky did not meet in the Final Four; they met in the Eastern Regional finals. The winner would go to the Final Four. The loser would go home. In and of itself, the game isn't completely relevant to the central topic of the 1966 game. However, it is worth discussing here because the game itself is a legend, and also because it makes for a good historical comparison to the 1966 game to see what happens if Duke plays Kentucky to go to the NCAA championship and Duke's second leading scorer doesn't get sick; it gives us a very useful reference as to what would have been the impact in Kentucky (and Duke) if Duke had had Bob Verga and had won the 1966 game, where we will see that the difference in both locations would have been truly remarkable. In 1992, the game turns out differently, as history appeared to have been on Duke's side that time around, as twenty-six years later, instead of tobacco and racism, Duke actually represented medicine and progress.

Speaking as an ardent lifetime Duke basketball fan and a long time ACC basketball observer, I am actually not quite convinced that this was the greatest college basketball game ever played. The 1974 NC State-Maryland ACC championship game, played on March 9, 1974, is the other one that is usually mentioned. That game, while also not completely relevant to the central theme of this book, was so remarkable that it is worthy of discussion here in and of itself. That game, which occurred nearly fifty years ago at the time of this book's writing, is one with which younger college basketball fans are not likely familiar. Since it did not have any endlessly-replayed signature plays like Laettner's shot, and was not seen on national television, it is in danger of being forgotten by history. By introducing it to a new generation of readers, it is my hope that the game's well-deserved legacy for excellence will be preserved. It will also help to give some actual comparison of games to determine whether the 1992 Duke-Kentucky game really was the greatest, and to give some better historical context to the 1992 game as Duke in 1992 was trying to become the first team to repeat as champions since NC State made history and broke the UCLA dynasty after the Maryland game in 1974.

There were four good NBA players on the 1974 Maryland team: Mo Howard and All-Americans Tom McMillen, Len Elmore, and John Lucas, a future number-one NBA draft pick in 1976. McMillen had been on the cover of *Sports Illustrated* as the best high school player in America in 1970. Lucas grew up in Durham, the son of my high school principal who used to announce Lucas's statistics on the school P.A. after Maryland games, and who, like every Black resident in Durham, had been cheering for Texas Western in 1966. He is widely considered to be the best player ever to grow up in Durham. There were three NBA players on the NC State team. They included the legendary six-foot-three David Thompson, the 1974 and '75 NPOY, who soared high above much taller defenders for alley-oops and jump shots; five-seven Monte Towe, who zipped up and down the floor as point guard; and human beanpole seven-three Tommy Burleson somehow running the floor and shooting well-coordinated hook shots (Towe and Burleson were the shortest and tallest players in the NCAA that year, respectively).

Thompson still holds the NC State scoring average record of more than twenty-six points per game, scoring over twenty-three hundred points in only three years. Had he played with freshman eligibility (freshmen were not allowed to play on the varsity until 1972), he may have scored more than three thousand points during his NC State career and become the all-time ACC scoring champion. His legacy outside the ACC has largely been lost, as drug and alcohol issues shortened and dampened his NBA career. Thompson once scored seventy-three points in an NBA game in an end of the season scoring contest with George "The Iceman" Gervin for the 1978 NBA scoring title. "Ice," hearing of Thompson's feat, promptly poured in sixty-three of his own to claim the title. Due to both his amazing highlight-reel athletic plays at NC State and incredible championship-winning performances in both the Maryland and UCLA games in 1974, Thompson remains a legend in the state of North Carolina. Many observers, including myself, believe that Thompson still stands as the greatest in-college basketball player in ACC history, over such players as Christian Laettner, Tim Duncan, Ralph Sampson, and Michael Jordan. His NC State career was the inspiration for Wilmington-born Jordan.

The 1974 NC State team won the national championship by defeating the great Bill Walton-led, John Wooden-coached UCLA in double overtime in the semifinals. UCLA had won every NCAA championship since Texas Western beat Kentucky in 1966, who in 1974 were actually finally on the verge of returning to prominence the following year with quality Black players under Joe B. Hall, beating number-one ranked Indiana in an all-time great NCAA tournament upset. Thompson put forth a truly remarkable effort in the 1974 UCLA game, scoring effectively over six-eleven UCLA Hall of Famer Walton (the picture of him on the cover of *Sports Illustrated* shooting well above Walton, who was eight inches taller, is truly amazing). Walton had scored forty-four points on twenty-one for twenty-two shooting (none of them dunks) in the title game against Memphis State the year before. Maryland's loss to NC State that year also meant that the 1974 college basketball journey of Grateful Dead devotee Walton, often seen by the author at their concerts, would not end at (Maryland) "Terrapin Station" either.

The '74 NC State-Maryland game also had an incredible emotional and physical intensity level because back in that era only the ACC tournament champion played in the NCAAs. For NC State, this was the only time during the Thompson-Burleson era that the two were eligible to play in the NCAAs together; NC State had been undefeated the year before, but ineligible to play in the NCAAs due to recruiting violations around Thompson. For Maryland, it was the last time All-American Lucas would play with seniors McMillen and Elmore. The trio had failed in five previous attempts at beating NC State with Thompson and Burleson, losing by a total of twenty-seven points; this was their last try, with everything on the line.

This meant that for both teams the game was all or nothing that year; either the number-three or number-one ranked team in the country would not be in the NCAA tournament, with no chance of playing together again the next year, depending on who won the game, so the loser was faced with the prospect of going home for all time with nothing. This was just as number-two ranked Duke would have done in 1966, had Mike Lewis missed his free throws at the end of the 21–20 ACC tournament semifinal against North Carolina. In fact, 1974 was the last year that happened; the NC State-Maryland game forced the NCAA to allow more than one team to play in the NCAAs from each conference, which they did the next year along with raising the number of tournament teams from twenty-five to thirty-two. Maryland, who lost the game, declined an invitation to the National Invitation Tournament, thinking that they might lose on an emotional letdown and thereby end their season on a negative note after the incredible NC State game.

The 1974 NC State-Maryland game was simply a wonder to behold. It was a virtual forty-five-minute highlight reel, one play after another being flawlessly executed between two very good defensive teams; Maryland scored effectively inside despite playing against seven-three Burleson. The game, which NC State won 103–100 in overtime in an era without either a shot clock or the three-point shot, was famously played at an incredibly high level from start to finish. Four Maryland starters played the entire forty-five minutes. The game flowed up and down the court at a high pace, in a timeless display of beautifully run basketball plays.

The 1974 game featured great team play as well as truly remarkable individual performances. Thompson leapt above defenders six and seven inches taller than him for high arcing jump shots. Towe almost singlehandedly defeated Maryland's defensive pressure with amazing displays of behind-the-back full court ball handling. There were perfectly timed alley-oop passes from Towe to Thompson, (together they had invented the play by accident at an NC State practice a few years before), who soared above the rim like an orbiting satellite, gracefully dropping the ball in the basket because he was forbidden to dunk. Six-three John Lucas ran Maryland's fast break with pinpoint passes to Mo Howard, streaking in for layups. Burleson vengefully scored against Len Elmore (and six-eleven Tom McMillen) with sweeping jump hooks (and also throwing a bounce pass between McMillen's legs) after being passed over for ACC first team in favor of Elmore. Elmore and McMillen valiantly battled the giant Burleson (and also bruising Tim Stoddard, a future major league pitcher), nearly five inches taller than either of them, for rebounds, as they triggered the Maryland fast break with strong outlet passes and responded to Burleson's thirty-eight points with forty of their own in Maryland's more balanced attack. Lucas and the entire Maryland team sprayed the ball around the floor for one quality shot after another, as Maryland's All-Americans poured in basket after basket with hot shooting from all over the court (they hit ten of their first twelve shots), desperately trying to keep pace with NC State's incredible Towe-Thompson-Burleson highwire act. Maryland shot over 60 percent for the game from the field, scoring one hundred points, and *still* lost. During the game, according to John Feinstein, legendary official Hank Nichols, realizing he was seeing history, turned and said about a certain call to another official, "Not in *this* game!"[1] At the end of the game, the entire stadium, who realized they had witnessed a truly incredible performance, gave both teams a standing ovation.

A number of people who saw both games still thought the 1992 Duke-Kentucky game was better (it should be noted that the comparison was made immediately after the game, as it was clear no other game besides NC State-Maryland '74 was worthy of comparison). Having seen both 1974 and 1992 games, I agree with 1974 Maryland center Len Elmore—who played in the first and did the television commentary for the second—that the '74 game was a better game overall from start to finish (usually only the last third of the Duke-Kentucky game is considered great). However, the game was not seen by most people in the country because it was only regionally televised in the mid-Atlantic ACC region (the Carolinas, Virginia, Maryland). Unlike the 1992 Duke-Kentucky game, whose ending has been replayed many times nationally since 1992, the legacy of the NC State-Maryland 1974 game, which did not produce an iconic, game-winning shot, has largely been lost outside the original ACC region, where it remains a legend.

In addition, the greater prior and subsequent national success of the two programs in the 1992 game—NC State and Maryland have won only three NCAA championships between them versus thirteen for Duke and Kentucky—gave the 1992 game more lasting historical significance, as the two programs have been among the best in the country for most of the nearly thirty years since that game. That is especially true when considered against the historical backdrop of the 1966 Final Four, Kentucky's 1989-1991 probation (which made the Kentucky team of mostly in-state seniors truly special in the hearts of Kentucky fans), and the 1992 Duke team (widely considered to be the best Duke team of all time) trying to make history by being the first repeat NCAA champion in nearly twenty years.

The ending of the 1974 game was also somewhat anticlimactic. Maryland point guard John Lucas, tiring from playing all forty-five minutes of a fast-paced game, threw a bad pass over wide-open Len Elmore's head to end the game, thereby depriving Elmore of the chance to make his own iconic game winning shot, in stark contrast to Christian Laettner's incredible shot that ended the 1992 game. Lucas had dreams (or nightmares) about the last play of the game decades after it happened. According to Lucas, "There's Lenny Elmore. He's open! I'm so tired. . . . And I throw it over his head."[2] Elmore actually didn't think the Duke-Kentucky game was better overall, but the ending in overtime was more dramatic—the ending building with shot after shot, each one bigger than the last, finally ending with Laettner's all-time game winner. So, in the end, he concluded that the Duke-Kentucky game was more significant. According to Elmore, "I think ours was better for the intensity and the level of talent. But ours didn't end with the drama this one did."[3] Elmore's analysis appears to be correct; it is essentially the *last fifteen seconds* or so of the 1992 game in overtime that made the difference. Without Sean Woods' incredible one-handed apparent game winner and Laettner's even more incredible response, the game would almost certainly not be considered the greatest. Had Grant Hill's pass sailed over Laettner's head the same way that Lucas's pass for Elmore did in 1974, State-Maryland '74 almost certainly would have retained its title as the greatest game ever played.

So the 1992 Duke-Kentucky game—which was nationally televised between two of the all-time great programs and had the more dramatic, endlessly-replayed ending—clearly had the greater impact and has gone down as the game most often described as the greatest game ever played. This is even despite the fact that the NC State-Maryland game may have had greater historical significance, in view of NC State's subsequent dynasty-ending defeat of UCLA, who had won the previous seven national championships. In all objective fairness to the 1974 NC State and

Maryland players, I would describe the 1992 game as the greatest in terms of most emotionally intense or having the greatest impact, while reserving "best" strictly in the basketball sense for NC State-Maryland 1974.

From the point of view of the Duke faithful, remarkably enough, the two games also framed the worst ('74) and best ('92) points in the history of Duke basketball. The '74 NC State-Maryland game occurred at the all-time nadir of the Duke basketball program, just a week after the incredible eight points in seventeen seconds loss to North Carolina, and Duke had also just finished last in the ACC under one-year coach Neil McGeachy with a 10-16 record—the worst Duke record of all time. The NC State-Maryland game was especially painful for Duke fans to watch at the time, as it served as a jarring reminder of how far the Duke program had fallen in the eight years since the 1966 NCAA semifinal game (although it should be remembered that Duke had somehow beaten number-three ranked Maryland with McMillen and Elmore the year before, on an incredible thirty-nine point performance by Duke guard Gary Melchionni, '66 coach Bubas's last recruit at Duke). The '92 Duke-Kentucky game, by contrast, came the week before Duke became the first team in twenty years to make history by repeating as NCAA Champions. When we Duke faithful compared the two games, we were always reminded not only of how great Duke basketball was in 1992, but also how bad the program was in 1974.

The 1992 game is also historically noteworthy in that almost all of the players were four-year college players. The 1992 NBA draft class members, an especially good one with two future NBA Hall of Famers and a number of future NBA All-Stars, were mostly seniors. Even the great Shaquille O' Neal stayed through his junior year before going pro. This was near the end of "college player teams," with legitimate *college students* who actually stayed, completed their classes, and graduated: all of the Duke players on the 1992 team stayed four years, and all of the Kentucky players did except for Mashburn, who left after three. According to Grant Hill about the 1992 game, "I also feel like it was symbolic of an era that is no more. What I mean by that is, that was right before the mass exodus began, with guys leaving early."[4] The departure of most of the Fab Five from Michigan the next year as sophomores, the team Duke and Carolina both ultimately played for the championships in 1992 and 1993, marked the beginning of that change. The 1992 game occurred at the end of the era of college basketball, which is why it may never be replicated; in today's era of one-and-done NBA players at Duke, Kentucky, and elsewhere, the concept of players as actual college students now seems almost unrecognizable. Both the 2012 Kentucky and 2015 Duke NCAA championship teams started mostly freshmen who then went to the NBA, as both teams mostly have ever since—an ironic change from 1966 when freshmen couldn't even play. Given the players who were on the floor that night in 1992, who they represented, the history of the two programs, and the incredible way the game ended, it seems possible that the game may stand for all time as the last great *college* basketball game, with actual four-year graduating college student players.

So how did it go down in history that way? At the outset, it didn't look like it would. Unlike the NC State-Maryland game, where NC State was nationally ranked number one and Maryland number three, the two teams didn't appear to be that evenly matched. Duke came into the game as the defending national champions, having beaten the defending champions University of Nevada, Las Vegas (UNLV), the year before in a major upset (my brother and I exchanged primal screams on the telephone after Duke's victory), and had gone wire to wire as number one, even though they had lost two games—one to Wake Forest and one to North Carolina. They had on their team one present and one future NPOY (Christian Laettner and Grant Hill), both of whom were also future NBA All-Stars, and another eventual first team All-American Bobby Hurley, who also set the all-time NCAA assist record. They also had three other eventual NBA players on the team. Duke was coached by the legendary Mike Krzyzewski, who would later go on to set the record for most career wins by a college coach. The 1992 Duke team is generally considered to be the greatest Duke team of all time and one of the all-time great college basketball teams.

Not only was it a great team, but the players on the team also knew it. Everyone in *America* knew they were a great team. There was no let down with Duke after winning the championship the year before in 1991. The 1991 championship, Duke's first ever, was remarkable in and of itself. In the semifinals, Duke had upset the number-one ranked and undefeated UNLV team 79-77 in another truly amazing game. Duke came from behind by five points in the last three minutes on an incredibly clutch three-pointer by Bobby Hurley with about two minutes to go—often labeled by Duke faithful (myself including) as the most important shot in the history of Duke basketball—and won the game on two Christian Laettner free throws. I had the privilege of being present for the final game against Kansas, where I got to see Grant Hill throw down a jaw-dropping one-handed alley-oop dunk off a half court Bobby Hurley lob, which still stands as the greatest Duke dunk of all time; the camera angle on the video replay doesn't do it justice, although the 1991 *Sports Illustrated* article photograph does, as Hill was nearly twelve feet in the air when he caught it, and he slammed it falling away from the basket.

The Duke team in 1992 had no intention of resting on their accomplishment from the year before; they came ready to play every game. They knew that their quest to repeat as national champions, which no team had done since UCLA in 1973, would indeed put them on the list of all-time great teams. Once the players on the team realized that greatness was within their capabilities, they redoubled their efforts from the previous season. Led by their senior Christian Laettner, the team played even harder than the year before. Practices were more grueling.

The team competition was even harder. They played with an intensity almost unmatched by other previous champions.

And everyone in the country knew who they were too. Duke had a huge national following that year. They were articulate, photogenic (especially center Laettner), and likable. Women loved them: They sent them roses and baked them cookies. They sent them love letters and sometimes serenaded them at their off-campus housing. Bobby Hurley, the point guard, in particular, received piles of fan mail. It is hard to find any college basketball team in the past forty years that inspired the level of national emotion (both positive and negative) that that team did. As Duke player Brian Davis said, "If there was a Fab Five, it was us. We had the biggest following in college basketball history."[5] According to Grant Hill, "We were on regular television so much in our years at Duke, it was like we were regular programming."[6] Duke was in the NCAA finals three out of four years both Hill and Laettner were at Duke, spanning an era of six seasons. When I personally saw them get off their team bus at their hotel in Minneapolis after winning the national championship in 1992, they came out like rock stars into a huge adoring mob, with camera flashbulbs going continuously.

At the time of the Kentucky game in the regional finals, Duke had been playing well. They had had some injury problems earlier in the season; Bobby Hurley had broken his foot in February, but it was finally healing, and Grant Hill was picking up the pace at point guard in his place. The team was finally healthy, playing well down the stretch. Their last loss had been several weeks before, and they had beaten Seton Hall (with Hurley's brother Danny) in the Sweet 16 game before the Kentucky game with some, but not great, difficulty.

The Kentucky team, on the other hand, was clearly an underdog in the game. They had only one future (good, but not great) NBA player in six-nine sophomore Jamal Mashburn, also a future All-American. The rest of the main players consisted of a couple of decent, though not great, college guards in Sean Woods (who had actually excelled later in his Kentucky career after he realized he was *not* a great shooter) and Richie Farmer, and some average six-seven college forwards in John Pelphrey and Daren Feldhaus, with a respectable bench forward in six-eight Gimel Martinez. They were coached by Rick Pitino, who would coach Kentucky to his own national championship a few years later. Before the Duke game, they ranked sixth in the final regular season AP poll.

That particular Kentucky team was actually quite different than most recent Kentucky teams, before or since, for two other reasons: the starters were almost all seniors and most were actually from the state of Kentucky. They were in many ways a throwback to the Rupp era (and yes, three out of the five starters were White). Unlike in the Rupp era when most players came from in state, the fact that they were mostly local was truly unusual. Three of the four of them were from Kentucky proper, and the fourth, Sean Woods, was from nearby Indianapolis. They were all local high school heroes (Farmer had been named Kentucky high school player of the decade) who represented the state school as actual Kentucky residents. They were the incarnation of Adolph Rupp's statement "When a Kentucky boy is born, his mom wants him to be president, like another Kentuckian Abraham Lincoln. If not president, then to play basketball for the University of Kentucky."[7] The cover of Richie Farmer's book *Richie* features him waving to tens of thousands of fans in Rupp Arena—the personification of every Kentucky boy's fantasy, just like in Rupp's quote.

There was a reason that this team had such an unusual composition. Kentucky had been put on probation by the NCAA in 1989 for some significant recruiting violations and had to forfeit two years of NCAA eligibility in 1990 and 1991. The violations which occurred under coach Eddie Sutton, had been quite serious. Some had involved illegal payments. Others had involved fake transcripts. There were eighteen in all. The program was clearly in trouble. In addition to the loss of NCAA eligibility, the program was taken off TV for a year, and also had scholarships reduced. It was among the most severe penalties ever handed down for any program, just short of completely closing the program for two years.

It was made even worse by an extensive *Sports Illustrated* article "Kentucky Shame," which described the program's infractions. The article, written by Curry Kirkpatrick (a UNC journalism school graduate, whose name I had the privilege of chanting in 1991 when he walked in front of the Blue Devil faithful in Indianapolis after Duke won their first national championship), said, "Proud elegant Kentucky stood threadbare, stripped of its medals and conceits, dispossessed of image and reputation, exposed as a common NCAA felon."[8]

Once the extent of the sanctions became clear, many players on the Kentucky team started leaving. The Kentucky record dropped to 13-19 in 1988-89, the first losing record in more than sixty years, since before Adolph Rupp had come to Kentucky in 1930. Some Kentucky players such as Chris Mills and Leron Ellis transferred, but others, especially local players from Kentucky such as Richie Farmer, elected to stick out the probation in hopes of doing something for Kentucky in the NCAAs their senior year. The probation triggered the departure of players only interested in playing in the NBA. Kentucky would be off television for a year and out of the NCAA tournament for two years, which reduced their NBA draft exposure. So the Kentucky program in 1992 featured, for probably the last time ever, bona-fide four-year college students. They used their scholarships to attend class and graduate, knowing that their education and subsequent non-NBA careers really did matter, much as they did for most of the players on Rupp's teams. The probation, and the fact that they were mostly local players and seniors, gave this team a very special relationship with the people of Kentucky, one on the same level as Rupp's Runts from 1966.

So, this was the Kentucky players last and only chance to play in the NCAAs. The probation had forged a very tight bond between seniors Farmer, Woods, Pelphrey, and Feldhaus, who had played together for almost four years, and had stuck it out together while the team was banned from the NCAA tournament. They were not good enough to play in the NBA, knew it (none were drafted by the NBA, and they had not been heavily recruited to transfer to other colleges during the probation either), and focused their efforts entirely on playing as a team and playing winning college basketball. As a result, they played together with a level of teamwork and intensity almost never seen on college basketball teams. However, their overall talent level was still only a little better than mediocre.

After Sutton left in disgrace in 1989, Kentucky hired Rick Pitino. Pitino worked hard to recruit quality players, but found the going tough, especially with Black players because of the NCAA sanctions and Rupp's legacy. In 1992, Coach Pitino became aware of the program's enduring negative reputation with Black players while recruiting Louisville high school players; there was still a passionate dislike for Kentucky basketball, which could be traced to Adolph Rupp and by extension, the 1966 Texas Western game. According to Pitino, "Certain things you can't change because they don't want to change."[9]

Pitino worked with the players that he had who were willing to stick it out through the probation, and the few quality recruits he was able to get, such as Jamal Mashburn. Pitino liked to run and press, a style that had worked well for Kentucky under Adolph Rupp. He also had brutal workouts in the Rupp tradition. Pitino believed that even though Kentucky had an obvious talent deficiency from the player departures, they could still win with superior conditioning, as Rupp's Runts had in '66. The workouts, the player chemistry, and Pitino's emphasis on running and his use of full-court pressure eventually paid off. The team achieved far beyond their talent level in 1992, just as the '66 team had done. At the time of the Duke game, they were playing at their peak: Their signature up-tempo game was going effectively, just like they played in 1966 under Rupp. They had, at one point, won thirteen of fourteen games down the stretch. They had dispatched Massachusetts in their Sweet 16 game without too much trouble. So they were clearly peaking at the right time.

Those were the two teams to play the 1992 game: both extraordinary, but for different reasons. However, they clearly had a significant talent differential. So when Duke and Kentucky lined up for the opening tip-off on that fateful day of March 28, 1992, it did not appear that this game would be anything out of the ordinary. Most observers expected Kentucky to put up a good effort, but they didn't appear to have the talent to play at Duke's level the whole game. I expected Duke to win by maybe ten or fifteen points, as did probably most other people. The point spread was about seven points, which was actually probably generous to Kentucky.

But Kentucky coach Rick Pitino had a plan. He thought he could win the game. He knew that Duke was going to underestimate the Kentucky team—it was only natural, as Duke was clearly more talented, and ranked number one. Pitino thought that they would not likely play as hard as Kentucky (at least at the beginning) and wouldn't have a sharp mental focus. In addition, he knew that Kentucky had decent depth and great conditioning, which Duke had too—their practices were almost as intense as Kentucky's, and their bench had quality players on it, many of whom would start on another Final Four team two years later to play Arkansas coached by Don Haskins player Nolan Richardson. He decided to save his team's full court press for the second half, when Duke was starting to wear down. He thought Duke might crack and fold under the pressure, and not having played that many close games, they might not be able to pull it out down the stretch, in the same manner that 1991 champion UNLV had folded at the end of a close game with Duke.

The Bob Verga Shift

To his credit, Pitino alone was probably the only person who understood the possibility of the game before it happened. Knowing who Duke was, and knowing of the incredible intensity, teamwork, and mental toughness of his Kentucky team, he believed his team truly had a chance. According to Deron Feldhaus, "Believe me, Coach Pitino had us believing we could win the whole thing. We were pretty big underdogs, but we didn't see ourselves that way."[10] In search of inspiration before the game, Pitino and a friend jogged up the seventy-two steps of the Philadelphia Museum of Art to the Rocky statue—the statue of underdogs. When they raised their arms up in triumph, the people around them looked at them like they were crazy.

It turns out Pitino was pretty sane. The game played out pretty close to the way he thought it could. In the first two-thirds of the game, Duke's talent differential appeared to be decisive. The level of play during this part was high, but not anything that appeared out of the ordinary. This was how most observers expected it. During the first half, Kentucky started out strong, but Duke quickly realized that they had underestimated them and rallied. After making adjustments, Duke had a five-point halftime lead.

However, Pitino liked the game at that point. He thought Kentucky was close enough to catch Duke down the stretch. But as the second half started, Duke played better than in most of the first half. They went on to build a twelve-point lead with about eleven minutes to play and were leading 67–55 in what appeared to be the way the game was supposed to play out. It looked like Duke was going to win a good, but not particularly notable game; the overall quality of play had been high, but unlike the NC State-Maryland game in 1974, not particularly outstanding. Some sportscasters, concluding that Duke was going to win as expected, were already starting to write their final story about how Duke had won the game.

However, in the second part of the game, history began. Pitino called time out. He was ready to go with his full court pressure.

That was when the 1992 Duke-Kentucky game that has gone down in history actually started. The Kentucky players, sensing that their season and their Kentucky careers were coming to an end, decided to put everything they had left on the floor and stage a last-chance comeback. From that point on, the game was played at an incredibly high level of intensity. The Kentucky players began pressuring the ball up the floor, and Duke, starting to tire, began turning the ball over and looking nervous. Kentucky went on an 8-0 run to cut the lead to four with about ten minutes to go. Duke, stunned by the abrupt loss of their lead, rallied again to lead by ten at 7:40, but Kentucky went on a 12-2 run to tie the game with about five minutes to go.

At this point, observers sensed that the game was turning into something special. With around eight minutes to go, Christian Laettner was fouled by Kentucky player Aminu Timberlake, who lay on the floor afterwards. Laettner then contemptuously stepped on his chest while he was lying on the floor of the arena. In a controversial no-call, Laettner was not ejected from the game. Years later, many people think he should have been. Pitino said, "Aminu Timberlake was the reason we should have won the game because Laettner should have been thrown out of the game."[11] John Pelphrey thinks so: "No way you'd get away with that today."[12] But Laettner stayed in the game, earning lasting enmity from many basketball fans.

As the Duke lead dwindled, word got around the country (since there were other sports broadcasts showing the score) that the game was getting close, and people started tuning in from everywhere, sensing a possible classic ending. In North Carolina, the game was on at one of the bars in the Triangle Dinner Theater, in which a play was being held. However, as someone went out to the dining room and announced that the game was going into overtime, the play was halted and the patrons all rushed out to the bar to see the ending; people realized they were seeing something special, something in real life more dramatic than any play. College basketball TV commentator Dick Vitale was dining out for dinner in Sarasota, Florida, at the time. Most of the patrons in the restaurant rushed into the bar, which had quickly become standing room only, to see what was happening, sensing something incredible. Announcer Jim Nantz, who was in Lexington, pushed back his dinner reservation at Bravo Pitino to see the end of the game. I was tense with excitement watching as the teams traded baskets down the stretch and could also sense that the game was becoming something special. What happened next was more dramatic than any play ever put on.

As the game went into overtime, the teams traded shots, each one looking harder than the one before, as suspense grew throughout the country. Finally, with about two seconds to go, six-two Sean Woods of Kentucky threw up a running, thirteen-foot, one-handed bank shot in the lane over six-eleven Laettner that somehow went in (Len Elmore, doing the commentary, exclaimed on television, "That was a terrible shot!"[13]), giving Kentucky a one-point lead, and which appeared to win the game. Coach Mike Krzyzewski called time out to set up the last play. He still believed Duke could win the game; he said to his players, as he drew up the famous final play in the huddle, "We're going to win the game, and this is how we're going to do it."[14] He later said, "Whether you believe it or not, you have to have that expression on your face and those words in your mouth."[15] Grant Hill said, "We were really confident coming out of the timeout. We really felt if we got Christian the ball we would win."[16]

As the players went out onto the floor for the final play, Rick Pitino elected to keep all of his players on the defensive end to try and stop the pass reception. The move was greeted with surprise by coaches watching the game because it is usually typical to put pressure on the player making the inbounds play. Grant Hill had actually failed to make a similar play in February when he was guarded along the baseline. Grant Hill, who was also astonished by the move, had a clear path on the far end of the court to throw in the ball. According to Hill, whose father, Calvin, had been a famous NFL running back, and who had seen the 1966 Kentucky-Texas Western game at Yale, "I would always trash-talk that I had football in my genes. I knew I could make that pass. We practiced that, not necessarily the play, but that pass every day."[17] But John Pelphrey thought it was the right way to defend it. Refuting people who believed that it had been a mistake to not guard Laettner on the inbounds play, Pitino pointed out that Laettner had not missed a shot the whole game, and Pitino didn't want the ball thrown over their heads for a layup. According to Pitino, "Think about a Hail Mary in football. Nobody goes man-to-man. . . . That's what we did. We went five on four. Grant Hill was not taking us out on that play."[18] In addition, Kentucky's tallest player (and best leaper), six-nine Jamal Mashburn, who might have had a good chance to deflect or intercept the pass had he been between Laettner and Hill, had actually fouled out just before Woods' apparent game winner, and Kentucky's second tallest player, six-eight Gimel Martinez, had fouled out earlier too. So there were no players taller than six-seven guarding Christian Laettner on the final play, giving Pitino's decision to put in more players to contest the pass catch more credence.

Throughout the country, people sat amazed, awaiting the final play. Sitting in Madison, Wisconsin, where I was finishing up some work on nuclear test ban verification, still a Duke fan twenty-six years after the 1966 game, I watched, almost praying, hoping for a miracle. The crowd at Bravo Pitino (whose crowd may not necessarily have cheered Pitino's decision on this occasion) in Lexington held their breath.

The referee handed the ball to Grant Hill. All the Kentucky players were between Christian Laettner and the basket; there was nobody fronting Laettner on the inbounds play to block the pass from Hill. Hill threw the ball the length of the court to Laettner, breaking out to the top of the key. The pass was perfect. Laettner went up and pulled the ball down over two shorter Kentucky players. According to Pelphrey, "The most miraculous part of that play was the throw and the catch, not the shot."[19] The moment Laettner caught the ball, I was convinced the game was over. When Laettner came down with the ball, he dribbled once and faked, as he knew he had a couple of seconds to do something. The Kentucky players fell away to avoid fouling (Deron Feldhaus did try to get a hand up, but it was too late), as Laettner was a deadly free throw shooter, having hit all ten of his free throw attempts in the game (he didn't miss any field goals that game either). Vern Lundquist made the famous final call, as the ball went cleanly through the net: "There's the pass to Laettner . . . puts it up . . . Yessssss!"[20] Grant Hill said, "I felt like I was watching Robert Redford in *The Natural*."[21] Krzyzewski said he thought the shot was good as soon as it left Laettner's hands.

As Laettner turned and ran down the court in his since eternally famous picture of jubilation, the Kentucky players fell on the floor in disbelief. The game was over; Duke had won. The television announcers, knowing that they were seeing something truly incredible, fell silent and stayed that way for nearly seventy-five seconds as the cameras panned the faces of the players, coaches, and fans. Duke player Thomas Hill's expression of total incredulity was particularly famous, covering his head in his hands. According to Hill, "My expression after the game, that's my indication of how great the game was, how big that game was. That was pure emotion. It wasn't scripted."[22] Thomas indeed had no reason to doubt Christian's shot. The shot was so iconic that virtually everyone who saw it can remember where they were or what they were doing at the time.

The *Boston Globe* writer Bob Ryan showed a note after the game to Cawood Ledford, who had broadcast Kentucky games for thirty-nine years, and who had broadcast the original 1966 Duke-Kentucky game. It read, "Best game ever?" Ledford, with his headset still on, nodded yes. Ryan later wrote, "No other college game has ever combined, in one package, this much meaning, this much expertise, and this much drama. Duke-Kentucky was the greatest college game of them all."[23] Everyone there knew they had seen history. One writer said, "I can die happy now because I've seen it all."[24] And a few minutes later, Ledford's final postgame radio broadcast ever in a thirty-nine-year career dating from 1953 (he had called both 1966 Final Four games for Kentucky), concluded with a quote from Adolph Rupp's farewell speech (Rupp was still a Kentucky hero in 1992): "For those of you who have gone down the glory road with me, my eternal thanks."[25]

For the Kentucky players who had stayed during the probation, the ending was indeed painful. Columnist Rick Bozich went into the Kentucky locker room intending to ask the players how they felt about the game, but he immediately changed his mind, seeing how devastated they all were, seeing them all crying by their lockers. "The emotion was so raw, and they were so hurt by losing the game, the end of their careers, not going to the Final Four."[26] In the Duke locker room, Bobby Hurley said, "I asked Pete Gaudet if I were alive or in a dream. He smacked me upside of my head and said, 'You're alive.'"[27]

Laettner's shot has since become infamous in Kentucky. Both players on the end of the game-ending play against Kentucky, Christian Laettner and Grant Hill, finished their careers as NPOYs, and both had their jerseys retired by Duke. There have been other great college games since, most notably the 2008 and 2010 NCAA championships, the latter in which Butler forward Gordon Hayward (playing against Duke) barely missed a forty-five-foot bank shot, which bounced off the front rim at the buzzer. If the shot had gone in, it would likely have eclipsed Laettner's game winner in 1992. But the 1992 game has retained its ranking as the most memorable. The Kentucky players were known locally as The Unforgettables, and no other game, before or since, has been played with that level of emotional intensity and with that kind of an ending with two teams of that level of stature. It has never been duplicated, and after thirty years at the time of this writing, it seems possible it never will.

The 1992 game has gone down in Kentucky history as a legendary loss, of almost equal if not greater significance than the 1966 loss. The outpouring of emotion from the Kentucky faithful after the game was remarkable. According to Pitino, "We went home, and we had fifteen thousand people waiting for us at the arena. . . . As I look back now, I'm not disappointed at all. It was a classic game, and I'm proud to have been a part of it."[28] Because of their willingness to continue playing during the probation period and the special effort the seniors (Woods, Farmer, Pelphrey, and Feldhaus) had put forth for the state of Kentucky in leading the program back from disgrace, the University of Kentucky retired their jerseys as a surprise during the athletic awards ceremony the week after the Duke game in front of a crowd of ten thousand people. UK athletics director C. M. Newton said, "Many players have scored more points. Many have won more individual honors. But no one can match what you've done. You truly put your heart into wearing the Kentucky jersey."[29]

Riche Farmer described it by painting a picture of a little boy crying from the loss, but the next day picking his ball back up and practicing his game "because someday he's going to be a Wildcat and it's going to be different. That next time Kentucky's going to win."[30] In the next NCAA tournament meeting of the two teams in 1998, they actually did win, in another memorable game played with Mr. Scott Padgett, who also remembered the 1992 game and evidently heard what Mr. Farmer said.

When I read what Farmer said about the kid crying, I was struck by that statement. It immediately brought back memories of that fateful meeting in College Park in 1966, which Duke had lost, and which ended with me, at age seven, on the floor crying. I thought back to a short-handed Duke without Bob Verga playing valiantly down to the wire, and ultimately falling short with the words, "Next time, Duke's gonna win!" I thought on the difference between the two eras: what Durham was like in 1966, back when it was a racist tobacco town, and what it was in 1992, when it had become a cornerstone of the Research Triangle and a leading medical research center. And I finally thought some on how things had turned out differently when Duke and Kentucky played the second time around, when it appeared that, this time, history was actually on Duke's side.

The 1992 game has not yet faded in memory, just as the 1966 Kentucky-Texas Western game continues to resonate. In Kentucky lore, Christian Laettner has gone down as the all-time Duke arch villain (would Bob Verga have if he had played in the semifinal and Duke had won?). Nearly thirty years after the game, Laettner is still despised in Kentucky. Kentuckians of all ages remember Laettner's heartbreaking shot. According to Mike Decourcy, that shot is burned so firmly into the psyches of Kentucky fans, it haunts their dreams: Laettner's endlessly replayed display of mouth-wide-open astonishment as he charges towards them in their nightmares. "His moment of ecstasy transformed into 20 years of agony not even two NCAA championships, five Final Fours and regular doses of Anthony Davis have completely erased."[31] So, when we examine how the 1992 Duke-Kentucky game ended, we do indeed have some idea of how events would have occurred if Bob Verga had not been sick: an incredible win—and possibly a national championship for Duke—and an enduring heartbreak for Kentucky.

I was lucky enough to get tickets from some old Duke friends for the 1992 Final Four, where I sat adjacent to the college basketball coaches. In the 1992 Final Four, Duke played a fairly close game with Indiana, in which they trailed in the first half but played better in the second behind some amazing defense, holding Indiana scoreless for an extended period to pull away and win. (During the off day between games, I went to see the movie *White Men Can't Jump* with my White friends from Durham.)

They then went on to beat Michigan for the championship in a game since vacated, as it was eventually shown that the Michigan players were being paid off. Rick Pitino was caught doing that at Louisville in 2017. (Wasn't he the Kentucky coach in 1992?).

At the end of the Michigan game, Duke was awarded the national championship trophy. When they gave it to Duke, I stood quietly, taking the moment in. There it was: the moment that history had denied Duke University in 1966. The greatest Duke basketball team of all time, the first team to repeat as national champions since the seven-year UCLA dynasty ended in 1974, was now standing on the podium receiving the NCAA trophy. A *biracial* team, which represented the City of Medicine, stood proudly before America as national champions.

As millions of Black Americans watched the 1992 Duke men's basketball team standing in front of them on national television, Black Duke players Grant Hill, Tony Lang, Brian Davis, Thomas Hill, Kenny Blakeney, and Ron Burt all happily smiled back at them, holding up their NCAA championship trophy. All of them would go on to graduate from the very university that was built on the backbreaking labor of their ancestors' compatriots, which their parents and grandparents had never been allowed to attend. I stopped on the steps leading away from the stadium and made one last look to see that it had really happened. I smiled, turned, and walked away down the stadium aisle steps, into the rest of my life. I haven't been to a Duke basketball game since.

After receiving their championship trophy, Duke went home to Durham. Folks in Durham were finally able to accept Duke as NCAA national champions in 1992. Both players on either side of Laettner's incredible play finished their careers as National Player of the Year, and both had their jerseys retired. While the local UNC fans and alums were not going to applaud Duke's 1992 victory (actually getting one of their own to cheer for against the same Michigan team the next year), everyone else was able to accept it. There was no one in hoods and robes to cheer for

Duke, and there was no one in segregated schools to jeer at them, as there had been in 1966.

By 1992, American Tobacco had closed their Durham operations, and Liggett and Myers, the last tobacco manufacturer in Durham, was scaling down operations, ultimately moving to a small factory forty miles away in Mebane, NC, in 2000. When the 1992 Duke basketball team came home to Durham holding the NCAA championship trophy, it was greeted by a city that was largely at peace with itself. A city that had made its way to a much brighter future than the dark world of tobacco and racism of 1966 that Durham and North Carolina were finally leaving behind. And that was a far better ending than could have been imagined if Duke had won the national championship in 1966.

CHAPTER 12

CHANGING THE VERDICT OF HISTORY

When we examine the 1966 Kentucky-Texas Western game, the historical verdict has always focused almost entirely on the championship game, which Kentucky clearly lost. There has been little discussion of the Duke game, which this book now shows had equal or greater significance. So Kentucky folks over the years have spent most of their time being concerned with losing the championship game rather than beating Duke in the semifinals.

When a team loses a game, there are three possible reasons. First, they lose because the other team is better, or just outplays them. That's usually the case with most college basketball games; when a team loses by ten or more points, it's because they were simply beaten by a better team. In closer games, they sometimes lose because they don't play up to their potential, or have a bad shooting game, or don't execute well in the clutch. Finally, in *very* close games, they sometimes lose due to the officiating; they do (or don't) get a close or judgement call, or maybe the officials have a home bias (which has been demonstrated) or maybe they're just incompetent.

In the Kentucky-Texas Western game, any reasonable observer would have to conclude that the first reason was the case in that game; Kentucky lost because they lost. Texas Western clearly outplayed them. However, to his dying day in 1977, Adolph Rupp didn't see it that way. He insisted, to the very end, that Kentucky had lost because they had a bad shooting game, or the flu bug, or they didn't get the calls, or Texas Western had used ineligible players, or the officials were biased. "That loss to Texas Western hurt me more than you can imagine," Rupp was quoted as saying after his retirement. "Years later I was wondering what I could have done to turn the tide."[1] Rupp used to wake up in the middle of the night thinking about it. Louisville's Butch Beard seemed to wonder too: "In the back of my mind I thought, 'If me and Wes had gone to Kentucky, would we have made a difference?'"[2] We'll never know for sure, but it certainly was not their fault that Kentucky lost. There's no way to know whether any Black players would have played for Kentucky prior to 1966, given that they would have had to actually integrate the entire racist SEC, a task which even mighty and stoic Wes Unseld would have found daunting.

But Rupp's own attitude had something to do with it too. Rupp couldn't accept the obvious reason that he lost to a better Black team was at least in part due to his own intransigent racist refusal to do more than half-heartedly recruit Black players, despite the repeated entreaties of university president John Oswald and a number of other people at the University of Kentucky. Rupp went to his grave bitter about that one championship defeat, even though he had won all four of his other championships. According to Tony Kornheiser, "For all of Rupp's victories, Rupp's most famous game is one he lost."[3] It was as if all his other national championships and more than 870 coaching victories were overshadowed by that one loss. He would never admit that Kentucky had simply lost to a better team.

Having lived near the Boston area for a while, the author has become aware that there are different ways of looking at winning and losing; is the glass half empty or is it half full? For example, in 1986 when the Red Sox lost to the Mets, what most Red Sox fans remember about that year is the incredible sixth game world series choke. (And no it wasn't the ground ball to Buckner that lost the game, it was the wild pitch by Calvin Schiraldi that lost it.) But how many of them remember Dave Henderson's two run homer in the ninth inning of the ALCS which saved Boston from losing the series before? They sure remember it in Anaheim! And Boston fans also only remember in 2003 how the Red Sox lost to the Yankees because Grady Little failed to pull Pedro Martinez in the eighth inning, while conveniently forgetting that the only reason they played the game in the first place was because Eric Byrne and Miguel Tejada didn't have enough sense to tag home plate in the *same inning* in the series before and knock the Red Sox out of the playoffs. They sure remember it in Oakland! But the point is, in Boston, the glass is always half empty; it's never half full.

So historically, the Kentucky fans have almost always viewed the 1966 Final Four through the glass half empty view of them losing the final game too. They have consistently failed to remember that the only reason Kentucky played Texas Western in the first place was because Bob Verga got sick before the semifinals. And the same even holds true for Duke fans too. Duke fans typically only remember losing the 1978 NCAA championship game to Joe B. Hall's Kentucky team. They hardly remember Duke winning their first-round game against Rhode Island by one point because a Rhode Island player missed a *wide-open* layup that would have won the game and knocked Duke out of the tournament, which 1978 Duke player Kenny Dennard (famous for performing the first ever reverse slam in an NCAA tournament game that year against Villanova) has never ceased to point out.

So the verdict on the 1966 Kentucky-Texas Western game, up until now, has always been the glass half empty one that Kentucky is the team that lost to Texas Western. But looking at the impact of them winning the 1966 Duke game, is that really fair? Should Kentucky really go down in history as racist losers, especially when many of the Kentucky players were making a good faith effort to recruit Black players and they should likely never have played the game in the first place? I'm not convinced that is fair to Kentucky. That gives only a negative view of what Kentucky did that weekend.

This book has carefully examined the potential outcome of a Duke-Texas Western game. After discussing almost every group likely to be impacted by the game, it is almost impossible to find any group that would likely have benefited from that game. The most likely outcomes of the game, either a close Duke win or a close Texas Western win, which might have had at least some value to the Black community, would have had little lasting positive impact on anyone's lives due to the troublemaking nature of the game. The outcome wouldn't have had a positive effect on Duke, who would not have been able to recruit quality Black players for a very long time, and who would have also gone down in history as racist villains, despite *their* good-faith efforts to integrate the program. It wouldn't have had a positive effect on Durham or North Carolina, which still had segregated schools and a very active Ku Klux Klan, as it would have divided and antagonized people of both races. It wouldn't have had a positive impact on Black athletes in the South and other Black youth who wished to attend college, as they would not likely have seen a clear Texas Western victory or an obvious villain to cheer against. It would not have promoted racial harmony in hundreds of cities around the country, many of whom would be facing significant racial disturbances in the next two years. And, in a final bit of historical cruelty, it would not even have had a positive impact on White America, as it would have symbolized the triumph of tobacco and racism, thereby encouraging the persistence of racist attitudes and smoking. In fact, the only groups who might have benefited from such a game would have been the tobacco industry, who would have been happy to turn the game into a cigarette commercial, and racial extremists, who would have been only too glad to use the game to further their troublemaking racist agendas. Bob Verga's chance illness and the UK Wildcats saved Duke, North Carolina, and America from a game that would have had almost no positive implications whatsoever.

Many people in Kentucky are still bitter about the Texas Western game, believing that it was a historical accident that their program was tagged as racist villains, while Duke was not. Many now wish that Duke had played the game instead of them, sparing Kentucky from carrying the historical burden of being known as the White team that lost to Texas Western (of course at time of the game almost all of them felt otherwise, since they thought Kentucky was going to win). According to the Kentucky sportswriter Harry Reed, it would have been better for Rupp if they had lost to all-White Duke in the semifinals. "Then maybe it wouldn't be quite as easy for today's revisionist historians to make Rupp such a scapegoat."[4] Joe B. Hall, pointed out, "The news made a big thing out of it, but Duke was an all-white team in the 1966 game and they didn't mention that."[5]

But the difference that the outcome would have had on the two regions is enormous. A Duke victory *or* loss would have had a far more negative effect on North Carolina, with its combustible racial situation, than was the actual historical effect on Kentucky, and also would have been of little benefit to Black America (although a Kentucky victory over Texas Western would have been an even greater loss). Duke, a late-integrating school with a long history of racist exclusion and poor treatment of Black employees, who had been champions for several years of the still largely segregated ACC, *clearly* deserved to lose. But Kentucky, led by a racist coach, who for thirty-five years had been the flag bearer of the still completely segregated SEC, deserved to lose *even more*.

But the biggest difference between the two programs was that while Duke, Vic Bubas, and the ACC were making a real effort to do something about the race situation, Rupp and the rest of the SEC simply weren't. Larry Conley thinks Duke would have been treated differently if they had been the ones to play Texas Western. "I think Coach Rupp was the pivotal figure in all of this. I think the focal point is him and what people think he represented."⁶ The fact that Rupp was unable or unwilling to recruit quality Black players before the 1966 game is likely equally the fault of Rupp and the virulent racism of the SEC schools of which he was the champion. It was almost impossible for him to find any Black player willing to deal with the brutal hazing one was bound to endure from the Deep South schools as the first Black player at Kentucky in the SEC.

For Duke to have played the 1966 championship game would have been a tragedy of incredible proportions for the program, for the state of North Carolina, and for Black America, in the classic Greek sense where events force someone to do something that they shouldn't have to otherwise. The game would have caused significant racial tension in the Durham community in an unwitting and unnecessary manner. It would have discredited years of hard work on both sides of town, by numerous people in Durham, to help change their way of life—including my own mother, who was a prominent civil rights activist in that era—polarizing the community in a lasting manner. In the end, justice was served; the coach and the conference that deserved to play the game even more than Duke and the ACC, Adolph Rupp and the SEC, were the ones to play it.

Looking back at what Durham was like at the time of the 1966 game—and what it had been a few years before—it seems hard to believe that things were really like that in Durham. Even at the time of the 1992 game, which was only more than a generation removed from the time when the 1966 game occurred, it seems incredible. Driving through the Triangle today, seeing the modern laboratories and pharmaceutical companies, visiting the world-class Duke Medical Center, and seeing an area rated as one of the best places to live in the country, it's hard to fathom that Durham was founded on tobacco and racial oppression. A place where the Ku Klux Klan held hate-filled cross burning rallies, attended by thousands of people, less than ten miles from my childhood home. It seems outrageous that, not very long ago, we lived in a world where people sat in separate areas of theaters or where Black kids had to go miles further across town to go to segregated schools. During my childhood, my family sat in Howard Johnson's looking out at Black people who weren't allowed to eat there, and it was just, normal. My high school teachers fought in WWII and came home to a Durham where a Black GI, who also fought for his country, was shot and killed on a bus by a White passenger for refusing to sit in the back—the bus driver was then acquitted by an all-White jury in twenty minutes. White boys in the 1940s risked being thrown in jail just for traveling across town to play a basketball game. How? How could our whole way of life in Durham have been built on marketing an addictive product to minors that would destroy their health and likely end their lives years or decades early? When people look at it now, it just seems outrageous that it could actually have happened that way; it seems like something from an episode of *The Twilight Zone*, a bad comedy, or even a horror movie. Even those who grew up there remembering it all, and mercifully watched it all die, find it hard to believe.

It was indeed a strange world in Durham back then, one which I found puzzling then and even stranger when I think back on it now. Even at the time, I viewed it as indeed a strange accident of birth that caused me to grow up there. The basketball team in my backyard, in the life chosen for me at random (which could have been any one of three hundred division one teams), just happened to be Duke. So, like most kids would, I became a fan of the local team. I can still remember listening to Add Penfield on the radio doing the Duke games back then. Since we were nearly three hundred miles from the nearest pro team, that was what we had. At the time Duke played the 1966 game, I was seven years old, in first grade. An age where kids strongly identify with their sports heroes. I loved to imagine that I was Steve Vacendak when I played basketball with my friends. When Duke lost the Kentucky game, I was simply devastated, inconsolable as only a little kid can be. Looking back on it more than fifty years later, it's painful even now to accept that Duke could not have played Texas Western without going down in infamy for racial troublemaking.

What made the Kentucky loss actually hurt so badly for us Blue Devil faithful in Durham was two things. First, Duke never made the NCAAs the entire time I was growing up in Durham, a span of twelve years, which included an ACC tournament where sixth-ranked Duke—a legitimate Final Four contender—lost 12-10 to an inferior NC State team coached by Norm Sloan, who apparently had learned something from Dean Smith's 21-20 game a couple of years earlier. It was All-American Mike Lewis's last game for Duke, described by one of the announcers as being as exciting as artificial insemination. A game so riveting that at one point an NC State player dribbled near midcourt doing nothing for nearly thirteen minutes. Year after year, my friends and I huddled in front of our radios during the era when UCLA won eight championships, listening to the Duke games, hoping that Duke basketball might someday reclaim its past 1960s glory.

As Duke slipped further into 1970s oblivion, the 1966 Kentucky game loss hurt worse over time, as it appeared that Duke would never reclaim the place it had held in the 1960s. There were no more recent NCAA victories, so it lingered in our memories for more than a decade. That era ended for me, fittingly enough, in 1977, with one last heartbreak my final year in Durham when Duke's Tate Armstrong, on a nationally ranked team that was a legitimate potential NCAA tournament Sweet-16 level participant, broke his wrist midway through the season, ending my final chance of seeing Duke play in the NCAAs before I left for college.

The second thing that made it so hard to take was the success of the UNC program only ten miles away. Unlike Duke, they

The Bob Verga Shift

were able to successfully recruit quality Black players back then. They even played for the national championship twice in that era—losing a championship game to Marquette they could have won in 1977 if their coach, Dean Smith, hadn't tried stalling in the second half. (Serves him right!) And, led by Art Chansky and Curry Kirkpatrick, the local media (most of whom went to UNC Hussman School of Journalism) rubbed it in ceaselessly, taunting and laughing at our beloved Blue Devils every chance they got. So, unlike the Kentucky folks, who were left alone for a decade after 1966 to ponder their loss and Rupp's humiliation, the Blue Devil faithful were constantly being reminded of how bad Duke basketball had become by UNC fans, who poured it on mercilessly while their team beat Duke on a consistent basis. Between 1971 and 1978, UNC won all but two of the games they played with Duke, most famously when they came from eight points down with seventeen seconds to go to win in 1974, tying the game at the buzzer on a forty-foot bank shot by Walter Davis (whose nephew Hubert ultimately became the UNC coach nearly fifty years later), a game I heard with my best friend from Durham, who later played in the Duke pep band when Duke played Kentucky for the NCAA championship in 1978.

What made it even more unbearable for us Duke folks was having to watch the UNC coach Dean Smith strut and preen in front of the local media, making snide remarks about Duke basketball while also running his infuriating four-corner delay offense (the same one he started using in the ACC tournament semifinals in 1966, when UNC actually started the game in the four corners), which also angered the rest of the teams in the ACC. It is the reason the NCAA added a shot clock several years later—see Carolina-Virginia 1982, when Michael Jordan, James Worthy, and Ralph Sampson did *nothing* the last seven minutes of the ACC championship game while Dean Smith ordered a stall and the entire stadium booed mercilessly. And in addition to running his infuriating four-corner stall offense, Smith was a notoriously poor loser who instructed his players to hack and foul at the close of games that were obviously already lost, turning the end of UNC losses into an endless and annoying parade of fouls, whistles, and free throws. Being next to UNC made the Duke fans hurt as much or even more over the following decade than it did for the folks in Kentucky, who had to endure the trauma of seeing their state idol be turned into a racist villain, while the Duke fans had to endure a twelve-year-long merciless barrage of taunting from the UNC folks less than ten miles away. Smith was even the US Olympic coach in 1976, putting four of his own players on the team (although admittedly, most of them did deserve to be on it) and not playing Duke's great shooter Tate Armstrong.

But if Duke had won the 1966 Kentucky game, the outcome might have even been worse. Would my family have been pelted by rocks and bottles in 1966 by the Black side of town at our victory parade? Maybe, but probably not, since it is not very likely there would have been one. When we integrated the schools a few years later, would the Black guys have remembered the game and given us grief about it? Would Gene Banks have ever come down to Duke and rescued Duke basketball from 1970s ignominy? Maybe, but probably not, given the negative impact the game would have had on Duke's recruiting. But in the end, I am eternally thankful to Pat Riley, Louis Dampier, and the rest of the 1966 Kentucky Wildcats that those are questions to which I never learned the answers. The author, at age seven, who was busy reading *Sally Dick and Jane* and adding two plus two, wasn't quite up to doing detailed sociological analyses of the effect of college basketball in 1966; he was mercifully spared by Kentucky of seeing his childhood idols be turned into the racial villains of his future classmates across town.

When we look back on the 1966 game together, it appears in the end that history wasn't on the side of either Duke or Kentucky; they were both playing at a moment in history when

White dominance of college athletics was drawing to a close. Both programs were going to have to adapt to a changing racial environment, which took both of them nearly a decade after the game to do successfully. They were going to have to accept that Black athletes and students had to be given their rightful chance to compete on the playing field and in the classroom—as free American citizens, it could not be denied to them.

Even now it's hard for Duke fans to accept that the national championship was likely taken away from us that weekend. However, history doesn't always see things the way that we do when events are unfolding. Time often renders a different verdict, sometimes even by ourselves as we get older and put time and distance between our past selves and past events. Even Pat Riley agrees that Kentucky did more good for more people by losing their last game that year than by winning it. "Only I think years later, can you really take a look at it, and say you know maybe they were playing for something a hell of a lot more significant. And if they were, then the right team won."[7]

And in the end, Duke did more good by losing that weekend too. Speaking as someone who grew up in Durham idolizing Duke basketball, who lived and died with all the games as a kid, who can tell you almost every Duke roster since 1965 and can remember virtually every significant Duke game ever played in that time, and who has kept up with his Blue Devil basketball team even to this very day, I have to agree today with the verdict of history: it was better that Duke lost the 1966 Kentucky game. There is no other way to look at it.

Sitting watching the game on the west side of Durham, I was completely ignorant and years away from comprehending what was actually happening in Durham or in the rest of the South back then. If I had known then the full extent of what Bob Jones and the Klan were up to in my hometown, how the Black side of town was likely to feel if Texas Western lost to Duke, and what the overall likely effects of a Duke victory would have been on

Black America, I would have been cheering for every Pat Riley field goal that night.

At the time the games were played, it seems clear today that almost none of the players on *any* of the teams involved comprehended that they were players in a larger drama. The Duke players—almost all of them from out of state (primarily from the non-segregated North), sitting isolated in West Durham, single-mindedly focused on their classes and on winning basketball games—knew almost nothing of how the Black community in Durham or the rest of the South was likely to see a Duke-Texas Western game. They were little aware that the North Carolina Ku Klux Klan, in the middle of a three-year reign of terror greater than anything occurring since the Civil War, would have very likely hoisted them on their shoulders as their White champions in the event of a Duke victory. The Kentucky players—concerned with their own classes and life goals, the idols of the White media and likely the most popular basketball team in the history of the state of Kentucky—came into the finals with the deafening screaming of "We're number one!" from thousands of fans in their own arena still echoing in their ears. They firmly believed that they were about to make history as Kentucky heroes and join the pantheon of the other four great Rupp championship teams. They had no idea that their state icon coach was being set up to play the villain in someone else's racial drama, or that the game would go down as the worst defeat in Kentucky basketball history. Most of the Texas Western players were focused on winning the game and their own agendas. They seem to have had only a slight understanding that they were going to make history in a game that would make them heroes to Black America and resonate for decades. Only Don Haskins, who to his eternal credit, understood that the game *did* have significant racial implications, and said so to his players before the game—and possibly David Lattin, who did seem to understand that something larger was going on—had any idea of the greater significance of what was to happen. None of the rest of the coaches and players did, including Adolph Rupp.

The verdict on Rupp appears to be a complicated one. On the one hand it is clear that Rupp was confronted for years with a very difficult and dangerous situation in integrating the SEC. As an old man with health issues, he did not want to deal with something that would have been an incredible distraction and difficult to deal with while traveling further south. On the other hand, there appears to be enough evidence that Rupp clearly made racist remarks on a number of occasions that the accusations against him of racism cannot be readily dismissed. In the end, probably the most accurate view of him is that his attitudes were typical of people of his age in that era and area of the country, as I can remember so many other Southern people of that age being like—like some of my relatives who lived further south. To expect someone in his sixties who had spent his entire adult life living and traveling in a world of racist segregation that almost no one can understand today and who was famous for not changing his mind about anything, to instantly turn into a civil rights activist near the end of his life would indeed have been a tall order. So the verdict on Rupp isn't so much a verdict on him; it's the verdict on his entire generation and the world they lived in, the same generation that attended Ku Klux Klan rallies in North Carolina and blocked the integration of Duke University. That is a verdict which subsequent generations who have examined the strange world of segregation Rupp and I lived in then and found it simply incredible, have rendered decisively in the negative.

And as for the verdict on the other famous figure in 1966, Senator Mitch McConnell, that will be one which future generations will get to determine as well. Examining his performance in the Senate as Republican leader between 2008 and 2016, it appears that he may indeed have learned something when he was at Kentucky in 1966 after all. When they read this book and examine how he proceeded during that time period, *they* will get to determine what it was he learned back then, and *they* will get to render their own verdict on what he did to American democracy. One wonders if McConnell has ever considered the incredible irony that he, who had actually been a civil rights activist at Kentucky in the 1960s, appeared to have behaved the same way in the Senate at a similar age that Rupp did back in 1966. But I doubt it.

But for the Kentucky players, it is clear that the verdict should have been changed long ago. It is time to revise the historical record to a better, glass half full view of the 1966 Final Four. History will actually show that Kentucky did indeed win the game that mattered. But it wasn't the Texas Western game; it was the Duke game. When Larry Conley, having soldiered through much of the game despite a 102-degree fever, with the last gasp of effort left in his flu-ridden body, drove the length of the floor to score the game-clinching basket, he helped save America from a game that likely would have been the single most racially polarizing and divisive college basketball game to ever be played.

When I think back on the end of the 1966 game, how I fell on the floor crying as Conley's layup ended the *only* chance for my team to win a championship (or even play in the NCAAs) when I was growing up, I still want to cry about it. But I don't want to cry for us Duke folks, even though it took twenty-five years for Duke to win a championship, during which time we wandered through the Dark Ages of the '70s, finishing last in the ACC four years in a row, and lost championship games to Kentucky in 1978 (coached by Rupp assistant Joe B. Hall), to Louisville in 1986 (on a rebound of a missed airball!), and to UNLV in 1990 (in a record-setting thirty-point-margin massacre) before finally winning one in 1991. In the end, Duke won their share of championships too.

I want to cry instead thinking of what would have been taken away from Black America that night if Duke had won. The 1966 Final Four happened at an important moment in history, a time when many Black Americans were trying to figure out how to proceed after the Civil Rights Act had been enacted. That game inspired thousands of Black athletes and students to go off to college and pursue their ambitions as free American citizens, a right that had been denied them for nearly one hundred years since the Civil War and several centuries before that under slavery. That game changed the course of history, all because of Bob Verga's chance illness. The game that Duke would have played would have given them almost nothing of any value to work with; only a trouble-making racist cigarette commercial, a tragedy of enormous proportions.

Cazzie Russell, who endured the heartbreak of losing in the previous two Final Fours with University of Michigan (one of them to Duke in 1964), before seeing his team lose to Kentucky in the 1966 NCAA tournament, said, "Possibly God had a plan. Sometimes we have to give up something to get something."[8] If his team had beaten Kentucky, the 1966 game would never have happened. The same statement may have held true for Duke as well. Was Bob Verga's illness a part of *Someone Else's* plan to ensure that Duke lost and that Kentucky would play the game? Only God knows.

Looking back on that Final Four, it seems very possible that the teams playing that weekend may have been pieces on His celestial chessboard. Larry Conley later on seemed to understand that the Kentucky players may have been fulfilling a larger purpose that night. Conley saw later how the game helped Black America and has not begrudged it for using it to advance their cause. Said Conley, "Whatever was created was created without us being involved. We were simply the pawns."[9] As Pat Riley famously said, "We didn't know we were going to take part of the Emancipation proclamation of 1966."[10] In the end, we can't know how He does things or what His purposes are. If that was how He saw things back then, and that was His purpose, it can't be contested or understood by Duke, Michigan, Kentucky, or anyone else.

So if the Kentucky players actually fulfilled some bigger plan, then they should be given credit for what they did, even if it may have been largely unintentional. Pat Riley, Louie Dampier, Thad Jaracz, Tommy Kron, and Larry Conley all had outstanding careers and went on to have a very positive impact on society. All five of them were motivated by that game to achieve at a likely considerably higher level than if they had won the national championship. All-Americans Riley and Dampier went on to play and/or coach as champions in largely Black leagues. So how can they go down in history as racist villains when their entire subsequent careers refute that? Even the Texas Western players didn't see it that way. According to the late Harry Flournoy, "The Kentucky players, every last one of them, were gentlemen," he said. "They got a bad rap. They've been looked at as bad guys."[11] The all-White Kentucky team was simply typical of that era; most other teams in the region were all-White as well, just like Duke. The late Tommy Kron was bothered by the fact that people actually believed that the Kentucky team was racially motivated. According to Kron, "That was certainly not the case at all. To me, that's ignorance and we didn't deserve that. All we cared about was winning the game."[12] They didn't deserve to lose any more than the Duke players did, and it is almost a certainty that the Duke players would have seen it the same way. The only person who deserved to lose in 1966 was Adolph Rupp.

For the Kentucky players, who clearly never deserved infamy in the first place, it is time to change the verdict now and for all time. The legacy of Rupp's Runts is not as the team that lost to Texas Western; they are the team whose game inspired a generation. Cheers, Kentucky! Let's raise a half-full glass! Congratulations on winning the Duke game! By winning *that* game, Kentucky transformed the 1966 championship into a game that inspired an entire generation of Black youth to step forward, go off to college, and claim the lives that their God given abilities gave them the right to have. And not coincidentally, Kentucky saved

Duke, Durham, and North Carolina from a game that would have racially polarized the city and state for decades. Speaking for all who grew up in Durham in that era, thank you, Kentucky, for saving us from ourselves. You saved us, from us! In 1966, that was salvation enough.

ACKNOWLEDGEMENTS

The 1966 final four has been the subject of numerous books and dozens of newspaper and internet articles. Consequently, it was actually not necessary to consult many of the participants personally concerning what happened, as many of them had been asked about it numerous times. The problem in fact, was actually of too many quotes and interviews about the games; it was a major effort to sort through them all and make sense of them. The web site "Adolph Rupp, Fact and Fiction" in particular showed not only how much material is available, but how obsessed people in Kentucky are about Rupp's record. However, there were certain areas where it was necessary to check with some of the original participants and subsequent authors concerning what happened to better understand the situation. Special thanks to Charles Martin, Lane Demas, and David Cunningham for helping better understand the implications of the games, and also to former Durham Civil Rights activist Dr. Howard Fuller for better understanding the situation in Durham. Also, thanks to former Duke basketball players Pete Moeller, Steve Vacendak and Bob Verga for helpful communications. Thanks to the Duke Library and the Rubinstein reading room for providing helpful files and articles. Thanks to the Duke and Texas Western athletic departments, the Raliegh News and Observer, and the Kentucky Special Collections Research Center for permission in using photos, and the University of Kentucky library for providing numerous newspaper articles about the 1966 Game and its aftermath. Also, a final thanks to the University of Louisville library for personally contacting Senator Mitch McConnell to help clarify his relationship with Adolph Rupp.

NOTES

Chapter One

1. Jackie MacMullan, Rafe Bartholomew, and Dan Klores, "How Basketball's Fight Over Racial Equality Remade the Game," *The Daily Beast*, February 18, 2021, https://www.thedailybeast.com/how-basketballs-fight-over-racial-equality-remade-the-game.

2. Jennifer Wells, "The Black Freedom Struggle and Civil Rights Labor Organizing in the Piedmont and Eastern North Carolina Tobacco Industry," (master's thesis, USF Tampa, 2013) 35-36, 59-60.

3. Smoking and Health: Report of the Advisory Committee to the Surgeon General of the Public Health Service, (Washington, DC: Executive Agency Publications, *1964*), 28.

4. William Sturkey, "Carr Was Indeed Much More than Silent Sam," *The Herald Sun* online, October 31, 2017, https://www.heraldsun.com/opinion/article181567401.html.

5. Breanna Edwards, "Duke University Will Remove Name of Virulent Racist From Campus Building," *Essence*, updated October 23, 2020, https://www.essence.com/news/duke-university-will-remove-name-of-virulent-racist-from-campus-building/.

6. Theodore Segal, *Point of Reckoning: The Fight for Racial Justice at Duke University* (Durham: Duke University Press, 2021), 14.

7. Scott Ellsworth, "Jim Crow Loses; The Secret Game," *New York Times Magazine*, March 31, 1996, https://www.nytimes.com/1996/03/31/magazine/sunday-march-31-1996-jim-crow-losses-the-secret-game.html.

8. Ellsworth, "Jim Crow Loses."

9. Michael Lenehan, *Ramblers: Loyola Chicago 1963—The Team that Changed the Color of College Basketball* (Evanston: Agate Midway, 2013), 87.

10. Ellsworth, "Jim Crow Loses."

11. Duke University website, "The Road to Desegregation at Duke," *Duke University Libraries: Exhibits*, accessed January 26, 2024, https://exhibits.library.duke.edu/exhibits/show/desegregation/before.

12. Melissa Kean, *Desegregating Private Higher Education in the South: Duke, Emory, Rice, Tulane, and Vanderbilt* (Baton Rouge: Louisiana State University Press, 2008), 62.

13. Kean, *Desegregating*, 66.
14. Kean, *Desegregating*, 148.
15. Durham Civil Rights Heritage Project website, "Martin Luther King Jr.'s Visits to Durham, 1956 to 1964," *Durham County Library* online, updated September 18, 2020, https://durhamcountylibrary.org/exhibits/dcrhp/events/martin_luther_king_jr.%27s_visits_to_durham_1956_196/.
16. Durham Civil Rights Heritage Project website, "Martin Luther King Jr.'s Visits to Durham, 1956–1964."
17. Alicia Sun and Isabella Arbelaez, "Who Was Oliver Harvey?" *Scalawag*, February 24, 2020, https://scalawagmagazine.org/2020/02/oliver-harvey-duke-civil-rights/.
18. Ken Smith, "Duke's 'First Five' Black Students Celebrate 50 Years since Integration," *WRAL News* online, January 24, 2020, https://www.wral.com/story/duke-s-first-five-black-students-celebrate-50-years-since-integration/12023048/.
19. Segal, *Point of Reckoning*, 43.
20. Segal, 44.
21. Segal, 46.
22. Harriot Quin, personal communication, 1964.
23. Duke University website, "King at Duke: King's 1964 Speech at Duke," accessed January 26, 2024, https://mlk.duke.edu/king-at-duke/.
24. Pete Moeller, personal communication.
25. Pete Moeller, personal communication.
26. Bill Brill, "The Legendary Vic Bubas," *Duke Athletics* online, January 29, 2001, https://goduke.com/news/2001/1/29/140839.aspx.
27. Bob Holliday, "Vic Bubas, 'A Man with a Lot of Brains,'" *WRAL Sports Fan*, April 21, 2018, https://www.wralsportsfan.com/vic-bubas-a-man-with-a-lot-of-brains-/17502029/.
28. "Stephen T. Vacendak," *Duke Athletics* online, December 14, 2005, https://goduke.com/news/2005/12/14/220809.aspx.

Chapter Two

1. Michael Lindenberger, "Louisville-Kentucky: Inside A Heated College Hoops Rivalry," *Keeping Score* (blog), *Time*, March 30, 2012, https://keepingscore.blogs.time.com/2012/03/30/louisville-kentucky-inside-a-heated-college-hoops-rivarly/.
2. Frank Fitzpatrick, *And the Walls Came Tumbling Down: Kentucky, Texas Western, and the Game That Changed American Sports* (New York: Simon and Schuster, 1999), 49.

3. Michael Lenehan, *Ramblers: Loyola Chicago 1963—The Team that Changed the Color of College Basketball* (Evanston: Agate Midway, 2013), 121.

4. Lenehan, *Ramblers*, 121.

5. Bob Carter, "Rupp: Baron of the Bluegrass," *ESPN Classic* online, accessed January 26, 2024, https://www.espn.com/classic/biography/s/Rupp_Adolph.html.

6. Rick Morrissey, "Past Imperfect; Future Intense," *Chicago Tribune* online, November 30, 1997, https://www.chicagotribune.com/news/ct-xpm-1997-11-30-9712020327-story.html.

7. Jon Scott, "Adolph Rupp: Fact and Fiction," *Big Blue History,* accessed January 26, 2024, http://www.bigbluehistory.net/bb/rupp.html.

8. Fitzpatrick, *And the Walls Came Tumbling Down*, 36.

9. Lane Demas, Personal Communication, 2020.

10. Dave Kindred, "Calling Rupp a Racist Just Doesn't Ring True," *Lexington Herald Leader,* December 22, 1991.

11. Curry Kirkpatrick, "The Night They Drove Old Dixie Down," Vault, *Sports Illustrated* online, April 1, 1991, https://vault.si.com/vault/1991/04/01/the-night-they-drove-old-dixie-down-in-1966-an-all-black-lineup-from-texas-western-beat-all-white-kentucky-for-the-ncaa-title-college-hoops-hasnt-been-the-same-since.

12. Bert Nelli and Steve Nelli, *The Winning Tradition: A History of Kentucky Wildcat Basketball,* (Lexington: University of Kentucky Press, 2014).

13. Scott, "Adolph Rupp: Fact and Fiction."

14. Scott, "Adolph Rupp: Fact and Fiction."

15. Joe B. Hall and Marianne Walker, *Coach Hall: My Life On and Off the Court,* (Lexington: University Press of Kentucky, 1999), 106.

16. Jeffrey McMurray, "In Defense of Adolph Rupp," *The Spokesman-Review* online, January 21, 2006, https://www.spokesman.com/stories/2006/jan/21/in-defense-of-adolph-rupp/.

17. Lenehan, *Ramblers*, 151.

18. John C. Thomas, "Looking Back at Loyola University's 1963 NCAA Men's Basketball Championship," *How They Play,* updated August 9, 2023, https://howtheyplay.com/team-sports/The-50th-Anniversary-of-Loyola-Universitys-Mens-Basketball-Championship-Season.

19. Larry Schwartz, "Robinson Has the Guts Not to Fight Back," *ESPN Classic* online, November 19, 2003, https://www.espn.com/classic/s/moment010828-rickey-robinson.html.

20. Scott, "Adolph Rupp: Fact and Fiction."

21. Hall and Walker, *Coach Hall,* 99.

22. Hall and Walker, 99.

23. Scott, "Adolph Rupp: Fact and Fiction."

24. S. Zebulon Baker, "'On the Opposite Side of the Fence': The University of Kentucky and the Racial Desegregation of the Southeastern Conference," *Register of the Kentucky Historical Society* 115, no. 4 (Autumn 2017): 563.

25. Hall and Walker, *Coach Hall*, 98.

26. Fitzpatrick, *And the Walls Came Tumbling Down*, 141.

27. Adolph Rupp, *The Rupp Tape: The Baron Tells His Own Story*, WHAS Productions, 1992, audiocassette, accessed clip online January 26, 2024, http://www.bigbluehistory.net/bb/Audio/rupp_on_oswald.mp3.

28. Greg Hoard, "The Great Wes Unseld: Owning His Own Ground," *Press Pros* online, March 3, 2019, https://pressprosmagazine.com/hoard-the-great-wes-unseld-owning-his-own-ground/.

29. Scott, "Adolph Rupp: Fact and Fiction."

30. Judith Egerton, "UK Ponders Its Racial Image–On Film and in Real Life," *Louisville Courier-Journal*, January 6, 2006.

31. Scott, "Adolph Rupp: Fact and Fiction."

32. Fitzpatrick, *And the Walls Came Tumbling Down*, 63.

33. Scott, "Adolph Rupp: Fact and Fiction."

34. Adolph Rupp, *The Rupp Tape: The Baron Tells His Own Story*, WHAS Productions, 1992, audiocassette, accessed clip online January 26, 2024, http://www.bigbluehistory.net/bb/Audio/rupp_on_oswald.mp3.

35. Scott, "Adolph Rupp: Fact and Fiction."

36. Fitzpatrick, *And the Walls Came Tumbling Down*, 148.

37. Terry Pluto, *Loose Balls: The Short, Wild Life of the American Basketball Association* (New York: Simon & Schuster, 1990), 241.

38. Scott, "Adolph Rupp: Fact and Fiction."

39. John Clay, "25 Years Later, Kentucky's 'Runts' Still Special," *Baltimore Sun* online, February 17, 1991, https://www.baltimoresun.com/1991/02/17/25-years-later-kentuckys-runts-still-special/.

40. John Clay, "25 Years Later."

41. Keith Taylor, "Looking Back: Larry Conley, Joe B. Hall Haven't Forgotten UK's Memorable Tourney Run in 1966," *Northern Kentucky Tribune* online, December 29, 2015, https://nkytribune.com/2015/12/looking-back-larry-conley-joe-b-hall-havent-forgotten-uks-memorable-tourney-run-in-1966/.

42. James Duane Bolin, *Adolph Rupp and the Rise of Kentucky Basketball* (Lexington: University of Kentucky Press, 2020), 295.

43. Bolin, *Adolph Rupp and the Rise*, 295.

44. Tom Eblen and Jerry Tipton, "50 Years After Kentucky-Texas Western: College Basketball Has Not Been the Same Since," *Lexington Herald Leader* online,

March 14, 2016, https://www.kentucky.com/sports/college/mens-basketball/article65655382.html.

Chapter Three

1. Luis Gonzalez, "The Legacy of '66 50 Years Later," *The Prospector Daily* online, November 3, 2015, https://www.theprospectordaily.com/2015/11/03/the-legacy-of-66-50-years-later/.
2. Charles H. Martin, *Benching Jim Crow: The Rise and Fall of the Color Line in Southern College Sports, 1890-1980* (Springfield: University of Illinois Press, 2010), 114.
3. David Kingsley Snell, *The Baron and the Bear: Rupp's Runts, Haskins's Miners, and the Season That Changed Basketball Forever* (Lincoln: University of Nebraska Press, 2016), 214.
4. Snell, *The Baron and the Bear*, 61.
5. Saslchan, "Fifty Years of Glory Road," *NBA* online, February 22, 2016, https://www.nba.com/spurs/fifty-years-glory-road.
6. Alison Shaw, "Nevil Shed Discusses Adversity and Civil Rights," *DU Clarion* online, January 15, 2007, https://duclarion.com/2007/01/nevil-shed-discusses-adversity-and-civil-rights-3/.
7. Frank Fitzpatrick, *And the Walls Came Tumbling Down: Kentucky, Texas Western, and the Game That Changed American Sports* (New York: Simon and Schuster, 1999), 105.
8. Ray Sanchez, "Cager to Reveal How the 1966 Miners Really Won," *El Paso Inc.* online, July 27, 2018, https://www.elpasoinc.com/lifestyle/local_features/cager-to-reveal-how-the-1966-miners-really-won/article_65c61de8-91bb-11e8-a57f-3b5ee0e99361.html.
9. Mike Hutton, "Gary Native Orsten Artis Remembers His Best Friend Harry Flournoy," *Chicago Tribune* online, December 24, 2016, https://www.chicagotribune.com/suburbs/post-tribune/sports/ct-ptb-mike-hutton-column-st-1225-20161224-column.html.
10. Snell, *The Baron and the Bear*, 144.
11. B. J. Schecter, "Harry Flournoy, Texas Western Forward March 28, 1966," *Vault, Sports Illustrated* online, April 6, 1998, https://vault.si.com/vault/1998/04/06/harry-flournoy-texas-western-forward-march-28-1966.
12. Snell, *The Baron and the Bear*, 115.
13. John Coker, "Basketball Legend Nevil Shed on Overcoming During the Civil Rights Era," *KENS5* online, February 22, 2019, https://www.kens5.com/article/

entertainment/living-basketball-basketball-legend-nevil-shed-on-overcoming-during-civil-rights/273-4fa0201f-3029-44eb-8956-0df5f378ff25.

14. Nevil Shed, "Scared to Death," *The Players' Tribune* online, April 2, 2015, https://www.theplayerstribune.com/articles/nevil-shed-texas-western-ncaa-tournament-march-madness.

Chapter Four

1. Christopher Klein, "How Bobby Grier Integrated One of College Football's Biggest Games," *History Channel* online, December 22, 2021, https://www.history.com/news/bobby-grier-college-football-color-barrier-sugar-bowl.

2. Charles H. Martin, "Jim Crow in the Gymnasium: The Integration of College Basketball in the American South," *International Journal of the History of Sport* 10, no. 1 (1993): 75.

3. Ellen Gutoskey, "Good Trouble: John Lewis's Pivotal Role in the Nashville Lunch Counter Sit-Ins of 1960," *Mental Floss*, July 21, 2020, https://www.mentalfloss.com/article/626699/john-lewis-nashville-lunch-counter-protests.

4. Lou Freedmen, *Becoming Iron Men: The Story of the 1963 Loyola Ramblers* (Lubbock: Texas Tech University Press, 2014), 151.

5. Clay Risen, *The Bill of the Century: The Epic Battle for the Civil Rights Act* (New York: Bloomsbury Press 2014), 90.

6. "Everett Dirksen: Forgotten Civil Rights Champion," *Face to Face* (blog), National Portrait Gallery, accessed January 29, 2024, https://npg.si.edu/blog/everett-dirksen-forgotten-civil-rights-champion.

7. Everett M. Dirksen, "Speech to Senate on the Civil Rights Bill," *American Rhetoric Speech Bank* online, accessed January 29, 2024, https://www.americanrhetoric.com/speeches/everettmdirksencivilrightsbillspeech.htm.

8. Dirksen, "Speech to Senate."

9. Stan Mendenhall, "Everett Dirksen and the 1964 Civil Rights Act," *Illinois Periodicals* online, accessed January 29, 2024, https://www.lib.niu.edu/1996/iht319648.html.

10. Joshua D. Farrington, "The Republican Party and Modern Conservatism in Postwar Kentucky," *Register of the Kentucky Historical Society* 113, no. 2/3 (Spring/Summer 2015): 307.

11. Al Cross, "Opinion: McConnell Stayed True to Form; No Guardian of the Republic, but Ready for the Next Battle," *Hoptown Chronicle* online, updated November 11, 2023, https://hoptownchronicle.org/opinion-mcconnell-stayed-true-to-form-no-guardian-of-the-republic-but-ready-for-the-next-battle/.

12. Jane Mayer, "How Mitch McConnell Became Trump's Enabler-in-Chief," *New Yorker* online, April 12, 2020, https://www.newyorker.com/magazine/2020/04/20/how-mitch-mcconnell-became-trumps-enabler-in-chief.

13. Betsy Schlabach, "'Our Emancipation Day': Martin Luther King Jr. in Chicago," *Black Perspectives* (blog), *African American Intellectual History Society*, April 15, 2018, https://www.aaihs.org/our-emancipation-day-martin-luther-king-jr-in-chicago/.

14. "Black Power," *The Martin Luther King, Jr. Research and Education Institute, Stanford University*, accessed January 29, 2024, https://kinginstitute.stanford.edu/black-power.

15. Clayborne Carson, *In Struggle: SNCC and the Black Awakening of the 1960s* (Cambridge: Harvard University Press, 1995), 209.

16. "'Black Power!' A Slogan is Born," *Today in Civil Liberties History*, accessed January 29, 2024, http://todayinclh.com/?event=black-power.

17. Carson, *In Struggle*, 194.

18. Carson, 215.

19. "Here Is the Speech Martin Luther King Jr. Gave the Night Before He Died," *CNN* online, April 4, 2018, https://www.cnn.com/2018/04/04/us/martin-luther-king-jr-mountaintop-speech-trnd/index.html.

20. Dave DeWitt and Frank Stasio, "The Klan's Rise to Prominence in 1960s North Carolina," *WUNC* online, February 26, 2013, https://www.wunc.org/politics/2013-02-26/the-klans-rise-to-prominence-in-1960s-north-carolina.

21. David Cunningham, *Klansville, U.S.A.: The Rise and Fall of the Civil Rights-Era Ku Klux Klan*, (New York: Oxford University Press, 2014) 94.

22. Wendell W. Smiley, *The North Carolina Press Views the Ku Klux Klan from 1964 through 1966* (Greenville: self-pub., 1967), 425.

23. Smiley, *North Carolina Press Views*, 123.

Chapter Five

1. Rial Cummings, "Lewis Just Missed Exit to Glory Road," *The Missoulian* online, January 29, 2006, https://missoulian.com/sports/rial-cummings-lewis-just-missed-exit-to-glory-road/article_aab2274b-cb8d-5a01-b0b1-70991a4fbb5e.html.

2. Mike Waters, "Jim Boeheim's History with Duke Goes Back to 1966 as a Player for Syracuse Basketball," *Syracuse Post-Standard* online, January 27, 2014, https://www.syracuse.com/orangebasketball/2014/01/jim_boeheims_history_with_duke.html.

3. Waters, "Jim Boeheim's History."

4. "Bob Riedy Knows About Final Four," *Staff Report, Morning Call* online, March 26, 1991, https://www.mcall.com/1991/03/26/bob-riedy-knows-about-final-four/.

5. Jim Sumner, "What If: Duke Had Played Texas Western in 1966 Instead of Kentucky?" *Duke Basketball Report* online, https://www.dukebasketballreport.com/2020/6/19/21296579/duke-texas-western-1966-instead-of-kentucky-vic-bubas-bob-verga-don-haskins-adolph-rupp.

6. Frank Deford, "Go-Go With Bobby Joe," *Vault, Sports Illustrated* online, March 28, 1966, https://vault.si.com/vault/1966/03/28/gogo-with-bobby-joe.

7. Jim Sumner, *Tales From the Duke Blue Devils Locker Room* (Champaign: Sports Publishing, 2020), 89.

8. Bob Holliday, "Vic Bubas, 'A Man With a Lot of Brains,'" *WRAL Sports Fan* (blog), *WRAL News* online, April 21, 2018, https://www.wralsportsfan.com/vic-bubas-a-man-with-a-lot-of-brains-/17502029/.

9. James Duane Bolin, *Adolph Rupp and the Rise of Kentucky Basketball* (Lexington: University of Kentucky Press, 2020), 296.

10. Russell Rice, "Old Fashioned Poultice, Vaporizer, Milk Shake Vital In Kentucky Win," *Lexington Herald,* March 19, 1966.

11. Curry Kirkpatrick, "Clash of the Titans," *ESPN Magazine* online, December 17, 2001, http://www.espn.com/magazine/curry_20011217.html.

12. Larry Boeck, "UK Beats Duke 83-79 Shoots for Title Tonight," *Louisville Courier Journal,* March 19, 1966.

13. Boeck, "UK Beats Duke 83-79."

Chapter Six

1. Art Chansky, *Blue Blood: Duke-Carolina: Inside the Most Storied Rivalry in College Hoops,* (New York: St. Martin's Griffin, 2006), 104.

2. Chansky, *Blue Blood,* 105.

3. Art Chansky, "Dean Smith Era Began with Famous Three-Peat," *Chapelboro News* online, January 23, 2018, https://chapelboro.com/sports/dean-smith-era-began-famous-three-peat.

4. Al Featherston, "A Look at the Duke-Kentucky Series," *Go Duke* online, November 13, 2012, https://goduke.com/news/2012/11/13/205731187.aspx.

5. Jim Sumner, "Duke-UNC Memories: Missoula Mountain Always A Duke Man," *Go Duke* online, February 5, 2004, https://goduke.com/news/2004/2/5/146955.aspx.

6. "Still No. 1 in Our Hearts", *Durham Sun,* March 14, 1966.

7. Joe Wilson, "One of Rupp's Runts Remembers a Different Kind of Game," *Kentucky New Era* online, January 13, 2006, https://www.kentuckynewera.com/article_f7d2bc64-db7e-533d-9218-d303af6f8dd1.html.

8. Jon Scott, "Adolph Rupp: Fact and Fiction," *Big Blue History*, accessed January 26, 2024, http://www.bigbluehistory.net/bb/rupp.html.

9. Frank Fitzpatrick, *And the Walls Came Tumbling Down: Kentucky, Texas Western, and the Game That Changed American Sports* (New York: Simon and Schuster, 1999), 24.

10. David Kingsley Snell, *The Baron and the Bear: Rupp's Runts, Haskins's Miners, and the Season That Changed Basketball Forever* (Lincoln: University of Nebraska Press, 2016), 208.

11. Michael Bohn, "Texas Western's 1966 Championship Win Changed College Basketball 50 Years Ago," *Go Erie* online, March 17, 2016, https://www.goerie.com/story/sports/nba/2016/03/17/texas-western-s-1966-championship/25076679007/.

12. Fitzpatrick, *And the Walls Came Tumbling Down*, 208.

13. Fitzpatrick, 36.

14. Tom Eblen and Jerry Tipton, "50 Years After Kentucky-Texas Western: 'College Basketball Has Not Been the Same Since,'" *Lexington Herald Leader* online, March 14, 2016, https://www.kentucky.com/sports/college/mens-basketball/article65655382.html.

15. James Duane Bolin, *Adolph Rupp and the Rise of Kentucky Basketball* (Lexington: University of Kentucky Press, 2020), 302.

16. Scott, "Adolph Rupp: Fact and Fiction."

17. Eblen and Tipton, "50 Years After Kentucky-Texas Western."

18. Scott, "Adolph Rupp: Fact and Fiction."

19. Don Haskins and Dan Wetzel, *Glory Road: My Story of the 1966 NCAA Basketball Championship and How One Team Triumphed Against the Odds and Changed America Forever* (New York: Hachette Books, 2005), 183.

20. Adrian Broaddus, "Celebrating 53 Years: 1966 Championship Still Beams in El Paso's Heart," *600 ESPN El Paso* online, March 19, 2019, https://krod.com/celebrating-53-years-1966-championship-still-beams-in-el-pasos-heart/.

21. Jere Longman, "Forget the Glitter, Riley is a Coach of Substance," *Philadelphia Inquirer*, June 8, 1987.

22. Scott, "Adolph Rupp: Fact and Fiction."

23. Scott.

24. Paul McMullan, *Maryland Basketball: Tales from Cole Field House* (Baltimore: Johns Hopkins University Press, 2002), 31.

25. Scott, "Adolph Rupp: Fact and Fiction."

26. Scott.
27. Rial Cummings, "Lewis Just Missed Exit to Glory Road," *Missoulian* online, January 29, 2006, https://missoulian.com/sports/rial-cummings-lewis-just-missed-exit-to-glory-road/article_aab2274b-cb8d-5a01-b0b1-70991a4fbb5e.html.
28. Scott, "Adolph Rupp."
29. Scott.
30. Scott.
31. Reid Forgrave, "50 Years Ago, Texas Western Didn't Realize What It Set in Motion," *Fox Sports* online, February 5, 2016, https://www.foxsports.com/stories/college-basketball/50-years-ago-texas-western-didnt-realize-what-it-set-in-motion.
32. Rial Cummings, "Lewis Just Missed Exit to Glory Road."
33. Eblen and Tipton, "50 Years After Kentucky-Texas Western."
34. Dale Robertson, "50 Years Later, Texas Western's Win More than a Game for David Lattin," *Houston Chronicle* online, March 20, 2016, https://www.houstonchronicle.com/sports/college/article/Fifty-years-later-Texas-Western-s-win-more-than-6922933.php.
35. Ron Fimrite, "It Was More than Just a Game," *Vault, Sports Illustrated* online, November 18, 1987, https://vault.si.com/vault/1987/11/18/it-was-more-than-just-a-game-on-march-23-1963-loyola-of-chicago-and-the-university-of-cincinnati-met-for-the-ncaa-championship-and-college-basketball-entered-a-new-era.
36. Robert Weston, "Duke's Blue Devils Aim at Becoming King Tomorrow," *Northern Virginia Sun*, March 22, 1963.
37. Rial Cummings, "Lewis Just Missed Exit to Glory Road."
38. Frank Deford, "Now There Are Four," *Vault, Sports Illustrated* online, March 21, 1966, https://vault.si.com/vault/1966/03/21/now-there-are-four.
39. Jim Sumner, "Duke-UNC Memories: Missoula Mountain Always A Duke Man," *Go Duke* online, February 5, 2004, https://goduke.com/news/2004/2/5/146955.aspx.
40. Rial Cummings, "Lewis Just Missed Exit to Glory Road."
41. Haskins and Wetzel, *Glory Road*, 143.
42. Frank Deford, "Now There Are Four."

Chapter Seven

1. "Duke Has No Fear of 'Race,'" *Charlotte Observer*, March 22, 1963.
2. "Driesell to Bubas: Forget Cincinnati," *Raleigh News and Observer*, March 20, 1963.

3. Dick Barkley, "Duke's Cagers Off to Finals," *Durham Herald Sun*, March 17, 1966.

4. Jack Horner, "Crowd Turns Out to Welcome Cagers," *Durham Morning Herald*, March 19, 1966.

5. Tom Eblen and Jerry Tipton, "50 Years After Kentucky-Texas Western: 'College Basketball Hasn't Been the Same Since,'" *Lexington Herald Leader* online, Mar 14, 2016, https://www.kentucky.com/sports/college/mens-basketball/article65655382.html.

6. Eblen and Tipton, "50 Years After Kentucky-Texas Western."

7. Theodore Segal, *Point of Reckoning: The Fight for Racial Justice at Duke University* (Durham: Duke University Press, 2021), 113.

8. Segal, *Point of Reckoning*, 113.

9. Rebecca Spicehandler, "Assassination of Rev. Dr. Martin Luther King Jr. - Durham Responds with a Silent March," *Durham Civil and Human Rights Map* online, accessed January 31, 2024, https://www.durhamcivilrightsmap.org/places/23-assassination-of-rev-dr-martin-luther-king-jr-durham-responds-a-silent-march.

10. Spicehandler, "Assassination of Rev. Dr. Martin Luther King Jr."

11. Rah Bickley, "Durham Civil Rights Leader Returns," *Indy Week* online, April 19, 2006, https://indyweek.com/news/durham/durham-civil-rights-leader-returns/

12. "Duke's Cagers Off to Finals," *Durham Herald Sun*, March 17, 1966.

13. Joe Gergen, "Art Heyman Put Up the First Duke," *Newsday* online, March 20, 1999, https://www.newsday.com/sports/college/college-basketball/art-heyman-put-up-the-first-duke-x66477.

14. Wendell W. Smiley, *The North Carolina Press Views the Ku Klux Klan from 1964 through 1966*, (Greenville: Self-pub., 1967), 152.

15. Ray Sanchez, "1966 Texas Western College Title Revisited," *El Paso Inc.* online, November 17, 2018, https://www.elpasoinc.com/lifestyle/local_features/1966-texas-western-college-title-revisited/article_fadd0b92-e9e2-11e8-a8b9-3ffef6ce17eb.html.

16. Rick Cantu, "After 50 Years, Miners' Historic Victory Still Resonates in Basketball," *Austin American-Statesman* online, September 3, 2016, https://www.statesman.com/story/news/2016/09/03/after-50-years-miners-historic-victory-still-resonates-in-basketball/10125156007/.

17. Jeffrey McMurray, "In Defense of Adolph Rupp," *Spokesman-Review* online, January 21, 2006, https://www.spokesman.com/stories/2006/jan/21/in-defense-of-adolph-rupp/.

Chapter Eight

1. Matt Levine, "Impact of a Scholarship: Billy Jones," *University of Maryland Athletics* online, February 10, 2021, https://umterps.com/news/2021/2/10/terrapin-club-impact-of-a-scholarship-billy-jones.
2. Kurt Helin, "How the KKK Helped Earl 'The Pearl' Monroe Become a Knicks Legend (and Not a Pacer)," *NBC Sports* online, April 20, 2013, https://www.nbcsports.com/nba/news/how-the-kkk-helped-earl-the-pearl-monroe-become-a-knicks-legend-and-not-a-pacer.
3. Barry Jacobs, "Jacobs: Claiborne's Journey Helped Transform Duke Basketball," *Go Duke* online, February 22, 2008, https://goduke.com/news/2008/2/22/1394549.aspx.
4. Jacobs, "Jacobs: Claiborne's Journey."
5. Larry Keech, "In the Beginning...\ One March Night 30 Years Ago Changed the Face of Basketball Today," *Greensboro News & Record* online, March 6, 1996, https://greensboro.com/in-the-beginning-one-march-night-30-years-ago-changed-the-face-of-basketball-today/article_14f958ec-9b11-55a1-8a42-2f48efac86e0.html.
6. Keech, "In the Beginning."
7. Eric Tullis, "C. B. Claiborne on Being Duke's First Black Basketball Player," *Indy Week* online, February 13, 2013, https://indyweek.com/culture/archives-culture/c-b-claiborne-duke-s-first-black-basketball-player/.
8. Art Chansky, *Blue Blood: Duke-Carolina: Inside the Most Storied Rivalry in College Hoops,* (New York: St. Martin's Griffin, 2006), 109.
9. Rick Brewer, "Charles Scott's Career Capped by Naismith Hall of Fame Induction," *University of North Carolina* online, September 7, 2018, https://www.unc.edu/posts/2018/09/07/charles-scotts-career-capped-by-naismith-hall-of-fame-induction/.
10. Chansky, *Blue Blood,* 108.
11. "Michael Jordan Admits Racism: 'I Was Against All White People,'" *NBC News* online, May 7, 2014, https://www.nbcnews.com/pop-culture/celebrity/michael-jordan-admits-racism-i-was-against-all-white-people-n98971.
12. Jim Sumner, "Jim On Duke's Most Important All-Time Recruits (Part II)," *Duke Basketball Report* online, July 11, 2019, https://www.dukebasketballreport.com/2019/7/11/20689855/jim-on-dukes-most-important-all-time-recruits-part-ii-johnny-dawkins-art-heyman-gene-banks.
13. Daryl Bell, "Before Zion: How Gene Banks Paved the Way for Duke's Stars," *Andscape* online, February 26, 2019, https://andscape.com/features/before-zion-how-gene-banks-paved-the-way-for-dukes-stars/.

14. Bell, "Before Zion."

15. Daryl Bell, "Philly's Gene Banks Helped Create the Duke Mystique," *Philadelphia Tribune* online, Mar 12, 2019, https://www.phillytrib.com/commentary/darylbell/daryl-bell-phillys-gene-banks-helped-create-the-duke-mystique/article_40d3594f-c531-585d-8eeb-8f18aaef73c9.html.

16. Bell, "Philly's Gene Banks."

17. Rodd Baxley, "Brotherhood Starts with Dawkins," *Fayetteville Observer* online, March 23, 2019, https://www.fayobserver.com/story/sports/college/basketball/2019/03/23/rodd-baxley-dukes-brotherhood-started-with-johnny-dawkins/5634905007/#.

18. Tony Kornheiser, "To Tubby: May Best Man Win," *Washington Post* online, May 15, 1997, https://www.washingtonpost.com/archive/sports/1997/05/15/to-tubby-may-best-man-win/be3a5641-d165-46b0-9904-f4337dffc8f3/.

19. Jerry Tipton, "Spurned by UK in '60s, Wes Unseld to Coach in House that Rupp Built," *Lexington Herald Leader*, October 20, 1992.

20. Charles H. Martin, *Benching Jim Crow: The Rise and Fall of the Color Line in Southern College Sports, 1890-1980* (Springfield: University of Illinois Press, 2010), 236.

21. Don Haskins and Dan Wetzel, *Glory Road: My Story of the 1966 NCAA Basketball Championship and How One Team Triumphed Against the Odds and Changed America Forever* (New York: Hachette Books, 2005), 199.

Chapter Nine

1. Miki Turner, "Riley Remembers," *ESPN Page 2* online, accessed January 31, 2024, https://www.espn.com/espn/page2/story?page=turner/060112.

2. Tim Reynolds, "Miami Heat President Pat Riley Reflects on 50th Anniversary of Texas Western Win," *NBC Miami* online, March 16, 2016, https://www.nbcmiami.com/news/local/miami-heat-president-pat-riley-reflects-on-50th-anniversary-of-texas-western-win/84594/.

3. Tom Eblen and Jerry Tipton, "50 Years After Kentucky-Texas Western: 'College Basketball Has Not Been the Same Since,'" *Lexington Herald Leader* online, March 14, 2016, https://www.kentucky.com/sports/college/mens-basketball/article65655382.html.

4. Doug Brunk, *Wildcat Memories: Inside Stories from Kentucky Basketball Greats* (Lexington: University Press of Kentucky, 2014), 1.

5. James Duane Bolin, *Adolph Rupp and the Rise of Kentucky Basketball* (Lexington: University Press of Kentucky, 2019), 336.

6. Eblen and Tipton, "50 Years After Kentucky-Texas Western."
7. Michael A. Lindenberger, "Louisville-Kentucky: Inside a Heated College Hoops Rivalry," *Keeping Score* (blog), *Time*, March 30, 2012, https://keepingscore.blogs.time.com/2012/03/30/louisville-kentucky-inside-a-heated-college-hoops-rivarly/.
8. Woody Paige, "Orange Flush," *Denver Post*, January 6, 1997.
9. Lindenberger, "Louisville-Kentucky."
10. Frank Fitzpatrick, *And the Walls Came Tumbling Down: Kentucky, Texas Western, and the Game That Changed American Sports* (New York: Simon and Schuster, 1999), 220.
11. Fitzpatrick, *And the Walls Came Tumbling Down*, 219.
12. Sam Gardner, "Fifty Years Later, Kentucky Reflects on Impact of Being on Losing Side of 'Glory Road,'" *Fox Sports* online, Mar 22, 2016, https://www.foxsports.com/stories/college-basketball/fifty-years-later-kentucky-reflects-on-impact-of-being-on-losing-side-of-glory-road.
13. Bob Carter, "Rupp: Baron of the Bluegrass," *ESPN Classic* online, accessed January 31, 2024, https://www.espn.com/classic/biography/s/Rupp_Adolph.html.
14. "Players, Rupp Honored in Coliseum Ceremony," *Lexington Herald*, March 20, 1966.
15. Jon Scott, "Adolph Rupp: Fact and Fiction," *Big Blue History*, accessed January 31, 2024, http://www.bigbluehistory.net/bb/rupp.html
16. Jon Scott, "Adolph Rupp: Fact and Fiction."
17. Gardner, "Fifty Years Later."
18. Pat Forde, "Legacy of Rupp Slow to Recede Repercussions of 1966 Title Game Still Echo in Many Ears," *USA Today*, April 2, 1996.
19. Don Haskins and Dan Wetzel, *Glory Road: My Story of the 1966 NCAA Basketball Championship and How One Team Triumphed Against the Odds and Changed America Forever* (New York: Hachette Books, 2005), 194.
20. Haskins and Wetzel, Glory Road, 194.
21. Joe B. Hall and Marianne Walker, *Coach Hall: My Life On and Off the Court* (Lexington: University Press of Kentucky, 2019), 96.
22. Keith Taylor, "Looking Back: Larry Conley, Joe B. Hall Haven't Forgotten UKs Memorable Tourney Run in 1966," *North Kentucky Tribune* online, December 29, 2015, https://nkytribune.com/2015/12/looking-back-larry-conley-joe-b-hall-havent-forgotten-uks-memorable-tourney-run-in-1966/.
23. Billy Reed "Criticism of Rupp Went Way Overboard," *Lexington Herald-Leader*, March 18, 1997.
24. Scott, "Adolph Rupp: Fact and Fiction."
25. James Duane Bolin, *Adolph Rupp and the Rise of Kentucky Basketball* (Lex-

ington: University of Kentucky Press, 2020), 336.

26. Mark Story, "Rupp's Legacy? One Hundred Years After Adolph Rupp's Birth, the UK Coaching Icon Still Evokes Strong Feelings," *Lexington Herald-Leader*, September 2, 2001.

27. David Brock, "UK Missed Opportunity by Focusing on the Past," *Lexington Herald-Leader*, February 3, 2006.

28. Bolin, *Adolph Rupp and the Rise of Kentucky Basketball*, 336.

29. Jon Hale, "African-American and Africana Studies Faculty Ask UK to Change Rupp Arena Name," *Louisville Courier Journal* online, July 23, 2020, https://www.courier-journal.com/story/sports/college/kentucky/2020/07/23/kentucky-basketball-faculty-call-rupp-arena-name-change/5494349002/.

30. Sam Goldaper, "Adolph Rupp, Basketball Coach Who Won 879 Games, Is Dead at 76," *New York Times* online, December 11, 1977, https://www.nytimes.com/1977/12/11/archives/adolph-rupp-basketball-coach-who-won-879-games-is-dead-at-76.html.

31. Frank Fitzpatrick, *And the Walls Came Tumbling Down: Kentucky, Texas Western, and the Game That Changed American Sports* (New York: Simon and Schuster, 1999), 22.

32. Russell Rice, *Adolph Rupp: Kentucky's Basketball Baron* (Champaign: Sagamore Publishing, 1994), 205.

33. Scott, "Adolph Rupp: Fact and Fiction."

34. Scott.

35. Bob Moser, "Mitch McConnell: The Man Who Sold America," *Rolling Stone* online, September 17, 2019, https://www.rollingstone.com/politics/politics-features/mitch-mcconnell-man-who-sold-america-880799/.

Chapter Ten

1. Ron Thomas, *They Cleared the Lane: The NBA's Black Pioneers* (Lincoln: University of Nebraska Press, 2002), 123.

2. Sam Gardner, "Fifty Years Later, Kentucky Reflects on Impact of Being on Losing Side of 'Glory Road,'" *Fox Sports* online, March 22, 2016, https://www.foxsports.com/stories/college-basketball/fifty-years-later-kentucky-reflects-on-impact-of-being-on-losing-side-of-glory-road.

3. William Gildea, "I Covered Texas Western's Win Over Kentucky. Here's How I Saw History," *Washington Post* online, March 17, 2016, https://www.washingtonpost.com/sports/colleges/i-covered-texas-westerns-win-over-kentucky-heres-how-i-saw-history/2016/03/17/bab64bc0-eb87-11e5-bc08-3e03a5b41910_story.html.

4. Joe B. Hall and Marianne Walker, *Coach Hall: My Life On and Off the Court* (Lexington: University Press of Kentucky, 2019), 96.

5. Gardner, "Fifty Years Later."

6. Dale Robertson, "50 Years Later, Texas Western's Win More Than a Game for David Lattin," *Houston Chronicle* online, March 20, 2016, https://www.houstonchronicle.com/sports/college/article/Fifty-years-later-Texas-Western-s-win-more-than-6922933.php.

7. Kevin Armstrong, "Fifty Years Later, Spring Valley Coach Willie Worsley Recalls Texas Western's Upset Over All-White Kentucky in 1966 NCAA Championship," *New York Daily News* online, April 3, 2016, https://www.nydailynews.com/2016/04/03/fifty-years-later-spring-valley-coach-willie-worsley-recalls-texas-westerns-upset-over-all-white-kentucky-in-1966-ncaa-championship/.

8. SI Staff, "50 Years Later, Black Basketball Team's Victory Resonates," *Sports Illustrated* online, Mar 16, 2016, https://www.si.com/college/2016/03/16/ap-bkc-ncaa-1966-championship.

9. Jay Hinton, "TCU's Cash a True Pioneer, Visionary," Go Frogs, website of TCU Athletics, October 23, 2014, https://gofrogs.com/news/2014/10/23/TCU_s_Cash_a_True_Pioneer_Visionary.aspx.

10. Jay Hinton, "TCU's Cash a True Pioneer, Visionary."

11. Jon Scott, "Adolph Rupp: Fact and Fiction," *Big Blue History*, accessed January 31, 2024, http://www.bigbluehistory.net/bb/rupp.html.

12. Frank Fitzpatrick, *And the Walls Came Tumbling Down: Kentucky, Texas Western, and the Game That Changed American Sports* (New York: Simon and Schuster, 1999), 28.

13. Frank Deford, "The Negro Athlete is Invited Home," *Sports Illustrated*, June 14, 1965, 26-27.

14. Robin Norwood, "Black and White? Only Bluegrass Matters," *Los Angeles Times* online, January 15, 1998, https://www.latimes.com/archives/la-xpm-1998-jan-15-sp-8661-story.html.

15. Charles H. Martin, *Benching Jim Crow: The Rise and Fall of the Color Line in Southern College Sports, 1890-1980* (Springfield: University of Illinois Press, 2010), 304.

16. Barbara Ward, "Education in a Free World," *Vogue*, November 1, 1949.

17. Alvis V. Adair, *Desegregation: The Illusion of Black Progress* (Lanham: University Press of America, 1984), 1.

18. Joy Ann Williamson, *Black Power on Campus: The University of Illinois, 1965-75* (Champaign: University of Illinois Press, 2013), 5.

19. Dr. Harry Edwards, "Crisis of Black Athletes on the Eve of the 21st Century," *Society* 37, (2000): 9.

20. William H. Turner, *The Harlan Renaissance: Stories of Black Life in Appalachian Coal Towns* (Morgantown: West Virginia University Press, 2021).

21. Chris Surovick, "The Day College Basketball Changed Forever," *Bleacher Report* online, March 19, 2010, https://bleacherreport.com/articles/365633-the-day-college-basketball-changed-forever.

22. Don Haskins and Daniel Wetzel, *Glory Road: My Story of the 1966 NCAA Basketball Championship and How One Team Triumphed Against the Odds and Changed America Forever* (New York: Hachette Books, 2005), 183.

23. Robes Patton, "Miners Mission: Just Win Title Game 30 Years Ago Changed College Hoops," *Spokesman-Review* online, March 10, 1996, https://www.spokesman.com/stories/1996/mar/10/miners-mission-just-win-title-game-30-years-ago/.

24. Haskins and Wetzel, *Glory Road*, 183.

25. Nelson George, *Elevating the Game: Black Men and Basketball* (New York: Harper Collins, 1992), 137.

26. Pat Forde, "Legacy of Rupp Slow to Recede Repercussions of 1966 Title Game Still Echo in Many Ears," *USA Today*, April 2, 1996.

27. Perry Wallace, "Glory in Black and White," *CBS*, April 2002.

28. Mark Bradley, "The Losing Side of a Historic NCAA Upset," *Atlantic Journal-Constitution* online, March 18, 2016, https://www.ajc.com/sports/college/the-losing-side-historic-ncaa-upset/dEZGtDlEMCzsF1O3RQTuXl/.

29. Joe B. Hall and Marianne Walker, *Coach Hall: My Life On and Off the Court* (Lexington: University Press of Kentucky, 2019), 97.

30. James Duane Bolin, *Adolph Rupp and the Rise of Kentucky Basketball* (Lexington: University of Kentucky Press, 2020), 297.

31. Jon Scott, "Adolph Rupp: Fact and Fiction."

32. John Marks, "Doug Collins' Memories of the Gold War," *Chicago Sun Times* online, September 10, 2022, https://chicago.suntimes.com/sports-saturday/2022/9/10/23345590/doug-collins-1972-olympic-basketball-gold-medal-soviet-union-chris-collins.

Chapter Eleven

1. Ken Denlinger, "ACC Tournament," *Washington Post* online, March 2, 1981, https://www.washingtonpost.com/archive/sports/1981/03/04/acc-tournament/7377a4f1-c31d-439c-8684-6d625863eedb/.

2. Jack McCallum, "Losers Weepers," *Vault, Sports Illustrated* online, March 8, 1999, https://vault.si.com/vault/1999/03/08/losers-weepers-the-year-before-the-

ncaa-added-at-large-berths-to-the-big-dance-north-carolina-state-and-maryland-played-an-epic-of-a-winner-take-all-final-in-the-acc-tournament-for-the-terps-the-result-was-a-crying-shame

3. Alexander Wolff, "The Shot Heard Round the World," *Vault, Sports Illustrated* online, December 28, 1992, https://vault.si.com/vault/1992/12/28/march-28-the-shot-heard-round-the-world-a-miraculous-last-second-play-lifted-duke-over-kentucky-in-perhaps-the-greatest-college-game-ever-played.

4. Dana O'Neil, "From Hill to Laettner, 25 Years Later," *ESPN* online, March 21, 2017, https://www.espn.com/espn/feature/story/_/id/18905808/remembering-christian-laettner-epic-ncaa-tournament-buzzer-beater-25-years-later?curator=SportsREDEF.

5. Gene Wojciechowski, *The Last Great Game: Duke vs. Kentucky and the 2.1 Seconds That Changed Basketball* (New York: Penguin Group, 2013), 204.

6. Wojciechowski, *The Last Great Game*, 205.

7. Russell Rice, *Kentucky Basketball's Big Blue Machine* (Huntsville: Strode Publishing 1976), 5.

8. Curry Kirkpatrick, "Kentucky's Shame," *Sports Illustrated*, December 12, 1988.

9. Jerry Tipton, "UK Basketball Scrimmage to Benefit Urban League, Improve Race Relations," *Lexington Herald Leader*, October 9, 1992.

10. O'Neil, "From Hill to Laettner, 25 Years Later."

11. Glenn Logan, "Kentucky Basketball: Revisiting Christian Laettner's 'Stomp.' Was it Really?" *A Sea of Blue,* June 18, 2012, https://www.aseaofblue.com/2012/6/18/3094400/kentucky-basketball-revisiting-christian-laettners-stomp-was-it-really.

12. Wojciechowski, *The Last Great Game*, 204.

13. Chris Kent, "Elite Eight Battle Between Duke and Kentucky in 1992 Was a Classic Thriller," *Sports Then and Now*, March 24, 2022, http://sportsthenandnow.com/2022/03/24/elite-eight-battle-between-duke-and-kentucky-in-1992-was-a-classic-thriller/.

14. Malcolm Moran, "College Basketball; Kentucky and Duke: As Good As It Gets," *New York Times* online, March 30, 1992, https://www.nytimes.com/1992/03/30/sports/college-basketball-kentucky-and-duke-as-good-as-it-gets.html.

15. Moran, "College Basketball; Kentucky and Duke."

16. Steve Berkowitz, "Great Ending ... And That's Just the Beginning," *Washington Post* online, March 30, 1992, https://www.washingtonpost.com/archive/sports/1992/03/30/great-ending-and-thats-just-the-beginning/1ce27cd8-1f8d-4bf3-ab69-fc18f564c5e4/.

17. O'Neil, "From Hill to Laettner."
18. O'Neil.
19. O'Neil.
20. "Kentucky v Duke: Hill Pass, Laettner Jumper," *CBS* YouTube *channel, October 19, 2006,* https://www.youtube.com/watch?v=AY-iq58_0z4.
21. Rick Morrissey, "Past Imperfect; Future Intense," *Chicago Tribune* online, November 30, 1997, https://www.chicagotribune.com/news/ct-xpm-1997-11-30-9712020327-story.html.
22. O'Neil, "From Hill to Laettner."
23. Bill Brill, *An Illustrated History of Duke Basketball: A Legacy of Achievement* (New York: Sports Publishing, 2012).
24. Wojciechowski, *The Last Great Game*, 250.
25. "Cawood Ledford's Final Sign Off," *KY Clips* Facebook page, accessed January 29, 2024, https://www.facebook.com/KY.Clips.
26. O'Neil, "From Hill to Laettner."
27. Gary McCann, "Saturday's Was a Game for the Ages," *Greensboro News & Record* online, March 29, 1992, https://greensboro.com/saturdays-was-a-game-for-the-ages/article_408da92f-108e-5a62-baa5-9adc9cc4e92b.html.
28. O'Neil, "From Hill to Laettner."
29. Mark Story, "The Enduring Gift That C. M. Newton Left The Unforgettables," *Lexington Herald Leader* online, June 7, 2018, https://www.kentucky.com/sports/spt-columns-blogs/mark-story/article212746109.html.
30. Alexander Wolff, "The Shot Heard Round the World."
31. Mike DeCourcy, "Kentucky-Duke: The Greatest Game Ever Played," *Sporting News*, April 4, 2015, https://www.sportingnews.com/us/ncaa-basketball/news/duke-kentucky-christian-laettner-the-shot-1992-elite-eight-march-madness-ncaa-tournament/1i1ou2eypyw791046c6cv4c1v8.

Chapter Twelve

1. Frank Fitzpatrick, *And the Walls Came Tumbling Down: Kentucky, Texas Western, and the Game That Changed American Sports* (New York: Simon and Schuster, 1999), 225.
2. Alejandro Danois, "Hoop Realities," *Baltimore City Paper*, February 19, 2003.
3. Tony Kornheiser, "On Smith's Ocean, Relation Ships," *Washington Post*, March 13, 1997.
4. *Adolph Rupp: Myth, Legend and Fact,* directed by Dick Gabriel (Lexington,

KY: UK Big Blue Sports Marketing, 2006), DVD.

5. Shafin Khan, "Q&A with National Champion Joe. B. Hall," website of Shafin Khan, August 18, 2019, https://shafin-khan.com/2019/08/18/qa-with-national-champion-joe-b-hall/.

6. Mark Bradley, "The Losing Side of a Historic NCAA Upset," *Atlanta Journal-Constitution* online, March 18, 2016, https://www.ajc.com/sports/college/the-losing-side-historic-ncaa-upset/dEZGtDlEMCzsFIO3RQTuXI/.

7. Jon Scott, "Adolph Rupp: Fact and Fiction," *Big Blue History*, accessed January 26, 2024, http://www.bigbluehistory.net/bb/rupp.html.

8. David Kingsley Snell, *The Baron and the Bear: Rupp's Runts, Haskins's Miners, and the Season That Changed Basketball Forever* (Lincoln: University of Nebraska Press, 2016), 235.

9. Frank Fitzpatrick, *And the Walls Came Tumbling Down*, 219.

10. William Gildea, "I Covered Texas Western's Win Over Kentucky. Here's How I Saw History," *Washington Post* online, March 17, 2016, https://www.washingtonpost.com/sports/colleges/i-covered-texas-westerns-win-over-kentucky-heres-how-i-saw-history/2016/03/17/bab64bc0-eb87-11e5-bc08-3e03a5b41910_story.html.

11. Scott, "Adolph Rupp: Fact and Fiction."

12. John Clay, "The Runts: Still Special After All These Years," *Lexington Herald Leader*, February 9, 1991.

BIBLIOGRAPHY

Adair, Alvis V. *Desegregation: The Illusion of Black Progress.* Lanham: University Press of America, 1984.

Bass, Amy. *In the Game: Race, Identity, and Sports in the Twentieth Century.* New York: Palgrave McMillan, 2005.

Blauner, Bob. *Black Lives, White Lives: Three Decades of Race Relations in America.* Berkeley: University of California Press, 1989.

Brill, Bill. *An illustrated History of Duke Basketball: A Legacy of Achievement.* New York: Sports Publishing, 2012.

Braun, Eric. *Loretta Lynch: First African American Woman Attorney General.* Minneapolis: Lerner Publications, 2016.

Carson, Clayborne. *In Struggle: SNCC and the Black Awakening of the 1960s.* Cambridge: Harvard University Press, 1981.

Chansky, Art. *Blue Blood: Duke-Carolina: Inside the Most Storied Rivalry in College Hoops.* New York: St. Martin's Griffin, 2006.

Cobb, Charles E. *On the Road to Freedom: A Guided Tour of the Civil Rights Trail.* New York: Algonquin Books, 2008.

Cunningham, David. *Klansville, U.S.A. The Rise and Fall of the Civil Rights-Era Ku Klux Klan.* New York: Oxford University Press, 2012.

Farmer, Richie (1992). *Richie: The Richie Farmer Story.* New York: Antex Corporation, 1992.

Feinstein, John. *Forever's Team.* New York: Villard, 1989.

Fitzpatrick, Frank. *And the Walls Came Tumbling Down: Kentucky, Texas Western, and the Game That Changed American Sports.* New York: Simon & Schuster, 1999.

Freedman, Lew. *Becoming Iron Men: The Story of the 1963 Loyola Ramblers.* Lubbock: Texas Tech University Press, 2014.

Goldman, David J. *Jewish Sports Stars: Athletic Heroes Past and Present.* Minneapolis: Kar-Ben Publishing, 2013.

Hall, Joe B., and Marianne Walker. *Coach Hall: My Life On and Off the Court.* Lexington: University Press of Kentucky, 2019.

Haskins, Don, and Dan Wetzel. *Glory Road: My Story of the 1966 NCAA Basketball Championship and How One Team Triumphed Against the Odds and Changed America Forever.* New York: Hyperion, 2006.

Hynson, Colin. *Timelines: The Civil Rights Movement.* London: Arcturus Publishing, 2010.

Jewell, Malcolm E., and Everett W. Cunningham. *Kentucky Politics.* Lexington: University of Kentucky Press, 1968.

Jonas, Gilbert. *Freedom's Sword: The NAACP and the Struggle Against Racism in America, 1909-1969.* New York: Routledge Press, 2005.

Kean, Melissa. *Desegregating Private Higher Education in the South: Duke, Emory, Rice, Tulane, and Vanderbilt.* Baton Rouge: Louisiana State University Press, 2013.

Keesing's Research Report. *Race Relations in the USA 1954-1968.* New York: Charles Scribner's Sons, 1970.

Lenehan, Michael. *Ramblers: Loyola Chicago 1963—The Team That Changed the Color of College Basketball.* Evanston: Agate Midway, 2013.

MacGillis, Alec. *The Cynic: The Political Education of Mitch McConnell.* New York: Simon & Schuster, 2014.

Martin, Charles H. *Benching Jim Crow: The Rise and Fall of the Color Line in Southern College Sports, 1890-1980.* Springfield: University of Illinois Press, 2010.

Maraniss, Andrew. *Strong Inside: The True Story of How Perry Wallace Broke College Basketball's Color Line.* New York: Philomel Books, 2017.

McMullen, Paul. *Maryland Basketball: Tales from Cole Field House.* Baltimore: Johns Hopkins University Press, 2002.

Miller, Patrick B., and David K. Wiggins. *Sport and the Color Line.* New York: Routledge, 2004.

Moore, Johnny. *100 Things Duke Fans Should Know & Do Before They Die.* Chicago: Triumph Books, 2015.

Nelli, Bert, and Steve Nelli. *The Winning Tradition: A History of Kentucky Wildcat Basketball.* Lexington: University of Kentucky Press, 1998.

Pluto, Terry. *Loose Balls: The Short, Wild Life of the American Basketball*

Association. New York: Simon & Schuster, 1990.

Risen, Clay. *The Bill of the Century: The Epic Battle for the Civil Rights Act.* New York: Bloomsbury Press, 2014.

Segal, Theodore D. *Point of Reckoning: The Fight for Racial Justice at Duke University.* Durham: Duke University Press, 2021.

Smith, John Matthew. *The Sons of Westwood: John Wooden, UCLA, and the Dynasty That Changed College Basketball.* Springfield: University of Illinois Press, 2013.

Smiley, Wendell W. *The North Carolina Press Views the Ku Klux Klan from 1964 through 1966.* Greenville: Self-pub., 1967.

Snell, David Kingsley. *The Baron and the Bear: Rupp's Runts, Haskins's Miners, and the Season That Changed Basketball Forever.* Lincoln: University of Nebraska Press, 2016.

Sumner, Jim. *Tales from the Duke Blue Devils Hardwood.* Champaign: Sports Publishing, 2006.

Thompson, Edgar T. *Plantation Societies, Race Relations, and the South: The Regimentation of Populations.* Durham. Duke University Press, 1975.

Upchurch, Thomas Adams. *Race Relations in the United States, 1960-1980,* Westport: Greenwood Press, 2008.

Veazey, Kyle. *Champions for Change: How the Mississippi State Bulldogs and Their Bold Coach Defied Segregation.* Charleston: History Press, 2012.

Volponi, Paul. *The Final Four.* New York: Speak, 2013.

Ward, Jason Morgan. *Hanging Bridge: Racial Violence and America's Civil Rights Century.* New York: Oxford University Press, 2016.

Wojciechowski, Gene. *The Last Great Game: Duke vs. Kentucky and the 2.1 Seconds That Changed Basketball.* New York: Blue Rider Press, 2012.

ABOUT THE AUTHOR

Michael B. Layden grew up in Durham N.C. in the 1960s and 70s where he frequently attended Duke basketball games. His family helped participate in civil rights activities throughout that era. He is a devoted follower of his beloved Blue Devil basketball team dating from before the 1966 final four, having the privilege of attending in person both of Duke's first two national championships, and often posting in years past on Duke basketball report on various topics. He has continued following his Blue Devil basketball team to this very day, including watching Mike Kryzyzewski's last two Carolina games. He lives with his family in New York, where he works as a business consultant, and where the ratio of Duke to Carolina fans is somewhat more even than it is in North Carolina.

www.ingramcontent.com/pod-product-compliance
Lightning Source LLC
Chambersburg PA
CBHW032150080426
42735CB00008B/652